TOM WATKINS

with **Matthew Lindsay**

LET'S MAKE LOTS OF MONEY

SECRETS OF A RICH, FAT, GAY, LUCKY BASTARD

1 3 5 7 9 10 8 6 4 2

Virgin Books, an imprint of Ebury Publishing,
20 Vauxhall Bridge Road,
London SW1V 2SA

Virgin Books is part of the Penguin Random House group of companies
whose addresses can be found at global.penguinrandomhouse.com

Penguin
Random House
UK

First published by Virgin Books in 2016

www.eburypublishing.co.uk

A CIP catalogue record for this book is available from the British Library

Hardback ISBN 9780753541968

Printed and bound in Great Britain by Clays Ltd, St Ives PLC

Penguin Random House is committed to a sustainable future for our
business, our readers and our planet. This book is made from Forest
Stewardship Council® certified paper.

CONTENTS

1

A BLACKHEATH BOY, OR 'I DIDN'T KNOW HE WASN'T JEWISH!'

Let's get one thing straight (and it will be just the one thing). This isn't a story about a 'working-class boy made good'. Well, OK, it sort of is. I may hail from humble origins, but all that 'rags to riches' nonsense bores the pants off me. I am, pure and simple, a self-made, man-mad man. Scoff if you like, but I am truly one of the last pop moguls: one of a dying breed, the kind that did it in style.

Call me old-fashioned, but I was at the top of my game when it was still fun, before all those talent-show dullards started pulling the strings. I love art and money in equal measure. I loathe boredom and boring people. I've acted like a fool most of my life, and outsmarted most of them. If there is one thing I have always possessed, it is real charm. If one thing has eluded me, it is real love.

I'm Tom Watkins: Svengali; entrepreneur; designer. I don't think it's too much of a stretch to call me a living legend.

I was born Thomas Frederick Watkins on 21 September 1949 at St Alfege's in Greenwich, London, which had just recently become an NHS hospital. The midwife held me up, turned to my mother and, in her thick Jamaican accent, said, 'Lady, this boy is going to be something!' That woman was not wrong, that's for sure.

I grew up in Blackheath, a village nestled in south-east London on the borders of Greenwich and Lewisham. When we were at school, we always believed Blackheath acquired its name from all the bodies buried there during the Black Death in the fourteenth century. Apparently that's not so. The moniker actually comes from the darker colour of the heath compared to the fields it overlooks by the Thames. I can't remember much about the debris left behind by the Second World War, only that rubble from the bomb-sites was used to fill in the various holes on the heath that hadn't been turned into ponds.

Despite being a rather posh 'bucolic enclave' in the city, Blackheath had a history riddled with rebellious troublemakers – a bit like me, I suppose. In the fourteenth and fifteenth centuries, the peasants were always revolting there. It was the stretch on the road from London to Dover that travellers feared, as many a highwayman would strike there. As a kid, I was regaled with tall tales of Dick Turpin in Blackheath. It was a place of adventure and infamy, perfect for yours truly to grow up in.

My mum, Patricia Daphne Diet, had fourteen siblings. There were so many of them that I can hardly remember all my aunts and uncles, except Ronnie and dear old Joyce. As a teenager, my mother befriended a woman named Rosie Truder, a member of a local entrepreneurial family in Greenwich. The Truders were a smart bunch and they had that neck of the woods well and truly stitched up with businesses.

Mum may as well have been part of the clan. She worked in their ice-cream factory and in their café in Catford. That was where she met Frederick Joseph Watkins, my father. Many years later, she worked the counter at Gambardella's, a Truder-owned café that was used as a hangout by the local boys in Squeeze.

Dad was a man's man, a no-nonsense grafter, 'one of the roughs' as Walt Whitman would say. He enjoyed racing pigeons, gambling and playing football for a team called Surrey Dockers. His mum, my Grandma Watkins, worked in Greenwich's Slipper Baths, which were a life-saver for the locals without washing facilities in their homes (there were quite a lot of them).

Dad was originally what was called a lighterman, ferrying people back and forth across the River Thames on a flat-bottomed barge. He was always on the make, and sold his passengers meat sandwiches for snacks. Unknown to them, the meat was Chappie dog food. It was a practice more common than you might think. These were the days before health and safety. Nobody ever complained. Nobody, as far as I know, ever got sick. Everybody around me was always out to earn a few bob. We may have been poor, but everyone I grew up with was hungry for more from life. I guess you'd call us aspirational.

Having said that, Dad and I never saw eye to eye. He was hostile to what he saw as my arty-farty ways and used to call me a 'big girl's blouse'. Sadly, as I got older, the gulf only got wider. Let's face it; I was no sportsman. And if I am brutally honest, I resented the fact that I came from such peasant stock.

It used to irk me that Dad toiled his whole life and never really got us out of our threadbare existence. He made money, but it never stayed around for too long. He was forever lending the wages to his mates who never paid him back. He was always late with the rent. Even when he tried his best, things went awry. One Christmas Eve when I was a little kid he tried to creep into my room with my gifts. Our pit bull was guarding me and attacked him. It was a harbinger of how doomed our relationship would prove to be.

After a few early years on a street called Armitage Road, we rented the downstairs flat of a house on Westcombe Hill owned by Aunt Joyce and her husband, Fred Wallington. Uncle Fred had bought the 1840s Victorian brick-built property for the princely sum of £1,050, making extensive renovations to it. Fred and Joyce were far better formative influences than either of my parents. They shaped so much of what I came to be. Without them, I don't know if I would have amounted to much at all.

Mum was a gregarious and charismatic lady. Later in life, when I had made it big, she took full advantage of all the cultural pursuits that wealth affords you and became something of an opera aficionado. Back then, though, she was heavy-handed Pat, fastidiously clean herself but a stranger to housework.

The dirty dishes would pile up and Mum would be sitting on her chair in the backyard, feasting on crab. She would hold court to an endless procession of visitors, puffing relentlessly on a Guards fag and swigging a lager and lime. Let me tell you, it was not a pretty sight. But Mum had a magnetic personality – something I probably inherited from her. Joyce would wait in vain upstairs for visitors that never came, because Mum had diverted them into her lair.

Dad was by then done with working the river and had become a coal merchant based in offices just up the road. He would arrive home from a hard day's work and have to scrub our scullery floors. He routinely attended to all the chores that Mum had neglected, as she entertained, oblivious to the domestic carnage in her wake. If anything, I felt contempt for Dad's chronic inability to assert himself.

I had grudging admiration for Mum, though. There was a peculiar skill to how she could do so little yet be so commanding. She doted on me, although as I got older her overbearing manner made me wince. She was always down the caravans with my Uncle Ronnie, dressed up in gypsy garb like a caravan-site Carmen Miranda.

Our home was a few notches up from Dickensian squalor. It looked like it was furnished with bric-a-brac from a charity shop. This was because it was. Everything came from a Greenwich warehouse store called Lawrence's and was bought on their tab, which was known as the tallyman. We got all of our furniture, household goods and clothing 'on the tally'. In those days it was a big, dirty secret if your school blazer came through these means – as mine always did.

The shame shaped my life. From that early age, I made a vow to myself: whatever it took, I would crawl out of this humdrum, dead-end world of poverty and never be poor or in debt ever again.

Aunt Joyce helped my mum by hunting for clothes for me. In contrast to our grimy pit, Joyce and Fred's apartment upstairs was a palace. They had wallpaper, and quality carpets. They liked nice things and worked hard to get them, then maintained them impeccably. Fred was the manager of the butchery department at the Co-op, in those days an enviable position. It meant that their place always had good cuts of meat on the table, rather than the daily diet of egg and chips that my mum served up.

My aunt and uncle were refined, cultured people. Fred was suave and Joyce was glamorous: she had even been Miss Ramsgate in 1947! They were working class but literate. Fred was an avid reader, especially of J.M. Barrie and Lewis Carroll. Through him, I developed an early love of literature. Historical novels were my passion, and I devoured the works of Geoffrey Trease and Rosemary Sutcliff.

Joyce was a skilled mathematician and particularly good at mental arithmetic. She took evening classes in bookkeeping and looked after the accounts wherever she worked. For a while, she had the best job that any boy could hope for a relative to have: working in Sidney Ross' toyshop on Greenwich High Road.

This meant that I had all the latest gifts and gadgets: Hornby train sets, Bayko building sets, Triang scooters, stilts and roller skates. You name it, Joyce got it for me. I will never forget how she used to beam and grab my chubby cheeks, always delighted to see me, whenever I came into Ross' shop.

One of my bizarre early recollections is dressing up as a clown on Sundays and making everyone sit on the lawn so I could perform for them. I told them I was going to run away and join Billy Smart's Circus, which regularly appeared on Blackheath. Joyce used to put all my clown make-up on for me.

You know what? Nothing has really changed. I just don't wear such heavy make-up these days.

I could read and write well beyond my years, thanks again to the tutelage of my aunt and uncle. They instilled in me a sense of pride about working hard and surrounding yourself with luxuries, the fruits of that labour. They also indulged my exhibitionist streak, enabling me to evolve into the larger-than-life character I most certainly became.

However, on a deeper level, they also provided me with a feeling of curiosity and wonder for *objects* that has never deserted me. That child-like excitement for toys persists in my inexhaustible thirst for art collecting, much of which, let's face it, just looks like overpriced toys anyway. Most of the houses I have designed and built too just hark back to those early years playing with all the wonderful gifts that Joyce would bring home.

Let's not forget that I have spent a lifetime styling pop stars and bands; not just dressing them but also presenting them to the public. It is often harder work than you would imagine, especially given some of the frumps I have had to make-over. Again, Uncle Fred was a man of exquisite taste and style, having a particular penchant for Italian tailoring. Suits, silk shirts and ties were all arrayed neatly in the bedroom. His belts and shoes invariably matched.

Fred's sartorial exactitude was awe-inspiring. I would sneak into their bedroom and gaze at his endless rows of shoeboxes, all systematically arranged, all labelled. I think the seeds were being sown right then and there for all my future endeavours in style and design. They had even inherited an Art Deco bedroom suite. It was certainly a refuge from the penurious world of the Watkins household downstairs.

Uncle Fred and Aunty Joyce didn't just expand my intellectual horizons. They were always taking me out of the city to the seaside, to Margate, Ramsgate and Hastings. Fred had an aunt who owned a farm in Hastings, the town I now live so close to.

We might have been poverty-stricken but we were never bored. Probably because, to quote my later charges the Pet Shop Boys, 'We were never being boring' (there again, they nicked it off Zelda Fitzgerald, thank you very much!). From the ages of four to seven, I attended Invicta Road School. It was literally a stone's throw from my backyard: I could even wave to all my relatives from the playground. At seven, I moved to Sherrington Road School around the corner until I was eleven. I was a precocious pupil and excelled at most subjects. So much so that I couldn't wait to get out of there and pursue my own hobbies and interests, of which there were many.

I would buy my comics from Mrs Klein's shop on Bramshaw Avenue. I loved reading *Hotspur, Beano* and *Dandy*. Then I discovered Marvel Comics, swiftly becoming part of the Merry Marvel Marching Club. I had a huge tin badge and wore it proudly, a fierce and mighty emblem of my allegiance to the great pantheon of super-heroes. There was Spiderman (that outfit was soooo tight!). The Incredible Hulk (I suspected that there was a strong family likeness). Howard the Duck (he was quackers, apparently). I loved all the giveaways from comics.

Years later, at a comic book convention in my late teens, I met the great Marvel Comics main man Stan Lee himself. I was with three mates, Barry Smith, Ian Gibson and my cousin Steve Parkhouse, who all ended up getting jobs with Marvel. Stan Lee signed my collectors' book and I got a badge and a ringer t-shirt! This may have been where my early obsession with merchandising began.

On Saturday mornings as a kid I would go to the pictures at the Roxy in Blackheath. I loved all the legendary film characters like Roy Rogers, Tarzan and Flash Gordon. You had to be accompanied by an adult unless the film was U-rated, so we used to stand outside and ask grown-ups to escort us in. Can't imagine that happening now, can you? To make a bit of pocket money, I sold the classified papers announcing the day's football results in Blackheath on a Saturday night.

Looking back, it all seems like a dream, as I guess so many people's childhoods do. Every season brought with it a whole slew of activities and adventures. In the winter, our neighbour Mr Russell built his son and me real sledges for tobogganing, making us the envy of all the other kids with their corrugated iron and tin trays. We would slide down from General Wolfe's statue in Greenwich Park to the Naval College as snow blanketed the world around us, and our frosty breath hung in the air.

Mum told me that as a girl she had skated across the pond outside the Hare & Billet pub on Blackheath. Given my girth, I was never going to follow her lead. Even as a nipper I was a bit of a corpulent chap. It didn't help that I often had two breakfasts: one at home with Mum and then another in a café with Dad. Pretty ironic considering that Mum's maiden name was Diet!

What I did enjoy was toy-boat racing in the pond by another Blackheath pub, the Princess of Wales, on Sundays. That was always a laugh. And between Pond Street and Paragon Place lay wild marshland. We would often go on school nature walks through it. It was full of newts that we captured in our nets, put into jam jars and then made to 'walk the plank' across lolly sticks. Poor little buggers!

At Easter, Mum and Dad would man Truder's Ice Cream Van at the Heath Fair as punters rode donkeys on the heath. The summers felt full of golden sunshine and went on for ever. I would spend hours up on the heath, feeling like I was on top of the world.

Autumn would find us in Shooter's Hill Woods collecting conkers. Being, as my dad had informed me, a 'big girl's blouse', I was initially petrified of the Guy Fawkes in November, although the Blackheath bonfire was a big deal locally.

I was far happier swimming in Greenwich Baths and buying a penny bag of chips afterwards. As it was just a short walk from the swimming bath, a few mates and I would kill time in the Maritime Museum. I was in awe of the scale of the place: the architecture, the history, the vistas and the streaming light. There were so many sea behemoths that dwarfed us and were often frighteningly huge.

There was a lot of Nelson in the museum. Then there was the *Cutty Sark*, with its history of fast voyages across the world carrying precious cargos of tea. Dry-docking and preserving this famous ship were prodigious feats of engineering. My visits gave me a passion for all things nautical that lasts to this day. Nowadays I co-own a restaurant that I also designed, the Ship, and its aesthetic is all about those boyhood afternoon museum visits, gazing at the relics of seafaring life. It was also the only interest I shared with my dad, who had been on the water himself in his lighterman days.

Viewed from today, my youth is a distant, far-off land. To young people it would seem like ancient history. The Blackheath of my childhood was still a place with a horse-drawn Dairy Express milk float; still a village that the rag-and-bone man wandered through. We had so little. Yet millions of pounds, mountains of cocaine and several ex-husbands later, it seems like so much to me now. It's true: the past is a foreign country.

At eleven, I was interviewed for the local posh grammar school, John Roan. Mum and Dad came to the interview. My mum looked like an overdressed publican's wife and my dad an extra from *Steptoe & Son*. I longed for Fred and Joyce to accompany me instead, and my dad could tell. After the interview, he scowled at me in the corridor, clenched his fists and said with real venom: 'Tommy, you're nothing but a spoilt snob.'

How right can a man be?

In any case, by then my sister Sally had been born (she was seven years my junior) and she was the apple of my dad's eye. In a fight, my mother would invariably take my side and my father would always support Sally. They dressed her like a gaudy 'Baby Jane' in cheap clothes. Our squabbles were the usual sibling warfare. She would wreck my room and then blame me for it.

Years later, I would become Sally's chaperone and we would be very close. So close, in fact, that it would cost me dearly.

I failed the interview for grammar school and ended up attending Raine's Foundation School in Tower Hamlets. It was a charitable Church of England secondary school, reaching out to all creeds and walks of life. It had been opened in 1719 by old Henry Raine, a man of faith from Wapping who had made his fortune from booze. He wanted to give kids from lesser backgrounds, such as myself, the chance to advance and learn the three Rs.

Every day I caught the 108 bus from the Blackheath Standard into the Blackwall Tunnel and to school. Raine's had a lot of Jewish schoolboys and I fitted in: they thought I was one of them. God knows why, but they did.

Two streets away from the school lived the Kray twins. We schoolboys were in awe of our local gangsters. I saw them a couple of times when I was buying fish and chips. I hadn't fully explored my sexuality at this age but I felt attracted to them. The danger, the power, the bespoke tailoring: I have to admit it, even then I think I loved the idea of being a gangster's moll.

Yet for now, my pursuits remained bookish. I was firmly entrenched in the realms of academia and not in the clutches of some nattily dressed underworld thug. Raine's developed my enthusiasm for art history. I was intrigued by stuff like the change from the Arts & Crafts movement into Art Nouveau, all giving way to twentieth-century Modernism. There were such radical paradigmatic shifts in style, from the florid Victorian age to Art Deco/Modernism's more pared-down, geometric forms. It was a major aesthetic overhaul to accompany the violent political turbulence of the new century, I guess.

Either way, my eyes and imagination were hooked. I fell in love with the order, clarity and sleek shapes of Modernism, particularly the work of the Bauhaus movement. In its way, it represented a leap from the vestiges of Victorian decay that defined my poor childhood. Even now I abhor the sight of Victorian architecture. It just reminds me of everything I ached to be free from.

A few years later, my sister Sally befriended a girl named Kim Moore. Kim was the daughter of one of the Krays' henchmen, Ray, who I got to know a little bit.

Being a part of the Kray's inner sanctum, Ray was feared and revered by all. Yet I knew a softer side to him. He loved how conversant I was in art and culture and would listen to me intently as I showed off all my knowledge. I sensed – I *knew* – that this erudition, combined with my ability to play the clown, would open doors for me. It would be my passport out of the land of dog-food sandwiches, grotty flats and the tallyman.

Unfortunately, things didn't work out quite so well for Ray Moore. When he came out of the pub one night, someone pumped him full of lead.

2

TARGET-TIME TOMMY

I am a maddeningly contradictory character. I always have been. Even as relatively studious as I was, Raine's was not a place that thrilled me for long.

Nor was my life outside education any more exciting. At home, every first Sunday in the month we would pour into my father's Standard Vanguard Battleship-Grey Road Tank, or whatever the bloody thing was called, and head off to nearby Charlton to take late tea with Dad's Great-Aunt Dolly. She was a cook at the local Angerstein pub so her culinary treats of shellfish, sausage rolls, trifles and red toffee apples were something to savour.

At these high teas, various distant members of Dad's family would gather like a small clan. It was there that I first met my distant cousin Steve Parkhouse, who was only a few months older than me. He had an amazing ear for music and he was a fine artist, already making plans to go to art school in East Ham.

Steve and I kept each other amused by sketching and giggling together about anything and everything. He lived in Wanstead Flats, where I had gone fishing a couple of times, and when his family invited me over during half-term holidays I leapt at the chance. The prospect of adventure, of spending time with Steve and his musical collections and artistic drawings, was too tantalising to refuse.

Steve, as I mentioned earlier, went on to become a staff illustrator and storyteller for Marvel Comics. He was later to introduce me to an entire gang of future Marvel staffers. For now, over a couple of years we traversed the Blackwall Tunnel and spent many fun-packed hours together.

Steve told me that he and a couple of his mates were going to take advantage of a slightly off-season holiday at a Warner's Holiday Camp in Hayling Island, Hampshire with the assurances of lots of girls and beat music in the camp club. Even by my early teens I knew my natural urges and the 'girls' bit filled me with dread. But I longed to spend extra time with Steve and his dreamy mates. I saved up like mad and, in fairness, my dad always gave me half towards most challenges that I set myself.

We all took our little brown suitcases on the coach to Hayling Island – Steve, of course, had a trendy duffel bag which I, of course, coveted. We were all determined to get a suntan, be rebellious and get laid (them by girls, me, I hoped, by them – fat chance!). Camp life was closely organised and the *free* time, as I called it, involved stripping down to our shorts and attempting to turn bronze instead of the milky white we all were. Steve had reddish hair and had to be careful not to burn. I simply roasted like a fine sow.

I will never forget lying on the lawn, pungent with the fresh smell of impeccably mown grass, on a cheap tartan blanket, intended for the colder nights in our cheap chalet. A party of girls joined us. One, called June, stole Steve's heart – and had a gleaming new transistor radio. One Monday afternoon as the sun beamed down, the radio crackled out a new song by a new band: 'Love Me Do' by the Beatles.

At that second, I knew exactly what I wanted from my life: music, art, fashion, boys and non-stop partying.

The world changed quickly. If my pre-teen years seemed torn from the pages of Enid Blyton, the emergence of rock and roll and my newly active hormones altered everything. Along came thrills, raised decibels and debauchery. It was an exciting time to come of age. It is often said that the world went from black and white to Technicolor in the sixties in England. It's a cliché but it is true.

The pop music explosion in Britain coincided with my burgeoning sex life. It was all starting to happen as I entered my teens. I've always maintained that sex is what drives and sells pop music and I defy anyone to disagree. It was the case back then, it was all through my career and it's still that way now.

Back then, rock 'n' roll was *really* sexy. It wasn't this twee indie-folk crap you hear now that sounds like it was designed to advertise insurance. It was dangerous. Elvis was my dad's favourite, so he was automatically out of bounds for me. But the Beatles were great. Hearing 'Love Me Do' for the first time was a total epiphany. They were where it all began for me. Yet even they were tame next to the Rolling Stones, who quickly usurped them in my fickle affections.

In no time, I was heading out to gigs. I caught Georgie Fame at the Flamingo Club, Rod Stewart (in his early band, Steam Packet) and Julie Driscoll (with Brian Auger and the Trinity). I saw the Who on their home turf at the Marquee. At the 100 Club, the Pretty Things were the resident band and I loved them.

But nobody could compete with the Stones. I saw them loads at the Crawdaddy Club, which moved from the Station Hotel to Richmond Athletic Ground as their audience grew. I loved the fact that they represented rebellion and stuck two fingers up to the establishment. Where the Beatles were that bit too squeaky clean, the evil Stones were a true incendiary force.

Mick Jagger only had to twitch his hips to generate hysteria. He was just so sexual. His preening, effeminate presence enraged my dad – good! – and excited me. Here was how provocative sex and music combined could be! This epiphany would obviously serve me well later in life, but in the early sixties all I felt was a fierce kinship with these modern gods.

It was a brave new world and I plunged headlong into it. It was all about being glued to the chart show on Sunday afternoons, then the advent of pirate radio, then *Top of the Pops*. There were occasional galas at the Lewisham Gaumont, and all the big boys played there: the Beatles, the Stones, the Who.

Not that you could hear a note they played. The cacophony of the crowd's cheers was almost terrifying, like mass hysteria. It felt as if my whole generation was having one collective, crazed orgasm! I heard that the Stones' manager, Andrew Loog Oldham, even orchestrated some of the din himself – an early note-to-self about the power of hype.

Like every self-respecting teen in the sixties I briefly joined a band. We were called Plain Facts and we formed at Raine's to try to raise money for church funds. The line-up was Paul Challenger on lead guitar; Martin Flatsman on rhythm guitar; Roger Dalliday on bass; some bloke called Dave on drums … and yours truly, Fatty Watkins, on lead vocals.

We were very much your identikit mid-sixties Brit-rock combo: a (very) sub-Stones mix of Muddy Waters and R&B covers. We played a gig in the hall and got a little mention in the school magazine for making the most money towards a new steeple, or whatever it was. I even got t-shirts with our name emblazoned on them. Even as a teenager, I was already well into merchandise and promotion.

Plain Facts also opened up exciting new avenues for me, if you'll pardon the phrase. Every Sunday night, one of the band's parents would go to the pub and I would take my maracas to his house for a supposed jam. We would end up shagging.

You wouldn't exactly call it very romantic, mind you. A year after I had left school, I saw the bandmate again at the Blackheath Standard. I tried it on with him and he threatened to give me a right-hander and said he 'wasn't like that any more'. I couldn't care less what he was like. I just wanted another shake of my maracas. After that, I never saw him again.

I also worked at our bassist Roger's parents' business. Dalliday's wallpaper shop was a quarter of a mile from Raine's and I would use my school bus pass to get through the Blackwall Tunnel on Saturdays. The Dallidays used to keep money in a paraffin can and sometimes I would nick some. They were an affluent bunch anyway, I figured.

My one other memory of the Dallidays was that they owned the first colour telly that I ever set eyes on. The first programme I ever saw on it was shown on Boxing Day 1967: the Beatles' *Magical Mystery Tour*.

There were monthly gigs at Greenwich Town Hall. I was there the night that JFK was assassinated. Yet even this hardly impacted on me. Suddenly I was lost to the world; on another planet entirely. My family receded into the background.

All I wanted to do was tape the latest hits off the radio with my reel-to-reel tape recorder then play them back at deafening volume, much to the consternation of my family (and, no doubt, the entire street). Dad would burst in in a fit of rage, bellowing, 'Turn it down, Tommy!' He might as well have shouted at the clouds. In fact, 'Get Off Of My Cloud' became my personal anthem. When I listened to it, I felt invincible.

A whole universe opened up, filled with the vibrant energy of all this new music. I would hang out at the Coffee House in Woolwich, where they played lots of great stuff on Tamla Motown and Atlantic: James Brown, Arthur Conley, Eddie Floyd, Aretha Franklin – the list of greats seemed endless. I loved soul, it was cool, it always put a real wiggle on my stride.

Everything was up for grabs and everything seemed like a revelation. A specialist stall in Woolwich Market sold reggae. I still remember so clearly buying 'Oh Carolina' by the Folkes Brothers. I loved Millie's early records, like the candy reggae-pop classic 'My Boy Lollipop', as well as all the Jamaican sounds coming out of Island and Trojan Records. There was just this great melting pot of soul, reggae, Motown and rock and roll.

I was not alone in this voyage of discovery. I had an accomplice, even if we made a slightly odd couple. I mean couple in the platonic sense of the word, as he was completely hetero.

Melvin Sharp was a younger friend of my dad's (they were both into racing pigeons). Melvin was a real Jack the Lad. I always suspected that he was the son my dad longed for me to be. Melvin was a scaffolder by trade and became a constant presence in the Watkins household. As different as he and I were, he picked up on my love of what was going on, and began to take me to the epicentre of Swinging London.

Melvin and I bought clothes from Carnaby Street, including John Stephen's famous boutiques. We were both dedicated followers of fashion and I became quite the dandy. There again, things went in very different directions when we hit the changing rooms.

Ever since I was a baby I have always been on the heavy side – it's a combination of being what they used to call 'big-boned' and loving my food. Where Melvin had no problem fitting into the latest threads, it was a different story for me. I would stare at the svelte peg-legged trousers he would effortlessly slip into with an envy that bordered on resentment. How could an aesthete like me be doomed never to fit into the very clothes I was so desperate to wear?

Yet I was always a resourceful stylist and I found things that I could tailor to my, ahem, 'larger' dimensions. Naturally, my father took huge exception to my new flamboyant attire, which delighted me. Every time I left the house, Dad would roll his eyes to the heavens and utter his perennial put-down of his only son: 'He's nothing but a big girl's blouse.' He was far too dim to work out that his good mate Melvin was facilitating my peacock parade.

Melvin and I frequented the cafés, bars and clubs of Soho together. I'll never forget speeding along on his ultimate Mod accessory: the Vespa scooter. Often it was in the dead of night, while everyone was asleep. Melvin and I would zoom off into the Smoke in pursuit of good times and good music. We always got both. My life suddenly seemed bohemian and cool.

Closer to home was El Partido, a great venue packed with both Mods and young Jamaicans, on Lee High Road next to the Sultan pub. It was over some shops, at the top of a vertiginous staircase, and I used to feel dizzy when I climbed up. But once inside, the sounds were the best in bluebeat, soul and Motown.

Bo Diddley played the Partido in 1965 and Jimmy Cliff the next year. To my eternal regret I never saw them but my own short-lived band, Plain Facts, also played a brief set there. We were so crap that they asked us to leave the stage. I'll never forget how embarrassed I was afterwards, when waiting to collect our equipment.

Plain Facts soldiered on. We renamed ourselves Bo's Children because of all of the Bo Diddley covers in our repertoire (not to mention the fact that, after the Partido debacle, our original name was now tainted with ridicule). However, my days as a frontman were numbered.

A lot of the Mods were Jewish boys that I knew. They reminded me a bit of Uncle Fred, with their impeccably coiffured hair and sartorial precision. Arbiters of general good taste, the Mods were forward-thinking and eclectic. Too much of later generations' perception of Mod stems from the late seventies *Quadrophenia*-inspired revival. It was all a bit stodgy and narrowly defined. The original Mods were open to anything – including fooling around with other blokes.

There were whispers in Soho that a few of the Mod 'faces' were rent boys to affluent older gentlemen. Some of these faces went on to become famous. Britain may still have been repressed in those days but in little pockets of London, a world away from buttoned-up, uptight, mainstream England, the possibilities seemed endless.

Drugs were a big part of the scene. You would take a purple heart to keep you up and party all night, buzzed on the music at gigs and in the clubs. I was eager to try everything, so I just gobbled up anything that was put in front of me.

Outsiders like me found a haven in the rock and roll scene. Jewish and gay men were the movers and shakers behind the screens. The first major pop Svengali I heard of was Larry Parnes, who groomed a stable of talent that included Tommy Steele, Billy Fury and Adam Faith. Beatles supremo Brian Epstein was gay and Jewish, too.

In fact, the list of gay managers in the sixties was never-ending and included Robert Stigwood, Simon Napier-Bell and Kit Lambert. The fact that I had been to a school with such a large Jewish population made me feel even more at home. It would be a few years before I was to venture into the world of pop management, but I like to think the synergy between these star-makers and the rock bands I loved rubbed off on me. Even then, naïve and wet behind the ears, I knew that I belonged in that world.

I suppose my first real exposure to the music industry was *Ready Steady Go!*, the first major pop show on telly, and I was determined to be where the action was. I even found a pretend girlfriend to accompany me.

This 'girlfriend', Myra Vosser, was introduced to me by another gay kid in Blackheath who used to collect antique silver snuffboxes. She was a Jewish East Ender and was Britt Ekland's cousin, no less! Well, she said she was. Her mum and dad ran the Terminus café where the buses stopped on Commercial Road. I used to go and have coffee there all the time. Myra came from the same world as me and we hit it off.

We would eagerly stand in line outside the TV studio before the show and the audience 'picker' would breeze past us. But we weren't going to give up that easily and we returned time and time again until they finally let us in. I think that the show's choreographer, Patrick Kerr, took a shine to Myra. Before long we were regulars on the programme.

Myra and I would practise our moves in the Vossers' flat on Stepney High Street. Myra could really dance well, and, despite my cumbersome bulk, I was a pretty nifty shaker, too. Once the show's producers saw this, we were permanent fixtures. Deep down, I always felt like the odd 'camp as Christmas' poof with his gal pal. It was all very *A Taste of Honey*. I was the chubby Murray Melvin to her Rita Tushingham.

Naturally, we took dressing up for the show very seriously. Myra was a kindred spirit, a DIY merchant who could whip up something snazzy with scant resources. She would make us Mod outfits, adding big bullseye targets to my t-shirts and painting designs on my jeans. To these customised garments I added the latest fashions: bowling shoes and turtleneck sweaters, or Caravelle's knitted three-button-necked fine sweaters. I bought this stuff with Melvin from Lord John in Carnaby Street.

What united a lot of the great British groups at the time was art school. So many came from that background. Pop art, the reigning aesthetic *du jour*, basically united my two great loves, and my leanings towards art and design came to the fore, galvanised by the sounds and visions around me.

I decorated my own room with ideas I had seen in current magazines and *In Your Room*, a very early forerunner of *Grand Designs*, the TV show that I would decades later feature on. *In Your Room* inspired me to get a huge Coca-Cola billboard and paper it on my wall. My room was a blank canvas and popular imagery was my palette. I had road lamps as bed lights and street signs on my wall. My bedspread had a big target on it and my ceiling light had a red bulb. Nowadays I suppose it would be dubbed 'kitsch', but in those days it felt like a breath of fresh air.

I was seizing the signs and symbols from the world around me (usually imported from America) to create my own little environment. My dad dismissed it as 'a junkyard'. Sometimes, even today, I wonder if the energy I threw into creating and designing was primarily a strategy to protect me from his rejection.

Because I didn't half feel rejected. My father seemed to contemplate my whole identity with disdain and disbelief. How could a son of his be this 'arty'; this 'girly'; this untutored in the rugged ways of his working-man's world?

Around this time I bought a camera, and I loved taking arty photos and having the chemist develop them. I would drag my sister Sally and cousin Toni on to the heath to pose for zany fashion-style shots. David Bailey, eat your heart out!

Even then, sneaky pictures of the odd labourer crept in. I was, you see, like my father, a man's man. I just extolled the virtues of masculinity in a rather different manner!

Not that anyone talked about being a 'queer' back then. Occasionally Mum might make an offhand remark about 'turd burglars' but that was about it. I knew that I was gay, but I never 'came out' to my dad. It wasn't even a conversation that I could ever imagine having. A lot of people used to say that homosexuality was a symptom of an absent father. I felt that Dad was absent because he knew I was gay.

Homosexuality wasn't even legal for most of my teenage years. The Wolfenden Report recommending the legalisation of homosexuality came out in 1957, but sexual acts between men over twenty-one weren't legalised until ten years after that. By then I was eighteen.

Yet, as I say, I always knew I was 'the other way' and I already had a wealth of experience to show for it. I posed as a straight for a bit. Even before I met Myra, I used to take my neighbour's daughter Brenda to the legendary Victor Silvester's ballroom dancing classes upstairs at the Gaumont. As we foxtrotted across the floor I felt an enormous burden weighing down on me. It sure wasn't Brenda. She was only a skinny thing.

Gay sex was hardly elusive. It was clandestine but it was everywhere. It happened in secret places, often very unlikely ones. My father had ventured into the motor trade by my teenage years. With his egregious brother Stanley, a loudmouth bully on his better days, Dad started selling and repairing cars. Soon he owned a fleet of delivery trucks with drivers. Quite how we remained so poor baffles me.

By now, we had moved out of Fred and Joyce's, due to an almighty row between Fred and Dad over Dad's inability to pay the rent on time. We didn't go far – just next door, in fact. Anyway, unknown to my father, I began fooling around with one of his drivers. At the time it gave me a wry sense of satisfaction that I was having it off with one of dad's sturdy blokes under his nose. But, looking back, I wonder if it was just a twisted way of seeking approval from him.

There were sailors, too, and men working on the ferries. I would pick them out at Woolwich Ferry terminal and relieve them. They used to give me a tanner (sixpence), the going rate for a wank. One sailor, who went on to captain a tug, had a wife who owned a café near East Greenwich Gas Works where my dad worked. He remembered me from my exploits down by the ferries (I didn't recognise him) and he told my dad he'd let me steer his tug (as it were).

Off we went as the captain took me up the river. In his cabin he came on a bit too forcefully so I rejected his advances. He got the hump and dropped me back early, warning me never to speak of it.

And I never have.

Until now.

With the money that I made from these encounters, I would furtively creep into the dodgy newsagents by the port and buy *Health and Strength* magazine. Finding a secret spot, I would rip open the shrink-wrapping and eagerly flick through the pages of male nudes with Herculean physiques. The models looked like otherworld deities: foreign, perfect and utterly inaccessible. Just the sight of the images filled me with intense feelings of longing. I passed them around certain boys at school, sometimes selling them for 6p.

Like I said, sex sells!

But school started to bore me as I progressed through my teens. The rules and regulations were stifling. There was no challenge to my advanced capabilities. I might have been arrogant, but everything that was going on outside of school was so much more stimulating and offered a more useful education.

I was an autodidact. I picked things up easily and school just seemed of no use to me. I wanted more: sex, money and rock and roll. School wasn't a route to any of these so I just stopped going. My record cards show a decline in attendance with each passing term. I would get up in the morning, leave the house and catch the bus and head into town. Once there, I threw myself into sexual adventures with other lads. I first had anal sex on top of a tower block. My high-rise induction into sodomy was a bit grim, but I knew I liked it a little rough.

Full gay sex was something I knew I had to get out of the way and so I just dealt with it. In any case, before AIDS homosexual sex was such a flippant, reckless thing. In the sixties it simply seemed to have no consequences whatsoever.

I didn't struggle with my sexuality or feel any of the tedious guilt and shame that afflicts others when they grapple with being gay. I knew I had an insatiable appetite and it needed feeding. It was as simple as that.

Or maybe my early rampant promiscuity was a way of exorcising the pain of never feeling I had a father who cared for me. Who knows? In retrospect, my journey from innocence to experience seems far too brisk and brutal. It did mean that I very quickly grew a skin that was as thick as a cow's hide. My feelings were a thing to be kept locked away – and that only got worse with the passing years.

Ultimately this premature emotional alienation was to prove more of a blessing than a curse. The music industry is no place for cheap sentiment (even if that is the product that it peddles!). I guess that my early years were the perfect apprenticeship for my later career.

3

LIFE CLASSES/LIFE LESSONS

It was the swinging sixties, London was a Day-Glo playground of thrills and sounds and school was a dull distraction. Just my daily seventy-minute journey to Raine's bored me rigid – but thankfully my time at the school was about to crash to a halt.

We used to wind up the supply teachers in German class something rotten. German is a very guttural language so we used to take the piss out of the teachers by repeating the words again and again. One day one of them lost it and whacked me around the head. Looking back, I can't say I blame him.

I stormed out of the class and went straight to Mr Broughton, the deputy headmaster, to make a formal complaint. He was not to prove a sympathetic audience. Fixing his eyes on me, he bellowed, 'Watkins, in all my years of teaching at this school I have rarely been confounded by a pupil so adroitly gifted yet utterly contemptuous of authority as you. You may be smart but you are a blot on the good name of Raine's!'

Fair enough. I felt that Raine's was a blot on my backside. Mr Broughton called my parents in to see him and suggested that I leave at the end of the summer term or right after I sat my first wave of GSEs. I did no revision and failed the lot – except for Religious Education. That subject had been so relentlessly drummed into us that it was inevitable I would pass.

Who cared? I told myself I knew better than the dour old teachers anyhow. It wasn't learning I deplored; it was conformity. I wanted to explore my passions and not have some staid curriculum forced upon me. A voracious reader, I scoured the libraries for books on art and architecture. Everything modern, slightly anarchic and bold captured my imagination.

At this precocious age, all of the various strands of early twentieth-century art transfixed me: Dadaism, futurism, Bauhaus, De Stijl. It was deeply serious but often playful. I picked up a ceramics restoration manual and started repairing Art Nouveau vases I had picked up in markets. My chubby fingers were never idle.

Nevertheless, after my exam failures the unwelcome spectre of work reared its head. Dad suggested I went to work in the butchery department in the Co-Op as I had done Saturday shifts there and Uncle Fred had prospered there. Naturally, I was allergic to any kind of daily grind: it just seemed like a dead end. But I knew I had to do *something*.

I landed a job as a filing clerk at the South Eastern Regional Hospital Board in Paddington: I lasted three months and hated it with a passion. I spent my time impersonating the other clerical staff and got caught mimicking my immediate boss's lanky, quirky walk. The day's highlight would be doing the *Daily Telegraph* crossword with one of the old-timers.

At lunchtimes and after work I'd call at a local vintage store called Hicks that was teeming with exotic artefacts. I purchased a snazzy zoot suit there. When I got it home, everybody laughed at me – but it was to change my life in the near future.

The Hospital Board had a field office in Greenwich, just a stroll from my house, and I set my sights on getting a job in the architecture department there. Art and buildings felt like my future so getting transferred was a major goal. Eventually I succeeded – only to find I was no more than a gofer there.

Realising I had made a terrible mistake at school, I set about retaking my O levels. Luckily, the department gave me a day release to study at Woolwich College. I re-sat Art, English Language, English Literature, History and Liberal Studies and got them all.

See – I could do it when I tried.

My next target was art college. This was fertile terrain back then for the most creative minds of my generation – in fact, it was virtually a rite of passage for British rock and rollers. It offered a viable route of expression and learning for those who were intellectually curious but stifled by formal academia – people exactly like me, I suppose.

Pete Townshend went to Ealing Art College; Keith Richards went to Sidcup; John Lennon went to Liverpool College of Art; Ray Davies went to Hornsey College of Art. So much of their music was really America's ignored blues heritage filtered through an Anglo art school quirkiness. As the decade progressed, art colleges grew increasingly radical, culminating in the 1968 Hornsey Art College sit-in. Indeed, 1968 was a year of political uprising across the western world and it intrigued me – although, to be perfectly honest, I was always too keen on getting ahead to be too concerned with what the longhairs were up to.

Also I found that most of the radicals I rubbed shoulders with were sanctimonious and bourgeois, cosseted by a privilege that allowed them to preach to working-class people like me. Truth be told, they invariably smelt, too. Like a future professor of mine, I never really felt art and politics made particularly compatible bedfellows.

I did know that to get to art college you had to do a pre-diploma, or foundation course, determining what area in art you were going to specialise in. I left my job and did mine at the Sir John Cass Faculty of Art, Architecture and Design in Whitechapel. I would sketch away in the life classes but I knew my interest lay more in architecture and interiors.

By no means a great painter, I nevertheless possessed what I suppose you would call an aesthetic sensibility. When I drew figures, my skill lay in composition and organisation: putting things together. (I mean, I used to look at the clothes that Mum and Dad dressed Sally in and know that I could do better!) Without being too pretentious, I had an appreciation of beauty. I would always rather have one great thing than twenty shit things. Plus – importantly – architecture and interior design seemed a more viable route to making money.

I remember that one of my mum's countless siblings, Aunt Doll, came over from America, where she had emigrated. She had married a Mexican doctor, leaving grey England for San Diego. Returning to England for a visit, she looked at the drawings I had been doing and really liked a painting of a woman I did with household paints on cardboard. Aunt Doll framed it and took it back to America, which meant a lot to me.

I was also honing a peculiar skill of my own. In my pre-diploma class I sat next to a guy named Tracy Edna, who was a brilliant artist and used to copy the Picasso drawings. And I watched him like a hawk and was soon copying him copying Picasso. Imitation is the fondest form of flattery, and all that ...

Yet when the time came to apply for my college place, I knew I wanted to study design. I applied to loads of places without success but was most keen on the Brixton School of Building and the London College of Furniture. The latter particularly appealed to me, but as there were only twenty-seven places on the course, I didn't think I stood a hope in hell of getting in. I applied regardless.

They asked me to go in for an interview. I gathered all my drawings in an old artist's portfolio, but they didn't look adequate enough to get me a place on the coveted course. Summoning all of my innate chutzpah, I decided that I had to make a different kind of impression. If my work samples weren't going to cut the mustard, then I would have to present myself as a masterpiece!

I grabbed the zoot suit that I had bought at Hicks in Paddington and assembled an outlandish and striking outfit, topped off with a highly snazzy and co-ordinated pair of shoes. As I left the house, the Watkins clan naturally chuckled derisively, with my dad leading the chorus. *Fuck them!* I said to myself as I waited for the bus.

It was one of those moments when all of my hopes and frustrations seemed to come together. I clenched my fists and gritted my teeth. *Nobody around me understands who I am or what I want to be.* I was nervous, and a rush of doubt came over me. Were they right? *Did* I look ridiculous? Would they laugh at me at the London College of Furniture, too? Who was I kidding even trying to get on the course?

The bus came and my nerves passed. I knew that I couldn't afford such lapses in self-belief. When I got there, I sauntered into the building as bold as brass. Nobody would have guessed how nervous I felt: I have always been good at fronting up.

In any case, I had no need to worry. The interview would bring me face to face with one of the greatest formative influences of my early life: the college principal, Bernard Gay.

This august but welcoming figure greeted me with a genial smile and I instantly felt at ease. We started a formal interview, but as soon as the Bauhaus movement came up, I was well away.

'You're familiar with Walter Gropius' vanguard art academy?' he wondered.

'Oh, yes! I've read extensively on Bauhaus: its 1919 origins in Weimar, then being ousted to Dessau where those magnificent buildings were erected and their final move to Berlin. It seemed the Nazis were chasing them wherever they went!' I gabbled.

I could hardly contain my glee at being questioned on a subject so close to my heart. We discussed all of the modern art I had so painstakingly read about and Gay was visibly impressed and took little notice of my old artist's portfolio. He could see that I was hungry and passionate about design. For the first time in my life I thought that the person looking back at me was really seeing who I was.

I was given a place on the course.

Now, decades on, I wonder if Bernard Gay embraced me because he could see someone eager to get out of the cul-de-sac of opportunity they were born into – and it felt familiar to him. Because the man had an upbringing, I was later to discover, that made mine seem positively aristocratic. Raised in an orphanage, he had been a gardener and sailor before educating himself and breaking into the academic world.

I guess he was a kindred spirit. I would go to lectures he gave outside the college and we would go for drinks afterwards. Bernard would tell me stories, including how Quentin Crisp had been a life-drawing model at Willesden in 1947. He said Crisp was a 'most extraordinary' model, able to hold poses for hours at a time and scolding anybody who lacked his discipline. Even then he sashayed around in fedora hats, cravats and flared velvet suits; a true trailblazer. It made me wonder if my flamboyant zoot suit had reminded Bernard of the Naked Civil Servant himself.

Crisp was to reprise his life-drawing-model role for us at the LCF. He stood in a loincloth, drank a Complan milky diet shake and was charming and contradictory. He complained of draughts in the studio and yet felt encumbered by the loincloth and would rather have modelled naked. Regardless of his quibbling, he was a real pro and even held his pose through the recess.

Bernard owned a lot of early Mondrian pieces and would bring them in and show us rarities that I had previously only seen in books. I adored Mondrian with his bold, simple uses of line and colour. The college had other lecturers that I liked such as Alan Hunt, John Bitmead and Alan Day, but Bernard Gay was my main man.

The college was on Pitfield Street, near to Old Street in the East End. It was a small, innocuous building that looked like a primary school and contained various sub-schools for the likes of silk-screen printing and weaving. Some of them were decidedly quirkily named: we learned about upholstery in the Tacky Tacky Bang School.

I applied myself to academia with a vigour I hadn't felt since my early days of school. The tedium of the antiquated curriculum at Raine's had sapped me of all my enthusiasm for education. The London College of Furniture revitalised it. It was a place full of bright young minds creating bright young things.

I was one of the brightest. I had always liked brash images: still do. I remember when I sat my O level, my art teacher had said, 'The trouble with you is that your work is vulgar and bold.' 'Tell that to Van Gogh,' I shot back.

One painter I particularly admired was an early twentieth-century artist, David Bomberg. Born into a large Polish-Jewish family, he had moved at an early age from Birmingham to the East End. Jewish, working-class and artistic, he was one of art's 'Whitechapel Boys' and came from the same world I had grown up in. I guess I felt he was a kindred spirit as well.

Bomberg was another *enfant terrible*. A true individual, iconoclastic and pugilistic, he had thrived against all the odds and took on the art establishment head-on. I liked and understood that. It was that Jewish determination that I had been at school with and it mirrored my own steely resolve. It was that fortitude of character that can only be shaped by someone who is part of a minority.

University was filled with people of a similar mindset. My first real mate at LCF was Glenn Harrison, a bespectacled little Jewish guy who was balding but very stylish. Glenn was a Jimi Hendrix fanatic and initiated me into him, as well as US folk and blues artists like Arlo Guthrie, Howlin' Wolf, Muddy Waters and Bob Dylan. Of course, they were also the deep roots of my beloved Rolling Stones.

Studying took up all my time and I soaked up everything around me. A woman called Roberta Clayton taught my liberal studies class. Bernard Gay encouraged anything that exposed us to all aspects of creativity and Roberta took us on trips to galleries and Hampton Court. If you were hard up, small funds were available to assist with travel costs.

She also introduced Glenn and me to Indian music (she knew Ravi Shankar, apparently). The Beatles had spearheaded a cultural shift towards the East and it was very hip to be running in those circles by the late sixties. By 1966's *Revolver* and 1967's *Sgt. Pepper's Lonely Hearts Club Band*, George Harrison had ensured the Beatles had become the chief emissaries of eastern philosophy and music.

It's hard to overstate what an impact this had on the flow of ideas between people in those heady days. Against my better judgement, I even dabbled in hippy chic myself, picking up a few kaftans and the Incredible String Band's classic album, *The 5000 Spirits or the Layers of the Onion*. Thankfully, it was a very brief flirtation. 'Tune in, turn on and drop out' was never really my mantra. I have to admit, though, I do still find myself humming the Incredible String Band's tunes from time to time …

Basically I was a sponge and wanted to absorb anything around me that was beyond the humdrum world from which I came. For the first year of university I was totally closeted with my studies. I did nothing else: even my sex life was barren. There was so much to explore and men were a low priority – at least, for the time being.

Glenn and I were very enterprising and set up a little silk-screen print works to print Hendrix images and the like on our fellow students' jean jackets and t-shirts. We'd do evening life classes at Whitechapel Art Gallery twice a week, and afterwards we'd go to his mum's flat just behind the Blind Beggar pub in Whitechapel.

This boozer was where Ronnie Kray had shot and killed George Cornell in front of drinking punters in March 1966. By then my own infatuation with the Krays was passing fast. Ronnie was becoming an erratic, unhinged character, and it no longer seemed so glamorous to be hanging around the outskirts of that world.

Glenn's mum Sally Harrison would help us knock up an omelette and she soon became a confidante of mine, my new

Aunt Joyce. By this time, Joyce and I had grown a little distant. She had moved a little further away and I only saw her at occasional family get-togethers. There again, I wasn't having much to do with any of my family.

Glenn and I were a wily duo. The LCF didn't have its own organised student union body, which meant that the live music at universities like the London School of Economics and North London Poly was far superior. So Glenn and I took it upon ourselves to act as de facto entertainment officers and nobody stopped us.

It was a lot of fun. We booked Cream, who were massive at the time. We met Eddie Chin, an American bassist who played in a load of bands, who took us to an authentic restaurant called the Lido in Chinatown that his Asian girlfriend recommended. I chowed down on duck's feet and pig's entrails and reflected that it was quite a gastronomic leap from my normal fodder of egg and chips. Clearly, hanging out with musicians could broaden my horizons.

I also became mates with a bloke called Ray, a Jack the Lad with a Mercedes convertible who was smart, well-travelled and loved the art-school scene. Ray was a real gift-of-the-gab salesman. His day job was selling carbon paper by the boxful to gullible customers. He was a proper wheeler-dealer: I have always had a soft spot for bad boys like that.

Ray would accompany Glenn and me on Saturdays on what we called 'romps' to Camden, rifling through bric-a-brac, having lunches and hatching plans. Ray was always nursing a hangover from the night before. We'd also head west to Portobello Road to pick up props, clothes and a regular cornucopia of arcana. The habit stuck: even today I still go to car boot sales and have a keen eye for a diamond in the rust; a jewel in the jumble.

Ray was as round as he was tall, a short bloke with shoulder-length hair, and a chain-smoker. I towered above both him and Glenn and we looked an odd trio. But we bonded over our love of junk and craft markets and always kept ourselves aware of fashions and anything fresh, young and exciting. We would pick up shells and bells to make into bracelets and necklaces and create funky little accessories. Of course, in later years Camden and Portobello became horrible tourist traps but back then they were a magnet for all things weird and wonderful.

Another regular port of call was Kensington Market, where Alan Mair and Freddie Mercury ran a stall. Mair was in a band, the Beatstalkers, and went on to join drug-addled new-wave band the Only Ones. I think it's safe to say that Mercury, of course, needs no introduction. David Bowie called at their stall, too. Things happened at those markets.

Ray, Glenn and I also visited Sheila Cohen, Nigel Weymouth and John Pearse's hippy King's Road boutique, Granny Takes a Trip, where I even managed to fit into a guardsman's jacket (cue *Sgt. Pepper*-style brass band!). London was full of little intersecting micro-worlds and as Ray had a motor we could zoom through the labyrinthine city with ease.

About now, I passed my own driving test and had my own car, too: a Triumph Herald Estate. I bought it with £140 I had saved from all my part-time jobs. My father told me I was an idiot for getting it as the suspension had gone. I used it after it was repaired, but I always preferred being in Ray's altogether more desirable vehicle.

Everything we did seemed to whisk us from our parents' stodgy world to somewhere more expansive and exciting. We would have lunch at singer Ronnie Carroll's stall in Camden where nouvelle hippy cuisine was opening up a new world of taste. Munching on falafel, humus and a bean salad felt like the height of sophistication.

Ray had even been to the legendary Haight-Ashbury district in San Francisco, which impressed me no end. Indeed, as the sixties progressed, London fell under the dreamy spell of visionary, counter-cultural America. I've never been a political animal, but even I stirred my stumps to go on an anti-Vietnam march to Hanover Square with my old friend Myra Vosser.

It was around then that my dad died.

He passed away on 22 June 1969. He had gone to have his valves replaced in his heart and died in the Brook Hospital, Shooter's Hill. On his deathbed he made me promise him that I would take care of Mum and Sally after he had gone, and that is a vow I kept.

Yet this isn't the part of the book where I get misty-eyed and sentimental. Don't bring out the violins. I had no relationship with Dad whatsoever. I didn't like him and he didn't like me. I wish things had not been like that – but that was how it was.

Dad was buried at Shooter's Hill Cemetery and I collapsed at the funeral. Believe me, it wasn't from grief. The burden of being the new family head just suddenly overwhelmed me. After the burial, Mum's sister Lil and her husband Len came to stay with us for a few days. We had no money for groceries and they cleared off sharpish as soon as they realised that the coffers were empty.

A few months after Dad died, I was playing my old recording of 'Get Off Of My Cloud' on my reel-to-reel recorder. When the song ended, Dad's reproachful voice appeared on the tape, as usual ordering me to lower the volume. It was a truly eerie moment. For a second, I did feel a twinge of sorrow as I realised that he was gone for ever and things would never be rectified between us.

But, like I say, that feeling only lasted a second. I buried it quickly, and I've been burying it ever since.

My sister and mother were far more deeply affected and Dad's mate Melvin Sharp was distraught. He was still part of the family and was eventually to marry my cousin, Christine Burwood.

Closer to home, my mum went off the rails for a while. Dad was the only man she had ever been with (or so she would have us believe) and the loss turned her world upside down.

When I graduated in that pivotal year, 1969, just two points beneath a distinction, I knew that I was going to have to do something big. The responsibility of the family rested on my shoulders. Dad was gone, the sixties were almost over and the world was waiting. It was a time for action.

4

GRANDER DESIGNS

If I am honest – and why would I not be, in my autobiography? – there was one very definite upside to my father's death. Having known for a long time that I was gay, I also knew what a shit-storm would have ensued if I had had to come out to Dad. As callous as it may seem, his death prevented this ugly confrontation.

My mum knew all about my leanings. Things came to a head not long after Dad died when I sashayed out of the house one morning in an outsize woman's fur coat and a tie-dyed granddad shirt. I topped off the outfit with the ultimate accessory: a shoulder bag deftly fashioned from a Kellogg's Corn Flakes packet.

Naturally, I got catcalls and whistles but I didn't give a damn. I felt it was my vocation in life to stir things up and get noticed with the most outrageous strategies. To quote a song I was to write years later, it was my job to 'set the cat among the pigeons'. My dear old ma didn't share this philosophy and was horrified to receive a phone call from a shocked neighbour as I paraded gaily up Westcombe Hill.

When I got home that night, Mum's conversational opener was not overly promising: 'Thank God your father's dead, that's all I'm saying!'

'It's just how I dress,' I explained. 'All cool, young people are expressing themselves like this. You should get out more, Mum.'

'Not all young people!' she snapped back. '*Just you queer lot*. Your father must be turning in his grave knowing you're a homosexuals.'

'*Homosexual*. We don't multiply independently! And I prefer the word "gay".'

'Well, anyway. Don't dress like that!' she concluded. 'You look like a hairy Hattie Jacques on funny pills.'

My mum and I had a strange relationship, full of contradictions. We were closer in many ways than my straight friends were to their mums. She always loved my stylistic flair and all my clichéd sissy sensibilities: all the things Dad had abhorred. After he died, she became a reader of the classics and educated herself and even bought me a copy of the collected works of Oscar Wilde. It was a cheap edition but perhaps a refined, cultured acknowledgement of her son's 'other way'.

However, once it became clear that I was gay, she baulked at it. She regretted my sexuality until the day she died and made the fact plain, both to myself and to others. But as politically incorrect as it might sound, I think our bond was strong *because* I was 'a fairy' (as she put it). Only the prejudices of her generation prevented her from realising that.

For a while after Dad's death, Mum just retreated altogether. As time went by, I coaxed her out of her shell. You can't spend the rest of your days haunted by ghosts and memories and I suggested she went to some singles nights in the nearby pubs. Reluctantly, she agreed.

It wasn't the best idea I ever had. Her first outing into the world of post-Dad dating was a singles night at the Black Prince in Bexleyheath. Melvin and I decided that we'd go down and spy on her for a laugh. We got to the pub to find her outside, crying in the rain, too afraid to muster the courage to go in. She looked scared and terribly alone and, as I comforted her and took her home, it dawned on me just how much she had lost.

Like they say, time is the great healer, and slowly but surely Mum came back to life. But the man she finally met was such a nerd that I wished she had stayed indoors – and she met him through my sister.

By now Sally was working in boutiques such as Jane & I in Blackheath (run by Jeff Banks and his wife). She would sneak the clothes off the rails, wear them out for the weekend and return them on her next shift. Done up in the latest threads, she would hang out at a local youth centre, the Samuel Montagu Boys' Club, where she met a lad called Andy Mason, whose father George was recently divorced. Sally played Cupid, and before long she and Mum were going on ice-skating double dates with Andy and George.

Let's be frank. By any standards, George was an unremarkable bloke. A joiner and carpenter, he was muscular and smoked a pipe. He had a parrot, also called George. I took against him from the start and thought he was evil: I definitely thought he was a freeloader.

My mother didn't share my misgivings and in 1971 she agreed to marry him – *she must be desperate*, I thought. On their wedding day, I told her that he was useless and we could get on better without him. In the official wedding pictures, I was hovering at the back with a strained, unconvincing smile on my face.

The reception was at Le Dolomiti, an Italian restaurant on the Sidcup Road. The owners were affiliated with the Truder family that my mum was close to. It reeked of that peculiarly English attitude to all things Mediterranean: slightly naff, slightly cosmopolitan. I loved it. I didn't love my new stepdad, though, and got so drunk at the top table that when George asked me what I thought of him, I told him: 'As far as I'm concerned, my mother's bent down and picked up a piece of shit.'

The entire table stared into their prawn cocktails. I guess any potential relationship between George and me died at that moment. It may sound like I was the archetypal gay stepson from hell, jealous of any man who got close to his precious mum, but George was a charisma bypass and as bland as beige.

He wasn't exactly a love machine either. Mum soon let it be known that every night in the marital bed he munched on an apple, pecked her on the cheek, rolled over and went to sleep. She quickly began tersely referring to her new husband as ''im'. At least I got on with his two sons, Andy and Tony.

Now I had left the London College of Furniture it was time to get into the world of work. I knew interior design was what I wanted to do, but the very concept was still in its infancy and nobody I knew was getting jobs, distinctions or not. Yet I got one quite quickly.

A man called Bob Simmonds hired me to work for Allied Breweries. There was a developing trend for pubs to have a 'corporate identity' and a standardised aesthetic regarding colours and the like. I thus got tasked with refashioning boozers like the Horseshoe on Tottenham Court Road that needed a major overhaul. It wasn't my dream job but at least it was a job.

I didn't stick it for long. After a year, and two or three renovations, I was bored and quit. I had made a rule for myself not to stay in a nothing job for any longer than that. There was a ladder to climb, and I didn't want to waste precious years designing identikit drinking dens.

No, what I really wanted was to work for a funky design practice. And I had one in my sights: Wolff Olins. This hip, relatively new design firm worked out of a studio in a mad warehouse building in Camden Town, and I paid Michael Wolff a visit there in the vain hope that there would be work for me.

We talked in his office, where he had a hi-fi with huge speakers made up of canvas bags, belted at the top, sitting on trolleys so he could have his sounds wheeled around wherever he liked. The walls were full of great art of a calibre usually only seen in galleries. Drawing boards were everywhere. It felt so cutting edge and impressive, and the scale of the place made me gasp with wonder as if I were a kid gazing at the *Cutty Sark* again.

Michael and I clicked but he had just taken on a designer from the Conran Design Group so had no vacancies. Michael called up Rodney Fitch at Conran's on the spot and asked him if there was an opening with them. There was! I hastily made my way from Euston Road to Hanway Place and presented Rodney with a portfolio culled from my days at the London College of Furniture. It was far more auspicious than the crap one I had handed to Bernard Gay.

My work samples included a plan for a toyshop named Cirque. I guess it was a cute throwback to the earlier, innocent days of Joyce and her gifts and me in my clown make-up. It also featured a standard detail for a modular housing concept and an exhibition stand for Olivetti. It was all very detailed and precise. Technical drawings were a skill I had acquired at the LCF and I had put my knowledge of surveys to practical use at Allied Breweries. Furthermore, I was now equipped to write a full specification on how a building should be constructed.

It was enough to get me the Conran job. This was a major step for me. Terence Conran and his design practice were the epitome of everything I longed to be. They were a quantum leap on from post-war austerity. Now this was more like it!

Terence Conran was the archetypal bon viveur, permanently puffing on a cigar, genial, magnetic but slightly aloof, even condescending at times ('If it's made with plastic, it's not a Conran!' he would proclaim). I probably uttered three sentences to the guy in the entire time I worked for him but he was everything that I aimed to be. An entrepreneurial polymath, the Conran credo was 'If you can't make it, then don't design it'. This chimed with me and felt like a modern distillation of Bauhaus and the Arts & Crafts movement.

Yes, Conran's business savvy and design genius made him a real role model: an aesthete with a bean counter's shrewdness. His practice was also a liberal working environment, a veritable hothouse of homos. Years earlier, when Rodney Fitch was arrested for being involved with CND, Conran had stood by him.

They hired me as an assistant initially and disaster nearly struck soon afterwards. The firm ran temporarily short of work and decided they would have to fire their most recently hired employees. It looked like my golden ticket was about to be snatched away from me.

Well, never underestimate the power of a good blow job! I used to get lifts back home with a senior employee. After I started helping him to relieve his day's stresses, he effectively got me my job back.

In fact, Conran's did wonders for my dormant sex life. Someone else that I worked with there had a fondness for S&M so I used to go around to his flat and beat him with a cane. I also got asked to take part in a threesome but I lost my nerve at the last minute. Call me old-fashioned, but too many queens do not a palace make ... and I've never been keen on group sex.

But rest assured, it wasn't all faggy frolics. All of the associates in the buildings had their own teams. There was a hierarchy that ran: project designer; senior designer; associate designer; and then the highest position, partner. Conran's had an intensive 'production line' mentality towards manufacturing. The lower-ranking designers did the nuts and bolts designs but were also expected to know how to build everything. Quite right, too.

Rodney Fitch had an assistant called Malcolm Ridell. They were both what were called 'flash chaps': regal fellows who were fully enjoying the freedoms afforded them by the new permissive society. I also loved Joanne, the archetypal cheeky cockney tea lady and mother hen in the kitchen. Joanne got on with everyone, posh or working class, and took a shine to me, the new tubby gay boy. She took me under her wing.

At Conran's, I was part of David Wren's team that designed a terminal at Heathrow. We came up with furnishings, checking booths, graphics, floor furnishes and colours for the airport. On the London Stock Exchange we devised funky little booths for trading. I felt like we were sprinkling the old world with a new, hip fairy dust.

Occasionally my imagination was allowed to run riot. I got to mastermind an exhibition stand for the concourse of Euston Station. The stand was a giant paint tube with big chunks of paint coming out of it and the cap was a giant circular seat with plants in it. That got me a D&AD (Design and Art Direction) Award. It also ensured that I got moved to the concept team, which was a definite progression as it meant I was taken off the routine chores.

While at Conran's I came face to face with Philippe Starck and Ettore Sottsass. Starck was my age and had formed his own company in France by the late sixties, producing largely inflatable objects. We helped to make a block of flats for him. We were also involved in Esprit prototype shops for Sottsass, who was already legendary by then.

Yet despite these exciting and exotic encounters, I still felt like I was 'neither here nor there'. Working at Conran's was a blast but I would come down to earth with a crashing thud every night. Wiping the exec's creamy cum from my lips like an overfed Cheshire cat, I would get into Mum's house and slump with despair at not having fully escaped.

I had been quietly stashing money away, and decided to take a trip to broaden my horizons. California was the hot new destination. The Beatles had split and London was going through a lull. And for a certain kind of English homosexual, the Golden State was the place to be.

Most recently, David Hockney had moved to Los Angeles. For him it was the place where the American spirit luxuriates and blooms in an almost Mediterranean setting. His paintings like *A Bigger Splash*, of clear skies and azure-blue pools, enticed me. I also loved *Peter Getting Out of Nick's Pool*, the one with the man's butt cheeks exposed; it felt like pop art updates of Michelangelo's *David* in a sun-kissed new world. It was all a damn sight more alluring than hanging out at Woolwich Ferry terminal waiting for randy sailors in the fog. Further upstate, San Francisco was becoming a mecca for gays from not just America but the whole world.

When I travelled there in 1972, Harvey Milk had just moved from New York to San Francisco and set up a camera store on Castro Street. He was to become America's first openly gay city supervisor. To be honest, I was oblivious to all this at the time, but I knew San Francisco was a hot spot for gays and I wanted to check it out.

I managed to give my trip a work cover story. Conran's held frequent 'lunch-ins' where food was provided and an employee would give a presentation. I spoke on San Francisco and they agreed to extend my three-week holiday trip for an extra week and deem it 'research'.

I started off in Santa Barbara, where I stayed with Aunt Doll, but boredom set in quickly and I was itching to make my way up to San Francisco. A Conran's co-worker had set up lodgings for me with a girl named Toni in Haight-Ashbury, the city's hippy epicentre.

San Fran was a wild, exciting city, unlike anything I had experienced. The topography alone blew my mind. The streets rolled on to infinity like massive slides with streetcars gliding up and down them. Palm trees lined the roads and every different angle you viewed the city from yielded new visual splendours.

There were awesome, majestic vistas! I walked everywhere, exhilarated by the sights around me. When English people come to America for the first time, it often feels like somebody has pulled back the curtains, opened the windows and shown them a bigger, bolder world. That was exactly how I felt.

It was July and I caught the queer drag troupe the Cockettes' final performance. They called it *Journey to the Centre of Uranus*. This was the year after Andy Warhol's obscene play *Pork* had caused a stir in London. Taboos were being busted left, right and centre. It was all a hoot.

Gay businesses were popping up all over San Francisco and the bathhouses were becoming the city's central meeting points for men to have sex. Trouble was that I didn't like these saunas. I felt uncomfortable walking around in just a towel.

Yet sex turned up for me in the unlikeliest place in the city. A married couple, Dan and Sylvia, lived in the same apartment block as Toni. Sylvia went off to work and Dan hung around (he made money through illicit means, if you get me). He drove me around the city in his Porsche, showing me all the landmarks like Fisherman's Wharf and Twin Peaks.

Early one morning I called in to his apartment. The door was wide open and I heard his distant voice beckoning me.

'Where are you?' I asked.

'I'm in the bedroom. Come in!' he replied.

'Oh, I'll just wait in the living room,' I stuttered.

'Don't be shy, Tom,' Dan coaxed.

I walked in and he was lying there stark naked. One thing led to another and we ended up going at it all morning. Afterwards I lay back and stared at the ceiling: satisfied but a little guilty. *I don't fancy myself as the other woman*, I thought. My mind was racing.

'Does your wife … ?' I began. Dan cut me off mid-sentence.

'Sylvia does what she wants, and so do I. This is San Francisco. We're pretty free here, man.'

Hell's bells, I thought to myself. These Yanks are something else! I mean, I had been with married men before, but it was always real cloak-and-dagger stuff. Dan's nonchalance was a galaxy away from the sordid goings on at Woolwich Ferry.

I loved this freedom and laid-back attitude towards sex with anyone. However, there was a dark side to the city. As much as San Francisco looked like heaven, some of its inhabitants were going through hell. Acid casualties roamed the streets, accosting you with deranged babblings. People close to my age wandered around, their faces ravaged by LSD, shabby and unkempt, haunted like Old Testament prophets on a bad trip.

I even got mugged by a gaggle of midgets on Haight Street in broad daylight! The city wasn't all flowers in your hair, that's for sure, and I was a little relieved when it came time to come home. A lot of the people I met seemed to have little ambition beyond a vegetarian diet and macramé. There's a good reason why people say San Francisco is where the young go to retire.

So I caught the Greyhound bus out of the city and stared out at the retreating Californian landscape. I didn't want to stay there but something about the place had rubbed off on me. Whatever it was, I was now determined to strive for even more from life.

I flew back to England, presented the Conran crowd with a slideshow and a discussion ... and left the company shortly afterwards. I found that I couldn't build up intimate client relations as the associates monopolised those. This was frustrating for me.

Before I left, I upgraded my motor. Conran's were involved in various car-exhibition stands and at one of those I came across a stripy Volkswagen Beetle. It was a sight to behold and I bought it on the spot. For many years, my Beetle become one of the regular sights of south-east London, routinely referred to by locals as 'the ice cream car'.

My next step from Conran's was an interesting one. I saw an advert in *Design* magazine for Tom Law, a smaller practice in Hampstead, looking for a designer. It seemed an opportunity to take things up a notch and foster a more intimate relationship with clients.

I got the Tom Law job and my most notable commission there was the Talk of the South, a nightclub in Southend. This was a huge concept based on penny arcades. It was the brainchild of the Manzis, an Italian family who owned much of Southend. They wanted the club to have themed bars: a Camelot bar, a disco, a Chinese bar. It was an ambitious undertaking with a tight budget.

Big Daddy Manzi was a cigar-smoking slob, had an air of a Mafioso kingpin about him but was completely legit. His son, Louis, took me out for dinner and quizzed me about being gay. Louis was completely straight but was intrigued by me. He was fascinated by my gayness, the way some people are. Or used to be. Straight eyes scrutinising a homo as if it were some alien, exotic life form ...

He asked me if I fancied him. When I said 'No', he was most offended. His assumption was clear: every homosexual must fancy every other man going!

I didn't, but while Talk of the South was being built I had affairs with a joiner and an electrician. One was a married man whose flat was only around the corner. Unsurprisingly, neither fling lasted.

Happily, the club was a huge success, becoming one of Southend's premier nightspots and hosting cabaret acts by luminaries such as Frankie Howerd. It still survives today, albeit in a much altered form and now simply called Talk.

Yet despite my career advances, I still wasn't satisfied professionally or financially. The journey from Blackheath to Hampstead was one more unwelcome trek. I didn't stay there for long – and I didn't last at my next job either.

Richard Ellis, an architectural and property firm, hired me as a team leader. While I was there, they secured a contract for London Corn Exchange. I hired an old university cohort, Frank Sawkins, and we had fun on the job, making it up as we went along.

However, our gay antics (well, mine were gay, Frank's were 100 per cent hetero) were cut short when a senior architect caught me looking at a book of male nudes.

'Tom Watkins, what on earth are you doing?' he asked me.

'I'm getting body studies to put in my visuals.'

'You must think I'm an arsehole!' he snorted.

'Yeah, I do, as it happens!' I confirmed. 'And you can't design as long as you have a hole in your arse.'

This was not the last time that my potty mouth or weakness for the male form would get me into hot water. Frank and I set up our own design practice and ran it from his living room. It was fun for a while but I wanted to put my knack of design and organisation to better use.

My love of money, sex and good-looking things was leading me to an inevitable next stop.

Pop music.

5

THE BOYS IN THE BAND

Charles Dickens was lucky enough never to see the seventies – the 1970s, that is – but if he had there is no doubt that he would have proclaimed them to be 'the best of times, the worst of times'. Surely no other era has ever been quite so divided and contradictory.

It was a decade of rising prices and rising expectations (not to forget rising violence, from the football terraces to Northern Ireland). If the sixties were permissive, the age of the dawn of sexual freedom, and the eighties were the money decade, the seventies was the awkward straddling ground between the two.

The decade was like a duel between a new world of freedom and sophistication and the old one of repression and rations. It was a time of strikes, shortages, three-day weeks and yet also decadent excess. Of glam rock and glum forecasts, Pan's People and Black Sabbath, Ziggy Stardust rock theatre and pub rock.

I started the seventies in design and ended it in pop music. The career change occurred in 1973 in the unlikeliest of places: the local Samuel Montagu Boys' Club, where Sally was still hanging out. After she hit the skids when Dad died, I began chaperoning her there in my rather conspicuous, head-turning stripy VW Beetle.

The Samuel Montagu was incredible, a bottomless pit of activity for a teenager to run riot in. When you pushed a button, a five-feet-high hydraulic stage emerged out of the gym floor. It had a boxing ring and a full woodwork room. Overlooking the gym was a gallery that housed three large snooker tables.

Each boy who attended was assigned to one of four houses. The club even got itself in *The Guinness Book of Records* for the longest five-a-side football match in history. From thirteen to eighteen the boys had fun in and out of the club, canoeing, trampolining, rock climbing and heading off on day trips out. They could even join an 'old boys' section when they reached the ripe old age of eighteen.

The club wasn't without its occasional ructions, especially during the seventies when a skinhead element came in and caused a bit of trouble, but for the vast majority of the kids who went there it was where they had their rites of passage: their first taste of freedom from their parents, the first time they got drunk, the first time they kissed a girl on the mixed-sex nights.

Or, in the case of two boys, Gary Deans and Jeff Barnes – the first time that they made music.

Jeff and Gary both lived within a stone's throw of the Montagu – in fact, Jeff was the groundsman there. He had been to John Roan, the grammar school that rejected me, but was more of an athlete and musician than he was an academic. After John Roan, he became a clerical officer but after eighteen months was bored to death and leapt at the chance of the Samuel Montagu job.

Gary came from a very loving home and was the first local kid to have a racing bike and a tennis-ball gun. He was charismatic and good-looking, lithe and athletic as a featherweight prize-fighter, with a face as striking as Freddie Mercury's, jet-black hair and piercing eyes. Sally was smitten with him. It made perfect sense that when Jeff started taking his guitar into the club and rehearsing with a band, encouraged by the music-loving deputy leader Mick Sullivan, Gary would be the singer.

Augmented by Jeff's brother Bob on bass, a lad called Dave Chumley on drums and a few hangers-on, they formed Wanted County. It was a name tinged with outlaw chic and all things country and western (lest we forget, 1973 was the year of the Eagles' *Desperado*). Two or three times per week, Wanted County would black out the windows in the soundproofed committee room and rehearse like madmen.

They were pretty good and even won a talent contest at the Royal Festival Hall run by the London Federation of Boys' Clubs. Lifted by this, they became what was known as a functions band, getting bookings via a talent agency called South East Entertainment in Catford and gigging at Masonic dos and various balls. Although they would play some C&W songs, they weren't really a straight country band. Their blend of country, pop, rock and covers of chart hits by the Fortunes and the Tremeloes lacked any real defining identity.

One night they played a pub called the Walmer Castle in Peckham and their van got nicked. They pursued it to Deptford and, when they got there, thugs swarmed around them. One of the band put in a call to local gangster Ray Moore. Within hours, the van was returned.

That was probably the most exciting thing that had ever happened to Wanted County – until they met me one evening on the roof of one of the buildings at the Samuel Montagu Boys' Club.

By now Sally was seeing Gary casually, and he asked her if she knew anyone who could photograph the band. My old LCF mate Glenn Harrison was a dab hand with a camera so we went along to take some pictures of them. After the photo shoot we stuck around and watched them rehearse, and it was evident that what they lacked in identity and original material they made up for in enthusiasm.

A light bulb went on in my busy little brain. This outfit could be the raw material for a new 'design' project. I could mould this motley bunch into something sexier and more palatable. I knew for sure that with my history as an entertainment officer I could book them for gigs. I also knew that I had the gift of the gab and the vision to make Wanted County far more dynamic and commercially viable than they currently were.

So I gave them a spiel to try to persuade them to let me handle their affairs. It wasn't hard. I was pushing at an open door. If anything they were grateful that somebody was offering to give them some guidance and direction.

First of all I went to meet their parents. If any of their mums or dads were uneasy about their lads being looked after by a (by now) openly gay manager, I allayed their fears when I bounded into the family living room. I was a bulky, denim-clad one-man charm offensive, dispensing beaming smiles and compliments about the decor of every home I visited.

Often the interiors were revolting (it was the seventies!), but if a little white lie could get their folks on board, who cared?

I loved the idea of managing a band and got right down to business. I began bombarding venues and student unions with phone calls and Wanted County promo packages featuring Glenn's photos and some breathless press blurbs I had written. It was my mission to turn the band from a semi-pro functions unit into a bona fide pop group.

I knew that they needed a dramatic style overhaul and a new name. Wanted County was too dusty and faux American for my liking. I suggested a few more in-your-face and poptastic names, but Jeff was a bit resistant so we settled on Love County Music. It wasn't the best moniker in the world but at least it was an improvement.

Then I set about sorting out their image. Most of the band were low-key, unassuming sorts, but I could see they had a star in their midst. Gary had amazing potential; he was magnetic and just the right side of flamboyant. Clearly he had to be the focal point for the band and they needed some razzmatazz to make them stand out.

The solution was obvious: glam!

I had loved glam rock as soon as I set eyes and ears on it. It was showbiz, theatrical, charged with sexual ambiguity and a real fist in the face of how dreary and 'mature' the rest of rock had become. Music had grown turgid, po-faced and wrapped in pretentious and pompous gatefold sleeves ... and all the people making it seemed to be strangers to deodorant and shampoo. Everyone had forgotten the simple thrill of rock 'n' roll, the bump and grind, the short sexy spurts of crude noise generated in the fifties and sixties by Elvis, Jerry Lee Lewis and Little Richard.

I had loved T. Rex's big 1970 hit, 'Ride A White Swan'. It was svelte, brief and boppy, the guitars were daubed in glitter and Marc Bolan's pouty poise evinced elegance and ambition. The singles that followed – 'Hot Love', 'Get It On', 'Telegram Sam' and 'Metal Guru' were all catchy as hell. They made rock music teenage again.

Bolan's friend and arch rival, David Bowie, had made it easier for gay men to breathe in Britain. His draping of an arm around guitarist Mick Ronson as he sang 'Starman' on *Top of the Pops* lifted a lid that would never be closed again.

I loved how the best glam rockers married pop and art. Bowie had absorbed the avant-garde, soaked in Japanese kabuki theatre and rubbed shoulders with the Warhol crowd. Roxy Music album sleeves credited stylists and hairdressers like the Golden Age of Hollywood and their music was a pop art collage, retro rock and roll meets squalling futuristic electronics. Like Bowie, they looked as if they were beamed in from another planet. Bowie and

Roxy spoke in a language I understood, bringing the kind of visual references I had decorated my room with into the mainstream pop charts. Bowie wanted to 'be a colour TV'. I loved that.

I was desperate to take my new charges down this route, but hit a problem that was to frequently repeat throughout my career – I wanted my artists to be Ziggy Stardust and they longed to be Joe Cocker! Love County Music were wary of my suggestions, feeling that glam glad rags would diminish their musical integrity.

To give you an idea of what I was up against: they were huge fans of the Doobie Brothers and Steely Dan. Yuk! Nonetheless, I was on a mission to smother everything in glitter.

At least Love County Music had one glam connection. A guy called John Springate had grown up on Invicta Road near me and was now enjoying success as the bassist in Gary Glitter's Glitter Band. Jeff and Gary befriended John before his success, when he played in a band called Elegy. Elegy would sneak Gary and Jeff into their pub gigs and placate angry parents when they got dropped home late because the van broke down or the gigs went on too late.

Now that John was in the hit parade he was a bit of a mentor for the pair and encouraging their songwriting. Another Glitter Band man, Gerry Shephard, would show them his specialised tunings on his star-shaped guitar.

Love County Music went to the Rainbow Theatre to see a Gary Glitter show, travelling from Greenwich to Finsbury Park in velvet flares, white t-shirts and platform heels. Gary Deans looked great, as ever. The rest of them looked like a bunch of hod carriers on the game. (Mind you, the first time I ever met Gary Glitter, I had to stop myself from laughing. He looked like an overstuffed Chesterfield sofa.)

The Glitter Band connection meant that my lads weren't totally averse to a sprinkle of stardust and glam slowly worked its way into the band's repertoire. They started dropping Gary Glitter, Sweet and Bowie covers into all the muso stuff. Even better, the drummer David Chumley's wife, Georgina, was a seamstress and made costumes for the boys.

Ray, Glenn and I were still heading off on our market-stall romps across London and I soon had the band dressed up in flared, sparkly outfits and platforms. Knowing that a band's big bass drum was always a focal point, I designed a drum skin with the group's name on it.

We even co-ordinated a colour scheme for them: red, green and white. This was the year of the iconic cover of *Aladdin Sane* and we liberally borrowed those Bowie image flourishes and daubed poor Love County Music in slap. It was all very campy and a few of the band members voiced severe misgivings (as had Mick Ronson, until Bowie told him that dressing up would help him to pull more birds).

Happily, Gary fully embraced the new image and was soon squeezing into tops that were slashed to the waist, accessorised with medallions the size of manhole covers. He was smart enough to realise that the bolder you looked, the more captivated the audience would be.

Gary's svelte figure meant that his skin-tight clothes fitted him like a hand in a glove. This wasn't true of the whole band. I found some beautiful lime-green sari material at Berwick Street Market and made a wild pair of trousers from it. One band member, a slightly portly chap who shall remain nameless, put them on and by the end of the show they had split at the crotch. He blamed the tailoring and not his fuller figure. As ever with musicians, it is always someone else's fault. (There again, I could sympathise with that particular plight.)

All the boys in the band thought that Sally was an amazing free spirit, full of vitality and beauty. But unknown to them she struggled for a long time after Dad died – his death had been even more traumatic for her than I had realised at the time.

She dated Gary in the band for a while then moved on to Jeff. Jeff was engaged at the time but fell under Sally's spell pretty quickly. She had agreed to do the boys' make-up for me, and the very first night that she did it Jeff fell for her.

Any man would have been seduced by Sally's voluptuous curves and effervescent personality, especially when she was done up in lip gloss, eye shadow and black velvet. She looked the quintessential Biba girl – and, indeed, was working there when she dated Jeff.

Actually, managing Love County Music was a real family affair. Mum also took a keen interest in my new endeavour, helping me to stuff envelopes to send to venues and student unions and often coming to the gigs with me. Her new hubby George did his own thing and she hated being alone. Getting attention from the band and the people around them made her feel young again.

Soon Love County Music were regulars on the pub rock circuit of south-east London: the King & Queen in Mottingham, the Montague Arms and Thomas a'Becket on the Old Kent Road and their old haunt of the Walmer Castle, Peckham. They were playing five nights per week and making more money than they'd ever seen. I was a hound, booking them and getting top fees for them.

Here was how it progressed: after one early gig at the White Swan in Crystal Palace, they went to Lewisham Wimpy bar. Within a couple of months, the post-gig eatery of choice was a posh steakhouse in Welling.

Yet if I have learned one thing in my life, it is that nobody is harder to please than a musician. No sooner did the band start making a name for itself than dissatisfaction set in. They grew tired of the glam tag and wanted to be 'serious' musicians. It was as predictable as it was wearisome.

Mini-fame went to their heads and they thought they were rock stars but they simply weren't stockpiling enough of their own material. Either way, it became clear that they wanted to sever ties with me. The buck always stops with the manager. If something is wrong, it must be your fault.

There again, their wish to get rid of me might have had something to do with a change in my attitude towards them. The better I got at handling Love County Music's affairs, the more bullish and dictatorial my stance became. I was no longer offering advice; I was giving them orders. 'You *will* do this,' I would tell them. 'You *will* wear this.'

Looking back, I suppose I can see why they bridled and rebelled, but I had such a burning certainty of what would work and I was obsessed with imposing my vision on them. Before long, Love County Music felt like an obstacle to achieving what I wanted to do with my life, not the means of achieving it.

But I soldiered on. I was *determined*. I always am.

6

THE EMPEROR OF ICE CREAM

The writing was on the wall for Love County Music. It had seemed like an advantage that Gary and Jeff were like brothers, a real double act, but now they were growing increasingly distant from the rest of the band – and from me. They were always off in a corner, talking quietly and conspiring.

The group played the Lord Nelson in Holloway Road in north London and the vibe just didn't feel quite right. The music was lacking its usual bite and the band weren't gelling. Even the charismatic Gary seemed to be going through the motions. At the bar during the interval, Gary and Jeff told a music journo they had had enough and were breaking up the band. By then the band's profile was so high that it became a news story in *Melody Maker*. That was how the rest of the band found out – even Jeff's brother, Bob. Unsurprisingly, they went mad.

However, I had heard that Gary and Jeff had been checking out and befriending a rival band, Jo Roadster. Jo Roadster were a slick bunch of musicians, probably superior to Love County Music but lacking the equipment that we had. Word quickly got around that Gary and Jeff were planning on joining up with Jo Roadster's bassist Steve Stroud, keyboard player Rob Norman and guitarist David Wells.

Sometimes in life you just have to use your chutzpah. I contacted the Jo Roadster trio, met up and did a number on them, stressing how many gigs I had got for Love County Music and how driven I would be to get them to the top. My nuclear charm offensive worked: they hired me. When Jeff and Gary turned up for a meeting with their new Jo Roadster colleagues, there was their rather familiar 'new' band manager: yours truly.

Gary and Jeff were shocked – they had hoped they were escaping me when they broke up Love County Music, and they said that the new band should sign with the Mecca Ballroom Agency, who wanted new acts for their halls. But that would have been a career cul-de-sac for the group, and Steve, Rob and David argued that I was too driven and effective to be discarded. Eventually Gary and Jeff had no choice but reluctantly to agree.

What's the line by the Who? 'Meet the new boss, same as the old boss … '

First things first: we needed a new drummer and a new name. The first bit was easy. We auditioned a guy called Jeff

Boltz who banged a kit with the force of John Bonham. He was the loudest drummer we had ever heard, and it was a no-brainer: he was in.

The name change was more problematic. Jeff Barnes wanted to shed every trace of the glam rock that I had shoehorned them into. It was thus no surprise that he hated my suggested name for the revamped group: Ice Cream.

For me, it was perfect. I wanted something fun, quirky and playful; a name that screamed out pop art. It was the right side of sexy and as sugary as the Sweet. I saw it – as I see most things – visually. Warhol had a sweet tooth and painted ice-cream cones with his blotted line technique. The cone was an instantly iconic pop art object. Jeff sulked and moaned, but he was overruled again.

Ice Cream it was.

For a merchandising maniac like me, the name was perfect and had so much potential. On a romp down the King's Road, Glenn, Ray and I saw mad Christopher Wray-designed badges of cracked eggs with the yolks spilling. Inspired, I designed similar ones using ice-cream cones. Love County Music drummer Dave Chumley was still on good terms with Gary and Jeff and was skilled at injection moulding, so he helped me lovingly and painstakingly to hand-paint badges with ice cream dripping down the side of a cone.

Having given up on my design agency jobs, Ice Cream became a full-on obsession for me. I very quickly got the taste for looking after a band, especially once I realised that I could make a lot more money getting gigs than I ever could from design commissions.

Initially it was very much a cottage industry. Working from my mum's kitchen table, I spent all I had on postage as she and I fastidiously assembled Ice Cream promo packages containing flyers and posters I had designed, upcoming gig lists, cassettes and t-shirts. I bombarded everybody with these parcels.

Tony DeFries was managing Bowie at the time and doing the same thing on a much grander scale. DeFries' whole ethos was that if you behave as if your act is a superstar, the world will come to believe it. I suppose he was quite an inspiration for what I was doing.

The pubs and venues of London were certainly unused to receiving so much publicity material and merchandise for up-and-coming artists. We even had a lighting rig: an outrageous set-up for a pub rock band! I quickly learned that if I was flamboyant and confident, that inspired confidence in promoters and venue managers.

Ice Cream gigged everywhere, from pubs and colleges to airbases. Actually, the latter were real money-makers. I booked them in through the NAAFI, the entertainment wing of the armed forces. The band always went down a storm and the soldiers really let loose on their nights off. The NAAFI officer I dealt with was big, blond Bob and I would take him to lunch, book the band into as many bases as I could and pay him a percentage of our fees from the shows. Bob didn't need much convincing to give Ice Cream shows, but the blow jobs I gave him in the bathroom after our lunches never did any harm. If rock and roll is prostitution, Ice Cream had the hardest working hooker in town!

Like big, blond Bob my bright ideas just kept coming, as I persuaded the band to work the old saying/chestnut 'I scream, you scream … ice cream!' into their live set. Whether they liked it or not, I sensed that it could be updated into a Glitterbeat chant and become a ready-made jingle for the band.

Let's not pretend otherwise: I was a total blagger. Half the time I was flying on the seat of my pants and I loved it. I'd open my gob, my spiel would spew forth and people seemed to like it. It got results. I quickly got a reputation for being 'larger than life' in every way. I was more than happy with that.

It certainly did Ice Cream no harm and they quickly became a bit of a sensation. The word of mouth spread that here was a hot act with a dynamic frontman. Original material was not emerging as thick and fast as I hoped it would, but they were skilled and clever interpreters of other artists' stuff.

When they did write original songs, they didn't suit my vision of how the band should be. Jeff came up with good songs like 'So I Can Be Strong' but its intricate muso melodies and harmonies didn't have the glam-bam appeal I wanted the group to have. Now and then I'd even get involved in the song-writing process, including penning lyrics for a tune called 'Electric Storm'.

With hindsight, the problem was that I was trying to push my artistic and commercial vision onto a group that it didn't fit. My promotional and merchandising material was still pushing the glam angle, and poor Ice Cream were left languishing in some nondescript midpoint between the Doobie Brothers and Marmalade. It was not a good place to be.

Naturally, the band didn't always like my creative input – they saw it more as interference – and Jeff particularly resented my involvement, which caused a major rift between us. Nevertheless, in July 1974 Ice Cream signed a singles deal with Fontana/Phonogram Records.

Hearing the buzz that I had painstakingly constructed around the group, the label's A&R men had checked them out. They were willing to take a chance, but only on a singles deal. The band were excited, and so was I – Fontana had been home to some of my favourite sixties artists including the Pretty Things, Scott Walker and Dave Dee, Dozy, Beaky, Mick & Tich. We also signed a publishing deal with Chrysalis.

The band had never been in a studio before. They went into Stanhope Place near Marble Arch and ripped through a scorching version of a gospel song, 'Jesus Is Just Alright With Me', which had previously been covered by the Byrds and the Doobie Brothers. It was OK, if you like that sort of thing, but I was far more excited by spotting Roy Wood, who had just formed Wizzard, tinkling at the studio piano.

John Springate came on board as Gary and Jeff knew and trusted him and he was an experienced guiding hand in the studio. Yet even with their respect for him, they mutinied when I decided their first single would be a cover of 'Shout It Out', a glam stomper that John had written for the Glitter Band.

The arguments went back and forth: Gary and Jeff protested that this was not who they were, and it wasn't the kind of music they wanted to make. But the first single was crucial for their fortunes and I was convinced that it would make a big splash with its raucous, catchy chorus. Eventually, John and I talked them into it.

We recorded it in the same studio (the baby-faced engineer was one Steve Lillywhite, who was to go on to be a legendary rock producer with the likes of U2). Neither John nor I liked what we finished up with. It just didn't have that glam feel: Norman's keys in particular sounded too much.

The next day John and I decided to re-cut the song and dragged just Jeff and Gary into Southern Music, a sixteen-track demo studio in Denmark Street, Soho's Tin Pan Alley. Unknown to the rest of the band, we wiped their band's contributions from the tape, with Jeff playing all of the parts except the drumming by the Glitter Band's Pete Phipps.

The B-side was to be 'Hold Yourself Tight', a tune that Jeff had knocked out with Gary in the Love County Music days. It was another very glittery number, a real Bolan/Bowie knock-off with lyrics like 'Maybe it's day, maybe it's night/Cross my mind like a cosmic light'. On the record it was credited as a band composition rather than to Barnes/Deans, which caused some tension in the group.

Indeed, the nearer we got to enjoying some success, the more time the group seemed to spend arguing over trifling quibbles. Our star singer Gary threw a diva strop and quit the band, complaining the gigging treadmill was tiring him out and things weren't happening fast enough. I think he wanted me to wave a magic wand and make Ice Cream superstars overnight.

Minus a singer, we staged emergency auditions at the Mecca Ballroom in Watford. I was panicking: Gary was the band's prime asset, they would be useless without him, and I had no real interest in being involved with Ice Cream without their showman. Even so, I knew I couldn't just pander to his every mood swing and hissy fit.

My fears were quickly allayed when the auditions began ... and Gary showed up! Doubtless worried about missing out on his moment in the limelight, he sat there in a pouty sulk while a few nondescript, unremarkable singers tried out. Then he agreed to come back.

It was my first major lesson in dealing with that self-centred, temperamental breed of overgrown toddler: the wannabe rock star. It was not to be my last.

When it came to the promotional material for the 'Shout It Out' single, my pop art obsessions went into overdrive. We shot press photos of the band looking a bit like glam-poppers Sailor, with Gary in a striped hat, rolled-up jeans and a neckscarf. By now, he was the only one I could convince to wear flashy clobber. The rest of them looked like off-duty farmers.

On the record sleeve, the band's name was spelt out in big, bold cartoon-style lettering as a bunch of illustrated ice-cream cones framed them. I nicked some bendy dots straight out of Lichtenstein's comic-book replicas. For the single's ad I went even further, drawing a rotund Italian ice-cream vendor with a speech bubble containing the single's title, pursued by a group of kids.

It was all meticulously conceptualised and illustrated. I felt as though the band were just my palette. Looking back, I was probably not just a control freak but also that most dangerous thing, a frustrated rock star, who knew that my bulk would never let me be a star in my own right. Was my control freakery a way of compensating? Yeah, probably!

Yet I was trying to flog a dying horse. Glam rock was on the way out even while I was obstinately clinging to it. Bolan's crown had been slipping for years and now he declared that 'glam rock was sham rock'. Bowie was setting sail for America and Philadelphia soul, while for Roxy Music feather boas and leotards were out and tuxedos and zoot suits were in. It was dying but I was in denial.

Ice Cream had the same agent as Leo Sayer and we got a support slot on his tour around the release of 'Shout It Out'. This was set to be our big breakthrough. We had already opened for Alvin Stardust, the Sweet and Capability Brown (covering one of their songs, which pissed them off). But now we had a single and were playing a full tour with a chart star, momentum was gathering and we really felt that the big time was around the corner.

Everybody was working so hard. The band slept and travelled in a three-tonne truck with their roadie. The itinerary was punishing. I pushed them to the limit. If they had a night off from the Leo Sayer shows, I booked them for another gig, sometimes hundreds of miles away.

One night on the tour we were playing Paignton before having a night off. I booked Ice Cream a gig in Middlesbrough that night and then the next night they were in Torquay and back on the Leo tour again: a 600-mile round trip! It was ruthless but paying your dues in the music business is no easy thing. I was dedicated, I had no personal life whatsoever and I expected the same level of commitment from the band.

Initially, the Sayer tour went well. Leo was an easy-going chap. His band had an amazing PA system and they let us use it. Ice Cream were good-looking, talented and ablaze with energy. People were starting to notice. The band were signing autographs for girls who couldn't stop screaming. It started looking as if Ice Cream could go all the way and be teen sensations with a heartthrob lead singer.

Then disaster struck. After the first five or six shows, we were tersely informed that we could no longer use Leo's PA. The reason was obvious when we arrived to play the theatre at the end of Hastings Pier. Parked outside was a beautiful white Daimler XJ6, regally positioned at the front of the pier. The owner was Leo's manager: Adam Faith.

Moving from centre stage as an entertainer in his own right to behind the scenes as a manager had clearly only swollen Faith's ego. He didn't want Ice Cream upstaging Leo Sayer, and even told them so directly: 'You can't be that good in front of my act.'

From Hastings on we were thus forced to play every show with just one microphone and everything unplugged. Night after night poor Leo would sit in the dressing room looking sheepish as Ice Cream trooped backstage after yet another weedy sounding set. We were learning the hard way just what a brutal world the music business can be.

Bad vibes began to set in – and, to be honest, my mind was already elsewhere. I was steadily and stealthily building a roster of talents that I was booking gigs for. After all, why waste a phone call trying to secure a gig for one band when you could promote another at the same time? My business was snowballing rapidly and I found the whole process addictive.

One band I became involved with was Burglar Bill. They were a cracking live act: a big harmony band with a versatile array of covers, like Ice Cream. One of their members, Mick Newton, had seen Ice Cream play and was impressed with the band's imagery. He said he wasn't used to seeing a band of that ilk being presented in such a high-concept way.

Burglar Bill had a big following. I checked them out at their residency at a club called the Double Six in Basildon. The sound was tapping into the same reservoir of influence as were Ice Cream: Steely Dan, the Eagles, Capability Brown. It was all defiantly un-glam, very transatlantic rock.

Nevertheless, I took them on and designed them a little cartoon logo – a burglar, unsurprisingly. Soon they were regulars on the London pub rock circuit. By now I was beginning to issue my bands with edicts and instructions: 'Facial hair is ageing, shave it off', or, 'Wear tighter clothes'. It was anything to make a band flash harder, stand out more and look sexier.

It was good that I had been slipping my fingers into a few other pies because Ice Cream were about to hit the skids. What happened next sealed their fate. They got pulled off the Leo Sayer tour and unceremoniously dumped by the record company for financial reasons that I still don't fully understand. The promotion for the single came to an abrupt halt and it vanished from the airwaves of Radio 1. They had seemed to be on the brink of success and it had been suddenly snatched away at the last minute.

Having said that, had they written eight or nine great songs it would not have been so easy for the industry to chew them up and spit them out. With hindsight, 'Shout It Out' wasn't the right song for them and I must take the blame for insisting they release it. It was a great Glitter Band song but maybe not the best showcase for Ice Cream's talents.

As ever, I had loved the 'superficial' aspects of pop music: the entertainment factor; the visuals. Music was the necessary evil I hoped the band would take care of. But Ice Cream never quite chiselled out an identity for themselves. I slopped my icing on the wrong cake. You can't turn the Doobie Brothers into Mud.

The Ice Cream fallout was bitter. They broke up in 1984 and Jeff and Sally split in the petty, acrimonious way that young lovers do. Jeff and I had been feuding for a long time by then and, truth be told, I was glad to see the back of him.

Yet even Gary and Jeff drifted apart. They had always been inseparable, in their own camp even within the group, but maybe they had spent too much time in each other's pockets. After the band imploded, the circuitry of that electric friendship blew altogether. Nothing is quite as jading to a young budding rock star as the disillusionment that comes from the industry's first swipe. They had shared a dream that was now in tatters. They could now only go their separate ways.

Jeff was incredibly proud of a Gibson Les Paul that he had customised and stripped away to natural wood just before Ice Cream finally melted. Penniless after the band split, he sold it for just £300.

Gary, Rob Norman and Steve Stroud soldiered on, forming a band called Sprinkler. After they split, Gary formed Risky Zips, the nadir of bad, bawdy seventies music taste, and went on tour with Dennis Waterman. He popped up on *New Faces* with Marti Caine, still hopeful that his big break was just around the corner. Rob and Steve joined Bucks Fizz's backing band and Steve went on to marry Cheryl Baker.

Yet Gary's story came to a tragic end. Ever since he got his first racing bike, he had always loved the thrill of tearing down the road at full throttle. He loved fast cars and frequently used to race around his local neighbourhood in them.

When he bought a gold Mercedes, it seemed a sign that maybe he was finally maturing and mellowing, but one Sunday morning in September 1986 someone offered him a test drive in a 3.5-litre Capri with a turbo, tantalising him with the promise that it was the quickest thing he would ever drive. His need for speed came racing back and he grabbed the keys.

Gary zoomed down the A20 and must have been going 80mph when he hit the big roundabout at Wrotham. The turbo kicked in on the bend and flipped the car over. It hit a tree. Gary had no seat belt on and his head hit the roll bar. There wasn't a mark on him but he died in hospital four days later at the tender age of thirty-four. A year later, his devoted dad Tom died of a broken heart.

Gary Deans was a natural star and he deserved better. I was too young (I started managing Ice Cream at just twenty-four), too easily bored and too eager to champion the next new thing to give him the guiding hand he required. I constantly needed a fresh face to champion and the shock of the new always beat the disappointment of the old.

I guess I thought that if I moved fast enough in as many directions as I could, those disappointments would never catch up with me. Well, they do. But when you are young and fuelled by mad ambition, nobody can tell you that.

Gary's death was incredibly sad and affecting. But when Ice Cream split, I was hell-bent on building an empire and I had no time to lick my wounds – or anybody else's.

7

CHUCKLE VISION

In fact, by the time that Ice Cream split, my plans for my next band to conquer the world were already well underway.

I had by now called my management company On the Corner Management. My stable of artists was growing and one band in particular were fast becoming the most likely contenders for fame and fortune. When I first met them they had the dodgy name Judy Blue Eyes, after a Crosby, Stills & Nash song.

In fact, they had had a few names. They were an Essex group who had started out as a proggy, jam-based band called Ocean (every town had a band named Ocean in those days), and then became a functions outfit called Still Water. It was clearly all about the H_2O for this lot.

The band had gone up a notch when they recruited a singer called Mal Corking from Clacton-on-Sea. Mal had put an ad in the weekly music papers, looking for a band to back him, and used the hip rock argot of the day to specify 'no breadheads'.

When Mal did an audition in one of the band's front room, they were blown away by the pint-sized cheeky chappie with the colossal pipes. He had the stature of an elf and the swagger onstage of a veritable rock god yet he was an instantly likeable character: wise-cracking, warm-hearted and utterly devoid of airs and graces. How many frontmen can you say that about?

Guitarist Jeff Carpenter, bass player Des Brewer and drummer Frog Goddard were all impressed by the little man with the big voice, and they gelled musically right away (once they ditched a keyboard player with a full-sized Hammond organ in an unwieldy Leslie cabinet). They played working men's clubs and entered a *Melody Maker* talent contest, making it to Southend Pier but no further. The name change to Judy Blue Eyes didn't really help.

They needed a dose of pizzazz and it was just around the corner. One day the band went to audition for *Opportunity Knocks* but gave up when the queue was too long. Disheartened, but determined not waste a journey up to town, Des said he had heard of a bloke called Uncle Tom (an occasional nickname of mine by then, despite my still tender years).

Des had heard that I was renowned for getting loads of gigs for relatively obscure, up and coming bands like Ice Cream. The band phoned up On the Corner Management's office, aka my mum's flat. I was out, but Mum invited them round for a cuppa. She loved them straightaway, and when I got home she was raving about this great bunch of lads who had called in, and told me that I had to go to see them play. I did – and was instantly blown away.

They were a powerhouse unit. As a live act, they took no prisoners, tearing through a mostly covers-based set with gusto. Jeff had all the makings of a guitar hero: a massive Eric Clapton-inspired sound that neatly matched Mal's lung power. Frog and Des were an ace rhythm section.

What's more, they were hard-working musicians who generally played seven or eight gigs per week. When I chatted with them, I was enamoured with their zest, eagerness and affability. I stuck them on a bill with the fast-waning Ice Cream, and as my interest in Ice Cream faded my focus on the new bunch sharpened.

Sensing that they were far more receptive to my ideas, I realised that this bunch of lads could be the putty that could be transformed into pop gold. They were malleable enough for a total makeover. At last, it was a chance to fully exercise my pop art/comic book aesthetic and vision.

We had to start with a name change. After all, they were from Essex, not bloody Laurel Canyon. They all had effervescent personalities, especially Mal, and they needed a name that reflected that. I soon came up with it.

Giggles.

They were a bit flummoxed by the new name but once they saw how fantastic it looked visually, especially when the initial G was blown up and emphasised, they quickly came around.

CHAPTER 7

It looked great on posters and it sounded bubbly when you said it.

Giggles!

It helped that they all thought I was hilarious. 'You need to be gay and Jewish to make it in this manager business, and I'm playing both cards!' I used to tell them. They seemed to have no problem with my sexuality, and neither knew nor cared that I wasn't really Jewish.

For me, Giggles were natural entertainers and I envisaged them as more than just a pop group. They could be a whole entertainment package, like a British version of the Monkees! They could be a multi-faceted venture with a movie, TV show and comic book.

In truth, I was thinking outside of the box partly to sell them, partly for my own amusement and partly because the designer in me couldn't handle just looking after another bunch of musicians who trundled on and off stage every night.

It was all about packaging, framing and placing. That Bowie mantra kept coming back to me: go out and 'be a colour TV'. Giggles had a real gang mentality and that could be a marketing man's wet dream. Only I didn't need a marketing man, I could devise the whole thing myself. I just needed a gullible record company to help me fund my grand schemes.

In the meantime, Giggles kept gigging. Their set was a mixed bag of current glam, bubblegum hits and edgier stuff: they would throw in 'Liar' by Argent to flex their hard-rock muscle. But my favourite part of the set was their sixties soul and Motown covers, hurled out with the high-octane, amphetamine-fuelled frenzy of the Who in their prime. Tracks like 'Heatwave', 'Needle In A Haystack' and 'Dancing In The Street' left me all misty-eyed and remembering my youth in Soho with Melvin. There was a healthy dose of old-school, no-nonsense rock and roll: 'Johnny B. Goode', 'C'mon Everybody', 'Great Balls Of Fire' and 'Summertime Blues', sometimes squashed into a medley. A canny reviewer nailed it: they were 'not virtuosos, but entertainers'.

Giggles toured the usual pub rock circuit, basically rhythm and booze with snacks and strippers thrown in. At the Montague Arms in New Cross they performed with 'showgirls' who draped their bras and straps all over a beetroot-red Mal, who valiantly soldiered on while the punters leered. One dancer couldn't get her knickers off her high heels. Classy stuff. It was a rough old pub. Jim Davidson was the resident comic there, more often than not off his head on speed. He gave us his seal of approval in a radio interview.

People began to notice Giggles. They re-entered the *Melody Maker* talent contest and got through to the final at the Roundhouse. The paper's headline on the story inspired Jeff to write an original song, 'Giggle Wiggle'. To say its titular rhyme made it an identical twin to Donovan's 'Mellow Yellow' might be a bit too generous. But nobody could deny that Giggles were a good time.

Fired up, I began inundating the record companies and music press with my customary paraphernalia. The Tom Watkins hype machine fired into life. I informed the world that Mal Corking was 'a born star with a voice you haven't heard before'; Jeff Carpenter was 'destined to become one of the finest guitarists of the pop scene'; Des Brewer was 'going to break a million hearts'; Frog Goddard was the 'best drummer around'. I assured everyone, everywhere that 'Giggles are heading for the big time'.

We worked our way through a few images that never stuck. One day Giggles were draped in hippy-meets-glam-chiffon. The next they were in stripy hats sharpened with some *Clockwork Orange* psycho droog-style ultra-violence.

But my grand plan for Giggles was that they would be a comic-strip combo who exploited their gang vibe with posters and adverts based on the world of Marvel and DC comics. It would give the band a striking, heroic identity to set them apart from all the others. Boys would respond to the action-packed iconography. We could release cartoons rather than the standard boring press release, thus creating a sense of excitement. *Beano*-style promo material could weave a narrative and back story around the band, intriguing punters and pundits alike.

I thought the *Beano*-style imagery would endear them to people, but in no time it was all about Marvel. The Silver Surfer and Thor crept into band posters and adverts. An early Giggles poster was a Biba-style drawing of a Greta Garbo-like starlet: her corkscrew hair spelt out the band's name.

The band's comic-strip image had to be as visible onstage as it was in the promotional material: more so. Their outrageous stage clothes got more and more wild. I dressed Mal in Ziggy-style red and green wrestling boots, tights and skin-tight jeans cut off into daisy dukes. I even made him squeeze into a Freddie

Mercury-style harlequin ensemble that looked like a second skin. Jeff was decked out in fake snakeskin. A friend of mine stitched together a diamond-studded salad jacket: gastro-glam insanity! Jeans came with a snake entwined around the leg to the crotch. Really, I treated Giggles as the ultimate rock-group/art-school project, a living collage. And, unlike Ice Cream, they went along with it.

One night they played at the Kensington in Earls Court. It was pretty much the local of an EMI press officer called John Bagnall, who lived a few minutes' walk away. He happened to drop in and saw a prime Giggles set that mixed their own songs (Jeff had written a few by now) with puckish covers of chart hits.

As is usual for record label people, John was both enthused and sceptical. He realised Giggles were very pop-influenced, but felt that to be a hindrance rather than a selling point. He felt it might make it hard for them to build the vital 'musical credibility'.

Nevertheless, Giggles' own musicianship, personality and humour charmed Bagnall. He praised their 'zany' appeal, loved the elements of humour that reminded him of the Bonzo Dog Doo Dah Band and found them 'fresh and funny'. He declared himself equally impressed with my 'passion, self-belief, imagination and dedication'.

After the gig he briefly chatted with the band and told them that he would recommend the A&R men at EMI check them out. As he left, the lads rolled their eyes incredulously, scoffing that he was most likely the label's tea boy with delusions of grandeur.

They ate their words when the label signed them to a singles deal in a matter of days.

EMI's offices were in Manchester Square, north of Oxford Street, and immediately you got the sense that you were dealing with major players. After Giggles signed their deal I became a permanent fixture in the building, pleading, cajoling, flattering and ranting to try to get my vision across.

This didn't go down that well. I was banging my fist on desks trying to get advertising and marketing campaigns signed off, and I felt like I was banging my head against walls. There was a definite air of snobbery around the label and I was on the receiving end.

I got the distinct impression that I wasn't deemed the coolest cat in the alley or the hippest manager on the block. I was loud and overweight, I dressed in denim and I drove a VW Beetle striped like a Neapolitan ice cream. It hardly induced the EMI establishment to smile upon me.

What was more, for EMI it was 'album acts' like Pink Floyd and Queen who were the company geese laying the golden eggs. Giggles were perceived as just a slightly oddball singles band: a novelty. Nevertheless, the band and I were really excited to be signed to them. Initially they seemed lively, professional and dynamic.

Soon I was spending half of my life there (not that the label bosses were always that happy about that). My burgeoning reputation may also have begun to go to my head. One day I got out of a cab in Manchester Square and saw a swarm of female pop fans outside the building. One of the star-seeking missiles ran over.

'Can I have your autograph?' she asked excitedly.

'Sure,' I replied. I was baffled, but glad to have a fan of my own. Well, I suppose it was only a matter of time …

'I love your record, "Happy To Be On An Island In The Sun,"' she went on. 'It's knockout!'

My heart sank. My new disciple thought I was Greek man-mountain Demis Roussos, a man who was even fuller figured than me! But I signed the autograph as Demis. She didn't know the difference, and far be it for me to shatter the dreams of an eager fan.

EMI's Christmas parties were legendary. Even the doormen got drunk. Motormouth publicist Eric Hall was ever-present, puffing on a cigar, requesting a limo and extolling the virtues of the next 'monster' hit, usually by his beloved Queen. There again, I remember him declaring that 'Bohemian Rhapsody' would be an utter flop before it came out.

EMI indulged Giggles at first … to a point. John Bagnall put my idea into practice, writing their first promotional label biography as a comic-strip script which EMI got illustrated and printed. It had a strong streak of tongue-in-cheek humour and was all about the hopes and dreams of a struggling rock band, from the dole queue to their first meeting with a huge, shadowy Svengali (guess who, eh, readers?). They even made up some promotional t-shirts. It may not sound much, but it was more than EMI usually did for bands who were on singles rather than album deals.

The merchandising side of things might have been going OK, but the actual record-making was rather more vexing.

We went into the studio to cut proposed debut single 'Giggle Wiggle' with future production legend Mutt Lange. It was a pure glam rock stomper, right down its 'Hey, hey!' chant and big bawdy beat. Yet it was light on musical substance, nobody felt it really represented the band and it got shelved.

Indeed, from that very first session the band struggled to master the transition from stage to studio. They never fully captured the incendiary, raucous magic of the live sets. Every time they were in the studio I'd be with them, twitchy and chewing on a blanket to relieve my tension like Linus in the *Charlie Brown* cartoons. This odd personal habit flummoxed Giggles, who threatened to cut up its patchwork squares and sell them back to me.

The problem was that Giggles were a hard-rocking group with a bubblegum twist. Few bands carry this off: the Sweet did, but Giggles never had the calibre of material that Chinn and Chapman gave the Sweet. And, like Ice Cream, they never fully developed their own songwriting. On vinyl they forever languished between candy pop and hard rock.

Eventually an American songwriter and producer named Kenny Laguna came up with the goods for Giggles' debut 45. He came to them fresh from working with David Essex on 'Stardust'. Kenny gave the band his own 'Maria (The Enchilada Song)' and they backed it with Jeff's boogie rocker, the unashamedly derivative 'Your Mother Wouldn't Like It'.

Kenny already had a lot of 'Maria' down on tape and the guys laid their parts over his pre-existing backing track at an all-night session in Olympic Studios in Barnes. I loved it and thought it was going straight to the top of the hit parade. From its vintage 'Leader Of The Pack' street-corner handclapping intro to its doo-wop harmonies, 'Maria' was an irresistible confection, a perfect mix of snot-nosed attitude and candy retro American pop.

It fell victim to an internal reshuffle in EMI's A&R department that left us feeling distinctly short-changed. When it came out in September 1974, 'Maria' began by selling 400 copies a day, which meant that with a bit of radio play it could easily have become what Eric Hall would have called a 'monster'. However, EMI, in their wisdom, pulled it.

The second single the following April didn't fare any better. 'Glad To Be Alive' was a lightweight number penned by Brian Wade (who was to go on to work on kids TV show *The Munch Bunch*). Still, I liked it and it featured a great vocal – part Rod Stewart, part Paul McCartney – from Mal.

A version of 'Wouldn't It Be Loverly?' from *My Fair Lady* ended up on the cutting-room floor. Another unreleased song, 'I Want A Girl Right Out Of This World', featured a blazing guitar solo from Jeff, a real one-take wonder, only for the engineer to confess that he had forgotten to press the 'Record' button.

Yes, Giggles seemed jinxed in the studio. But they were still wowing gig audiences ... and they were about to take an old teenage haunt of mine by storm.

8

THE FILTH AND THE FUNNY

Giggles' big break came when I secured them a gig at the Marquee, my old stomping ground with Melvin. A bloke called Ulrik Prutz was part of the management team and was the go-to guy if you wanted to get your act a show there. I hassled him to book Giggles. He refused. I persisted. Ulrik remained doubtful that they were right for the place.

Divine intervention arrived when a band pulled out, leaving a gap in the bill on 8 November 1975, a Saturday night. Ulrik grudgingly let Giggles fill the slot. They were on top form, adrenalised and sharper around the edges than ever. The crowd went mad.

Ulrik was convinced and gave them a residency. It was to last nearly two years, the longest in the Marquee's history. By May

1976 they were playing every Sunday, a fact that I trumpeted in ads in *NME, Melody Maker, Sounds* and *Record Mirror*.

There was real kudos in playing the Marquee and word soon spread that Giggles' gigs were seriously hot. We would turn up in the early afternoons to load our gear in and find people already queuing up to see them. It swelled to a real Who-style frenzy. One reviewer even noted how girls were screaming at Giggles, a noise rarely heard in the Marquee.

It built and built. Audiences started showing up in the band's red, white and green colour scheme that I had rehashed from Love County Music. I even remember getting a teddy with a scarf knitted in these colours. On the Tube after gigs, there would be crowds in Giggles t-shirts.

I was convinced the band were heading for the top and the music press agreed, declaring Mal 'a star in the making'. And yet EMI's investment in the band was lacklustre to say the least. They had only released two flop singles in two years. There was a yawning chasm between the buzz they were generating at gigs and the pitiful state of their discography.

Still, the Marquee residency opened up a whole slew of venues that would have been otherwise closed. Giggles also got a support slot with the Sweet. On the road, they were a bit stand-offish. Well, Andy Scott and Steve Priest were friendly enough, but singer Brian Connolly was totally aloof.

There again, they had been through the wringer. Connolly had been beaten up on Staines High Street, an assault that led to treatment for his throat by Harley Street specialists. They were used to aggro – they wrote 'Ballroom Blitz' after they were bottled off stage for wearing their glam clobber.

At Salford University they never even showed up and Giggles braved the gig alone.

There again, that kind of iconoclastic confrontation would soon be ubiquitous in London. The same month that Giggles began their fruitful tenure at the Marquee, a band called the Sex Pistols also played their first show ...

Giggles relationship with punk rock was complex and so was my attitude towards it. I was fascinated by it and kicked myself that I hadn't capitalised on it. There was incredible energy around the bands and the fashions were a breath of fresh air. It was what pop and rock need every few years – a kick up the arse.

Even so, I wanted entertainment and fun and the whole thing just seemed too angry, hateful and *political* for me. Furthermore, I could see with the Pistols that all that 'anarchy' and 'nihilism' was being masterminded very expertly and calculatedly by Malcolm McLaren.

For all of Johnny Rotten's lyrical assaults on the establishment, it seemed to me the Pistols were a boy band, plucked, preened and positioned for pop infamy by their Svengali manager. I thought it was a bit of a hoax and I'm glad now that I didn't jump on the bandwagon too much.

Obviously Giggles heard about the violent hysteria occurring at punk gigs. Punters would come and tell them about the gobbing and bottle-throwing going on at the 100 Club. They thought it sounded horrible. Always genial and chatting to fans, Giggles felt alienated by punk. They couldn't understand how a group like the Sex Pistols could ever make it. How wrong they were.

(Interestingly, years later, one of Giggles ran into Gary Numan at Shepperton Studios. Numan opened a briefcase to reveal a picture of himself outside the Marquee waiting to see a 1975 Giggles show. Numan was a post-punk pop star, far more enamoured with Giggles' pre-punk showbiz than punk's rejection of it.)

Giggles had other setbacks. Frog Goddard abruptly left the group in late 1975. John Glasgow was brought in and briefly manned the drum kit but his blues-style playing lacked punch. In early 1976 he gave way to Paul Simmons, who was soon nicknamed Mad Simm. Paul wanted to be a rock star like the rest of the band. He quickly fitted in.

Paul had previously been in Sisters, an oddball glam rock act that had managed to get signed to Bell and Warners. They were devised as a drag band, an English analogue to New York Dolls and Alice Cooper. Jeff Banks had dressed them in his latest collection. Sadly, they never quite took off.

Paul wasn't the band's first choice at the audition but I talked them round to him. He was a very solid drummer and easy on the eye. Eric Hall promised to get Giggles on *Top of the Pops* if he could 'borrow' Paul temporarily. I don't think Eric had Paul's prowess behind a drum kit in mind. Paul politely declined.

Paul also had a great Bowie story. He had once visited his sprawling Haddon Hall mansion in Beckenham to help a friend return some amps. Bowie's mum Peggy gave them cucumber sandwiches while her lad, with his Ziggy mop of hair, held up a map and pointed out the places he was about to play in America. Paul was most impressed that they had a colour TV: the news reports from Vietnam looked so vivid.

When Paul joined Giggles they got a new lease of life. From Jersey to Blackpool and back to the Marquee, they did 135 gigs in a matter of five months. The college and university circuits couldn't get enough of them. They continued to be a major draw at colleges and always received warm letters of thanks from the student union officers.

This was all very well but they were still languishing in no man's land with no chart hits. As ever, I compensated for their crap discography by unleashing the full Tom Watkins hyperbole, complete with zany Slade-style misspellings and emphatic bursts into capital letters. It went like this:

The act, like many of their contemporaries, come from Essex. They play a brand of music that carefully avoids any form of musical classification – other than that of '76 and beyond. And – as well as their own excellent material – Giggles are somewhat renowned for their interpretation of standards.

Jeff Carpenter could well become one of Britain's Guitar Greats. An important member of the band, his image as he struts around the stage is one of DISDAIN. Mal Corking, Giggles' vocalist, represents a truly electrifying stage presence which is a forceful front for the band's powerhouse that LOOMS out of the spotlights. Des Brewer on bass and Paul Simmons at 'the kit' – an outrageous rhythm section who, with their stage theatrics, highlight the band's obsession with MARVEL COMIX.

Giggles have already left their mark when they toured Britain with the Sweet, and now they're back to the college and DOWN-TO-EARTH club circuits were they'll turn an evening out (or a quiet drink?) into a truly 'ROCK'-ETING experience.

Funny name, Giggles, rolls off the tongue, and it's easy to remember. A pleasant … nice little word, fun packed with laughs! But a comedy band they're NOT! Giggles spells ACTION!!!

Promotional material showed Marvel's Thor throwing his hammer, while a caption asked student union officers: 'Are your balls together or do they sag?' We shot a great press photo of the band flicking through comics with another comic strip as a backdrop. It was real cool stuff, I thought.

The shows also got more playful, too. A cover of Cher's 'Bang Bang' ended with Mal trying to strangle Jeff, which at times I thought was not a bad idea. At the song's final drumbeat, Paul would stand up from his kit and shoot Mal with a fake starting pistol. It was great knockabout stuff.

For Giggles' next single I played a more active role in the production, determined to get them that elusive hit. John Springate suggested 'Just Another Saturday Night', a track by an obscure Canadian glam band called Moonquake. Phil Lynott was often propping up the bar at our Marquee gigs and when I first heard the song it made me think of Thin Lizzy. Its tough-guy sneer sounded quite punky. *This might be the one*, I thought.

We cut it at Mayfair Studios, above a chemist's shop in South Molton Street. The Bay City Rollers had recorded there. The sessions were a hoot and we added a whole host of sound effects, including smashing bottles. Mal ran down the fire escape for dramatic footstep noises and even my trusty stripy Beetle worked its way in, with a mic by its exhaust pipe.

The B-side was a Giggles original, 'Bazooka', a jazzy striptease of a song full of naughty phallic wordplay. It was a definite leap for their songwriting and became a great live staple, when Mal would come out in a soiled mac and do a 'dirty old man' routine. I thought it was a great two sides of vinyl – probably the only platter that ever caught what an ace band Giggles were.

When it came out in August 1976 the reviews were promising. *Sounds* foresaw a bright future ahead for the band and gave them the 'star single' accolade, albeit a little grudgingly. It pointed out the tough lyrics about 'switchblades, backstreets, bars and brawls' and praised Jeff's guitar that impersonated a police siren and the song's 'lewd ideas and double entendres'.

Unfortunately, the powers that be at Radio 1 listened closely to the words, too, and the references to switchblades got it banned. It was another year, another flop single.

We gave a grim laugh in August 1976 when a gig-listing ad in the *Daily Mirror* plugged 'Rolling Stones in Knebworth, Giggles in Wigan and AC/DC in Brighton'. We would love to have been in such exalted company, but we felt a long way away.

By now, my stepbrother Andy Mason was a Giggles roadie and at my suggestion had taken to squeezing himself into a Spiderman costume and invading the stage. He would sweep the floor and throw out Bazooka chewing gum as they played 'Bazooka'. The crowds loved it and it became a visual gimmick. Soon Spiderman was getting billed as a special guest for his impromptu walk-ons.

Andy was a real tough nut. When he drove the band in the van for long stretches he would singe himself with a lighter to stay awake. One night he was zipped up into the Spiderman outfit so tightly that the zip dug into his flesh. He was in pure agony as he walked onto the stage yet like a real pro (or psycho) he carried on regardless.

We loaned the outfit from Marvel Comics UK who normally used it for PAs in shopping centre appearances to promote Spiderman. They complained that the suit was always returned filthy or in a state of disrepair and wrote reproachful letters threatening to blacklist Giggles.

The person behind these indignant letters was one Neil Tennant – the future Pet Shop Boy.

Neil was a history graduate who had moved down to London from Newcastle. After his degree he had become an editor for Marvel Comics UK, editing American copy for a British audience and covering up cleavages for the younger-than-the-US UK readership. Crucially, he also occasionally interviewed pop stars, his real passion.

I met Neil when I had to go into Marvel after he started writing to me about the Spiderman costume. It was a scruffy, cramped office and Neil was quite snooty and very earnest about comics … and about the costume. He complained it was snagged and said that as there was no spare, we couldn't borrow it all the time. I told him Giggles were great publicity for Spiderman and for Marvel.

Neil checked out Giggles but was far keener on the Sex Pistols at the Nashville. Even then, his tastes were impeccably 'correct'. Neil knew punk was the right thing to like at the time, but if you ask me he really wanted to star in a Gilbert & Sullivan operetta.

Despite this, I soon developed a grudging mutual admiration with this bespectacled, bookish character. I liked his eloquence and intellect, his dry wit and encyclopaedic knowledge. He knew that I was a hustler par excellence.

Yet at this time, when as far as I was concerned he was just the costume bloke at Marvel, he kept his musical ambitions very quiet. I had no idea that he was already composing songs and had failed an audition for Jonathan King. He seemed more likely a bank clerk ... or a monk.

Had I mentioned it to him – which I didn't – Neil would doubtless have recoiled in horror from my latest business enterprise: the Radio 1 DJ Package Deal.

Working in tandem with a company in Tunbridge Wells known as the Paradise Agency, I started selling Giggles and occasionally my other acts as part of a 'package deal' with a current Radio 1 star. The band would come out and warm up the crowd up and then a DJ would do a PA, sometimes spinning the latest hits, sometimes acting as master of ceremonies, cracking jokes and generally 'entertaining' in that quintessentially naff seventies British way. We even paid a streaker to run across the stage naked.

The venues could choose a DJ, a band, or both, with varying prices according to the package. It was tacky as hell but it was lucrative and I ended up charging fees in all directions. Nice!

I remember that Tony Blackburn charged a higher fee than the others. His jokes were abysmal. He would tell the crowd that if anyone wanted to swear at him, they should form an orderly queue. Once he caught a glimpse of Andy in his Spiderman outfit backstage and it freaked him out.

The DJs were the main attraction. I would book Kid Jensen, Annie Nightingale, my personal favourite, Paul Burnett, and Peter Powell. One straight DJ asked my sister for her phone number. In no mood to oblige and feeling contrary, she suggested he acquired mine ....

Some of the bands I stuck on these roadshows were atrocious. One band called Supercharge was fronted by a bald bloke who performed at an RAF base in a figure-hugging body suit that was part wrestling singlet and part ballerina tutu. I wonder whatever happened to him.

Once we broke down in Norfolk after a gig and the AA had to come to the rescue. When they towed our van away, a massive press stand that I had made, with a collage of Giggles' comic book paraphernalia, press cuttings and photos, was left standing in the road. Apparently it was there for months.

Giggles' make or break next single, 'Gone Away', was to be produced by Norman 'Hurricane' Smith, the famous Beatles engineer, Pink Floyd producer and occasional pop star. Jeff had written the number, which I thought had all the hallmarks of a hit. It was gorgeous, a big late fifties-style Roy Orbison-meets-Del Shannon puller of heartstrings. It needed a suitably exquisite production and I cajoled EMI to draft in Norman Smith.

Giggles spent a week with him at the legendary Abbey Road Studios. They were in studio two, full of memories of the Beatles. Bags of seaweed down the walls deadened any echo, while red-painted fluorescent strips created atmosphere.

Norman wanted to put a grand synth solo on the song, so he phoned up and got a massive Moog delivered. Nobody could make it work. Eventually an engineer somehow fixed it with a toilet roll. Giggles spent most of the week in the studio pissed.

Everyone who heard 'Gone Away' thought it was amazing. It was instantly familiar … and there was a good reason for that. At the very end of the session, just as they had nailed it, a passing engineer strolled in and breezily said, 'Sloop John B.'

He was right. It was so obvious that we had all missed it, but John had essentially rewritten the Beach Boys classic. George Harrison's legal copyright problems with 'My Sweet Lord' and its resemblance to the Chiffons' 'He's So Fine' immediately crossed our minds, and that was that. 'Gone Away' went away on the shelf – forever.

There were other botched attempts to record Giggles. EMI's Peter Ridley had done a stellar job of producing the banned 'Just Another Saturday Night' so I entrusted him to set up a mobile recording studio to record the band.

As Giggles were such a cracking live unit, we thought maybe the best way to record them was to bring the studio to the show. Mal hated the studio and always felt better on stage. We took Peter Ridley's equipment down to the Marquee but the mics were badly positioned and the technicians kept disrupting the flow of the show. The tapes were put in a van and were never heard again.

Meanwhile, Kenny Laguna had re-entered the picture. He offered the band a great new song cashing in on the skateboarding craze, 'Street Dancer'. It was that perfect Giggles mix of pop appeal and rock attack and sounded like a Springsteen song that threatened to turn into ABBA's 'Does Your Mother Know' at any point. We put it out. It was yet another flop.

As time went by, EMI seemed to do nothing to help Giggles' cause. My relations with the label grew increasingly strained and at the end of 1976 I sent them a letter outlining my beefs:

tom watkins

copies:-
Nick
Peter
Brian
Mike
RAK.
Kenny.

9th.December,1976.

Ref: As Ever.. GIGGLES.. the continuing saga.

Dear Nick,

I am afraid to say its blow up time again. As you were aware Kenny Laguna met Mike Thorn on thursday morning for an introductory chat and to play some of Kenny's american material., result-ZERO! Nick, I have three burnin' questions: 1. Why does everybody in the A+R department have this THING about Kenny- you are fully aware I'm sure of his recent track record ? 2. Why is there not, in Peter Ridley's future absence, any one person that the band or even myself can identify with as to the future direction of Giggles as a recording act. 3. If we have found an excellent producer (no doubt in our minds) and have found a hit single (four months in the finding) 100% backed by our publishers RAK, why the hell can't we get something together??

We are simply procrastinating. We have a single that has support from EMI staff/Management/Publishers/Band and fans, we have a strong imaginative producer again firmly backed by various other hit acts, simply bustin' a gut to work with the band. And what are you doing-NOTHING. We are being pressured to come-up with product by guys around the corner and yet still we find ourselves pleading for action.

Yet again we find ourselves taking a back seat in EMI politics and current happenings, yet again we are wasting the current wave of press success and touring situations by not having product on the market. Yet again we have no idea what you want us to do in the way of promoting/helping ourselves to hit material. Another question... Why the hell did you sign us for another year and advance us more money if you had no clear direction of our future. The band are enjoying every other kind of success they welcome the attention they have received from Peter,Lynn,Brian,Eric,Su,Diane but how about the all important A+R department Nick, when are they going to stop making pathetic excuses and showing really dumb prejudices towards'nouveau'ideas now forth-coming from a previously silent band. I have never heard the band, in the three years of management, moan and complain'bout giving up and going away and being bank managers and brain surgeons again.... You Guy's are breaking their Spirits.. ; and we are fucked off... (PUNK SWEAR WORDS).....

MANAGEMENT:DESIGN CONSULTANT
74a Westcombe Hill.Blackheath.London.SE.17 7LX.telephone 01.858 7439.

Reviewing a Giggles gig in Bristol at the end of the year, the *NME* also bemoaned the band's fate. Surely, the reporter sagely suggested, a tiny bit of the income that EMI had earned from Queen's *A Night At The Opera* would pay for a better PA for Giggles? The band said the crowd at that gig reminded them of Madame Tussauds. They even renamed one of their songs 'Friday Night At The Morgue'.

EMI were indeed still lavishing all their money on 'album' acts rather than poppy bands on singles deals such as Giggles. Even so, in honesty part of the problem lay with the band. They were cracking entertainers but their sound never found an identity as strong as the comic-book image. And, deep down, I was losing interest.

Giggles even tried to embrace punk. The results were predictably awkward. Southern TV in Southampton wanted to cover the 'punk rock phenomenon' and asked Giggles to take part. As they played, a young Siouxsie Sioux and Steve Severin, who were also on the show, pogoed.

Siouxsie flashed her boobs and ordered her dessert before her lunch in the canteen. She was very cool. She was doing a lot of telly at the time. Shortly after our low-profile show, she appeared behind the Sex Pistols when they abused Bill Grundy in the teatime TV incident that made punk rockers Public Enemy Number One.

In truth, for us it was all a half-hearted, desperate attempt to jump on a bandwagon. Mike Thorne, the A&R man who had signed the Pistols to EMI, had seen Giggles at the Marquee and the Pistols at the 100 Club and said that the two bands were equally vital and energetic. Yet when we photographed

Giggles against a wall at the Barbican then superimposed punk-style graffiti on the picture (including the band's war cry: 'Raarrggh!'), it looked false and contrived.

A few months later, they played Durham University. It was officially the worst gig ever. The punky crowd drenched Giggles in gob and lager and threw glasses at them. Paul jumped into the crowd and punched someone. It turned out to be a student union officer with their pay. After the gig, the band barricaded themselves backstage with a crate of Newcastle Brown Ale and a bottle of tequila.

When they played Northern Ireland they got the third degree at Belfast docks. The customs men suspected their supplies of tea and sugar contained drugs. Thankfully they didn't.

When we drove down Belfast's Falls Road, the sight of bombed-out telephone boxes in a sub-zero climate was chilling indeed. Everything about the Irish tour was eerie and unsettling. During a long drive between gigs, we encountered uniformed Scottish soldiers in a remote spot. They stopped and searched us, took a couple of beers from our stash and let us go.

We turned up at a hotel and had to bang on the bullet-proof window and promise the staff we were booked there before they would let us in. Rocks strewn across the road prevented cars from parking. After we set up at one venue, British soldiers came bounding up to the stage and told us we couldn't play there. The gig was moved to the safer side of town, inside the 'security ring'.

The tension was unbelievable. One night a guy came into the dressing room in a wheelchair. His kneecaps had been drilled. The IRA had discovered he was selling dope, which they saw as poisoning the bodies and minds of their young potential recruits. Grim.

The band tempted fate on that brief tour. During the rock and roll medley section of the set, they asked the crowd to chant along to 'One for the money, two for the show'. Afterwards, Des told the audience he was surprised they could count as people generally thought that the Irish couldn't. Surprisingly, he didn't get a deserved kicking.

One night, reckless as rock musicians always are, they drove along smoking joints, drinking and throwing the empty beer bottles into the ditch. Then they realised they were being followed by another vehicle. A uniformed man stopped them and issued a surprisingly lenient warning: 'I don't mind you drinking and driving and smoking spliff but please don't throw the bottles out the window!'

I phoned up *Melody Maker*, feeling the anecdote was perfect for their gossip column. The editors didn't believe me.

Somehow, Giggles made it back to England all in one piece. Yet very soon the band would be falling apart.

9

THE GRAND OL' OBIE

In the summer of 1977, Britain seemed obsessed by the Queen's Silver Jubilee. Opportunistic as ever, I wanted to cash in and swiftly organised the 'Jubilee Jump Roadshow'.

It might sound patriotic, but it was basically another of my dodgy package deals, with Giggles and the DJs this time joined by my latest discovery, Easy, who had been supporting Giggles at the Marquee. In line with the mood of patriotic fervour, I designed a logo of the Queen and Prince Philip having a little dance.

My bash was a lot less negative than the Sex Pistols and Malcolm McLaren's boat trip down the Thames that was meant to show their contempt for royalty. There again, it would be a stretch to say that I was pro-monarchy.

It was all about the moolah. Money was my ruler!

CHAPTER 9

I had liked the look of Easy supporting Giggles and soon took on their management. They were a slick, close-harmony group from Romford in Essex with a frontman called Colin Campsie, who oozed not just star power but musical confidence, and a guitarist called Rob Green who was just as proficient musically, and super-sexy to boot.

I took advantage of Rob's sex appeal at once and squeezed him into the tightest jeans I could muster. He could be a moody bastard right from the off, but the songs that the pair were writing sounded destined for the charts to me.

The bassist, Jerry, was a lovely bloke but not rock star material and I made a mental note that he had to go. We advertised for a drummer in *Melody Maker* and got a flashy, ambidextrous seventeen-year-old player called Colin Woolway. We gave him the job on the spot and dubbed him Junior to avoid confusing him with Colin Campsie. My sister fancied him.

After the Jubilee Jump Tour, I set about overhauling Easy. As usual, the first thing to go was the name. I wanted something that reflected their classy, sophisticated sound, and inspiration came to me when I was watching a 1932 Greta Garbo movie, the one in which she says, 'I vant to be alone.'

The film was called *Grand Hotel* and I decided that this would also be Easy's new name. They acquiesced easily enough. It was also time to lose sweet but unassuming bassist Jerry, and we drafted in a guy named George Macfarlane.

George had been in Sisters with Paul Simmons from Giggles but had more recently unwittingly gone for a far more heavyweight role. He had been called for an audition for an unnamed band and arrived to find Everests of Marshall amps everywhere. The band was AC/DC! George did well and just missed out to the guy who got the gig, Cliff Williams.

Their loss was our gain. Colin Campsie bonded with George from the second they met and the pair quickly began writing together and built up an almost telepathic musical bond. Both favoured soulful, funky music and were fans of Hall & Oates, Todd Rundgren, Earth Wind & Fire and the Average White Band, too. They honed a slick, Anglo-American pop-rock sound that I thought was perfect for the times. Of course, the punks hated it and called it Adult Oriented Rock.

As I worked on Grand Hotel, Giggles' star continued to wane. The failure of 'Street Dancer' had been bad news, and when an EMI A&R man told me, 'There's nothing wrong with them, there's just not much *right* with them either,' I found it hard to argue. As loveable as they were, they looked increasingly unlikely to break out of the 'cabaret' circuit and into the charts.

I tried everything I could think of, even swapping drummers and putting Paul Simmons in Grand Hotel with his old mate George, and trying Junior in Giggles. It didn't work out, musically or personality-wise, so I swapped them back. Junior was enjoying Giggles because they did more gigs and got paid more often, but he changed his mind after Jeff crashed their tour van.

Intuiting how big Grand Hotel could be, I decided to give them another string to their bow and add another member. I recruited a guitarist and songwriter named Ivan Penfold, who had been in a band called Conkers. Conkers' other members had just gone on to play in the backing band of a new starlet called Kate Bush.

Ivan was very much in the Kate mould: floaty, ethereal and hippy. His Woolwich home was pretty cosmic, which was a stark contrast to Grand Hotel's earthy Essex-boy humour. There again, the band contained very distinct, separate camps. Where Campsie and George dipped into funk and blue-eyed soul, Ivan simply wanted to be Paul McCartney.

Impressed by the long-term success of Giggles in the venue, Ulrik gave Grand Hotel a five-week residency at the Marquee beginning in September 1977 – the week before Giggles bowed out with their final Marquee show. Supporting Grand Hotel were a band with a Bowie-esque singer with a 'too fragile to fuck' beauty.

They were called Japan. Grand Hotel were not impressed with them.

One review of the Marquee shows seemed to hint that my reputation was becoming as big, if not bigger, than the acts I was looking after. 'Tom's stamp is all over this lot. He's obviously trained them well in his usual style,' the hack wrote. I felt a tingle of pride. It was true: I had never wanted to be the faceless manager, pulling the strings from behind the scenes; I wanted to be an impresario, as famous or infamous as my charges, maybe even more so.

The same reviewer saw through a song that we included in the set to try to seem relevant to the punk movement. It was called 'I Hate School' and in truth even some of the band didn't like it. It showed: the journo commented they were 'clean-cut kids who play with too much panache to be true punks'. A generally positive write-up ended with one note of caution: 'Grand Hotel are not "different" enough to be huge.'

For now, though, this was a lone voice of doubt. Everyone else's money seemed to be on Grand Hotel for future glory. I quickly set about creating a concept for the group. Their name conjured up for me mental images of bellboys, and I worked them into the group's posters and press pictures.

I even got involved in the songwriting. George Lucas's *Star Wars* had blown me away when I saw it in Leicester Square. I couldn't sleep that night, it was so exciting, and in a burst of inspiration I wrote some sci-fi lyrics for a Grand Hotel song that got called 'Light Years'.

It wasn't all roses in the camp, though. Rob and Junior were not getting on and it came to a head when Junior's overeager drumming led to a broken bass drum pedal during an important record-label showcase gig. Rob had to be restrained from physically attacking him.

Poor Junior had to go. A guy called John Dee stepped in temporarily before a real ace drummer, Graham Broad, joined the band. Record companies circled as Grand Hotel became a major draw on London's pub and club circuit.

Sadly, for Giggles the end was near. EMI dropped this hitless 'singles band' and one of my package deals with Radio 1's Peter Powell was to be their last gig. We drove back from an underwhelming show in the sticks in thick fog and silence. There wasn't much giggling.

After they split and I exited, Giggles ditched Des, renamed themselves Giants and signed to RCA. When that didn't work out, Mal carried on at the label as a solo act. He recorded a cover of Smokey Robinson's 'Tears Of A Clown' (a highlight of Giggles' live set) but the Beat, er, beat him to it and RCA's press photo got his name wrong, calling him Mal Cockran.

Oh dear. He deserved better.

Paul went off to work with Kenny Laguna for Joan Jett, which ended in acrimony over royalties (doesn't it always?). Jeff got involved with Sheena Easton's career, and last I heard he was playing ukulele in a skiffle band with original Giggles drummer Frog Goddard. Rumour has it he also wrote a book about tins.

Tins! I can't wait to read that page-turner!

Grand Hotel, however, were on the rise and soon CBS came knocking at our door. A bunch of the label's A&R men were interested. One was a guy called Jamie Rubenstein, one was Muff Winwood (brother of Steve) and one was Nicky Graham, a former musician who had played keyboards for Ziggy-era Bowie before Mike Garson.

CBS was serious big time, a colossal American record label. You felt it as soon as you walked through the door. I began negotiating a deal for Grand Hotel and using the cumulative nous I had gained from my previous dealings with EMI and Phonogram, I managed to get us a £1 million deal.

That wasn't all. I also got them to guarantee full marketing and promotional backing and hustled for royalty breaks on doing special sleeves and not losing too much money. This was a major breakthrough for Grand Hotel – and, more importantly, for me.

Record companies are political worlds and it was important to know whom to befriend. I began cultivating relationships accordingly. A&R men fed artists to all the label's disparate departments: marketing, press, radio/TV promotions. An important figure was the label manager, who set the budgets for all of these areas.

Who reigned over the label manager? The managing director – and CBS's managing director was the biggest daddy of all, the formidable and eccentric Maurice Oberstein, universally known as 'Obie'.

Obie hailed from a major American music-business dynasty. He had worked for Columbia in the US before relocating to London to start up CBS. A fully-fledged Anglophile and a maverick oddball, he would confer with his dogs over the merits of a musical act. When bored in a meeting, he would leave a sailor's cap on the table, suggesting that the executives in the room talked to that instead.

Obie was also gay and we got on right away ... well, as well as anyone could get on with a man like Obie. He had so many sides and you never knew which one you were going to get. He could be:

a) Loquacious, larger than life and brimming with generosity and largesse.
b) Hawkish and bellicose, his skeletal visage scrutinising you with utter disdain as if you had no right to be on the earth.
c) Utterly indifferent to you.

Sometimes, he could be all of those inside ten minutes.

Yet we had a good, lively relationship. My most vivid memories of Obie are all in his garden at his home. He would be sitting down, pulling weeds out of the ground and pumping me incessantly for feedback.

He was a different league from anything I was used to but it was a league that I wanted to join. He took me horse racing and fine dining. Once I tried to be flashy at a top-end restaurant and picked up the bill for the table of five. The exorbitant tab made my eyes water. Obie saw that I was struggling, puffed on his cigar and snarled, 'That'll teach you to try to be big-time, Tommy.'

I could never work out if he was being affectionate or contemptuous. But he had a point: *these things cost money.* Grand gestures need backbone. I was trying to be a big shot, but was then mortified by the bill.

The lesson I quickly learned? Don't make overblown statements that you can't back up.

Once I was going to stay at his house. Obie informed me bluntly that I couldn't sleep with him, which I found a bit presumptuous, as I wasn't remotely attracted to him. In fact, like so many gay men with too much money, power and a penchant for rough trade, Obie got into messy situations with boys off the streets. He let them in too quickly and they ripped him off.

Although from affluent stock, Obie had paid his dues and never fell back on his privileged background. He had risked being ostracised by his family over his sexuality. Maybe because I was also gay, he gave me a bit more guidance than perhaps he would have to others when it came to dealing with him from the other side of the table.

Obie said it wasn't up to me to negotiate the details of the deal and I should get a lawyer that I trusted to do it. Jim Beach at Harbottle & Lewis was suggested. Jim was so good that he became Queen's manager in 1978, around the same time that he expertly guided me through the CBS/Grand Hotel deal.

Straight, posh and never patronising, Jim became an invaluable confidant. He realised that I could become something major in the music business and was willing to nurture me. Once I called him at the swanky RAC Club when he was having lunch. I was terribly apologetic but he didn't mind; he never did.

Jim carefully guided and educated me, especially on music business contracts and legalities, which were renowned for being incredibly complex and convoluted. For worldwide deals, you had to learn the royalties in different countries. What was an advance? What was a recoupable advance? What was a reasonable deduction for packaging?

It was all a labyrinth, a minefield that Jim Beach helped me through, and I came out the other end a wiser player as a result. Grand Hotel's million-pound deal was a phenomenal triumph for a young, novice manager like me, and Jim was vital to clinching it.

The trump card was that the label wanted the band. Badly. I learned later that Obie had briefed his legal team, urging them to 'close this deal regardless of what it takes'. Grand Hotel were young, sexy and smart and CBS wanted them on their roster.

It was also in our favour that the in-house marketing team knew that the images and graphics I was coming up with would make their life easier. I was offering a complete package, a package even bigger than Rob Green's dick looked in his ultra-tight trousers. This band was pop-star material.

Around this time, another music-industry veteran that I came to know, Dick Leahy, also became a vital sounding board for me. As an A&R man and record-label managing director, Dick had worked with everyone from the Walker Brothers and Dusty Springfield to the Bay City Rollers and Donna Summer. When I met him, he was taken by my enthusiasm and, I suppose, naïvety and invited me to lunch.

He offered to take me to a charming Italian restaurant off Soho Square where he would offer me counsel. Although I was now moving in elevated circles, I had not totally shaken off my tallyman background and was still prone to bouts of vertiginous nerves and feelings of crippling personal insecurity with these sophisticated high-flyers.

Before my meal with Dick, I got shit-scared and had to phone the Truder matriarch to get her to talk me through lunch. She told me to order melon, antipasto and steak, and always to drink fizzy water (I did, and I still do). I need not have bothered: Dick could not care less what I ate or drank and was a mine of useful information.

However, the CBS deal was the most momentous from my personal point of view because it introduced me to the man who was to become my best friend: Paul Rodwell.

Paul was the label's head of business affairs, the in-house lawyer who was effectively against me. Well, I've always thrived on a bit of conflict and we hit it off immediately. Gay, as were Obie and I, Paul was as aspirational as me and had clawed his way up from a working-class background in Dover.

The three of us started socialising. Paul lived in a one-bedroom flat, a flashy bachelor pad that I coveted, in Portman

Square. Obie resided in nearby Church Road. This was the first time that I had ever really fraternised in a predominantly gay milieu. The fact that they were also such major music-business players made the combination heady and irresistible.

I took to Paul Rodwell instantly. He had all the qualities I desired and had tirelessly worked his way from CBS legal assistant to running the entire legal department. He was equally impressed with my efficiency and cut-throat tactics, and told me that I should be on the other, record-company side of the table the next time I came to negotiate a deal.

Stylish, dapper and driven, Paul was a tall, elegant gentleman but also an outrageous queen. We shared a sense of humour that had us giggling like schoolkids from day one. We began travelling extensively together, sharing suites or even beds; our bond was never sexual although neither of us was in a long-term relationship.

We quickly built a friendship on that most sturdy of foundations: trust. It's a rare thing in the industry to trust someone implicitly and remain steadfast and loyal to each other even when our business affairs conflicted. Paul's friendship was to take me to new places.

We were the gay mafia. Obie, Paul and I had comparable goals and interests, chiefly the pursuit of nice things at all costs. The help and guidance I got from those two, Jim Beach and Dick Leahy, at the end of the seventies was my apprenticeship – and it undoubtedly paved the way for what I would become in the eighties and beyond.

10

THE LOVE I LOST

Grand Hotel had got our deal with CBS. Now we had to make an album.

Before beginning work on the record proper, the band had cut some demos with Nicky Graham at Whitfield Street Studios. (One session had involved a troupe of strippers, one of whom gave someone in the studio a blow job as the musical parts were being laid down. Or so I was told: I wasn't there.)

However, the album was to be produced by Rhett Davies, who had engineered the first Dire Straits album.

We made the album that was to become *Do Not Disturb* at Basing Street Studios in Notting Hill. Back then this was still a dodgy area and potentially a very dangerous place. The studio had an in-house chef, Lucky Gordon, whose main function was actually to keep the peace and mediate with the local

Yardies. Lucky once told the band that he had got involved in kidnapping Christine Keeler during the Profumo scandal. Sounds like a right old load of bollocks to me …

While we were there, Bob Marley was cutting an album in the studio next door, invisible in a haze of ganja smoke. It was a great studio, but I just stood fretfully behind the mixing desk, chewing my blanket, taking notes and hoping the album would come out OK.

It was certainly very bass-heavy. George had a habit of sneaking behind the mixing desk whenever Davies turned his back and mischievously cranking up the bass parts on the faders. Davies was a great producer, but at that early stage he lacked the authority to harness the band's talents and tangents.

It also became clear that there were too many cooks in Grand Hotel's kitchen. The band had lots of ideas and energy and everyone wanted to take a turn to play a synthesiser, especially their new toy of a £3,000 Prophet 5.

Inevitably, friction developed. Ivan Penfold's Beatles-like songwriting was becoming too dominant in George and Colin's minds. They preferred their own, soulful stuff. Graham Broad's virtuoso drumming was also at odds with the danceable groove George and Colin were hankering after.

But mostly everyone was increasingly unhappy with Rob Green's moods. He was so sullen that even the studio staff complained when he was having an off day. At an emergency meeting called at Watkins HQ, aka my mum's flat, the band voted him out. Danny McIntosh came in to replace him on guitar. Suddenly, I realised that Grand Hotel wasn't such a sure thing after all.

To be fair to Rob Green, it probably wasn't all his fault. He just was not gelling with the rest of the band. The internal dynamics of any group are always precarious. The pressures of the business, the clashing of egos and many other factors cause line-ups to change. Rob just wasn't happy.

Grand Hotel often came down to hang out at Mum's. We had recently moved. A property developer bought our gaff so we moved down the road to a smaller flat above an electrician's. I was to buy it for the princely sum of £27,500. It became yet another design project, another shrine to Mickey Mouse and Coca-Cola, with a few Art Nouveau-style objets d'arts scattered here and there.

My clothes also reflected my perennial obsession. I was swaggering around in Mickey Mouse earrings, Superman t-shirts and red Kickers. I felt it was essential to make an impression. I did the same with money. I carried £50 notes in my wallet so that when I whipped out my cash I looked wealthier than I was.

People respond to the big lie. I have always believed that. Project an aura of being a success and in no time you will become one. Grand Hotel often said I was more like a football manager than a music boss. They may have been on to something. I was always at the gigs, cheering them on, being a mascot when needed, being a harsh critic when I thought it was required. I even got on stage at Woolwich Polytechnic on Colin's birthday and stuck a custard pie in his face.

After six months, *Do Not Disturb* was complete. The cover and promo material saw me go to town on CBS's largesse.

We sent journalists a suitcase, a white shirt smeared with lipstick traces, a 'Do Not Disturb' sign and a copy of the album.

This was totally my concept, as was the album art. We decided that no band member should dominate the artwork and instead we would use the band's logo of a bellboy. For the album-sleeve photo session, the model posing as a bellboy was a chap named Russell, who was then in a band I was starting to manage called Portraits (they later became the Fixx). Russell was model-handsome, and also slender enough to fit into his minuscule costume.

The album cover's final image was a little bit surreal with the bellboy standing both in front of and behind a dado rail, inside and outside of the room. The band's faces hovered anonymously on the wallpaper. Unfortunately the music, an uneasy mix of Average White Band and 10cc, was neither fish nor fowl and turned out equally anonymous.

Grand Hotel played a showcase at a CBS conference in a south coast seaside town. Everyone there raved about the record. But, let's face it: *everyone* raves about an album in the music business before its release. It's like some collective form of hype-hungry delusion.

The label was less eager about the band when the singles from the album failed to get airplay or any chart action. 'Secret Life'/'Light Years' sank without trace and the follow-up, the supposed sure-fire hit 'Double Vision', went the same way.

When the album came out, that tanked, too. When the press didn't ignore it, they slagged it off. Sadly, the verdict on Grand Hotel was unanimous. The big buzz was a big flop.

After this disaster, Grand Hotel split. They went in various directions. Graham went on to have a great career as a drummer for Roger Waters and Bucks Fizz. Danny McIntosh played in Bandit with Jim Diamond and then became Mr Kate Bush.

Grand Hotel main men George and Colin were to enjoy fascinating later careers, working on disco albums, becoming a songwriting and production duo who enjoyed big hits in the US and even, in Colin's case, writing for the Spice Girls.

It's no surprise that George and Colin were to do so well in the future. Even in their Grand Hotel days they always had their ears open to all the latest sounds in the clubs. Now and then they would go with me to the Embassy Club on Old Bond Street.

The Embassy was the nearest that London came to its own Studio 54. Its compact dimensions increased the sweaty, hedonistic disco fever. It was often crammed with famous faces of the day, rock aristocracy like Jagger and Bowie, while behind the bar were faces that would be famous for fifteen minutes in the next decade: Limahl and Marilyn (the latter's friend Boy George often dropped in, too).

I loved the Embassy. Like Studio 54, it had scantily clad busboys for you to ogle in their red and white satin shorts. Best of all, you could eat and drink all you wanted at the Embassy for £4. I could satisfy all of my hungers and urges in there.

Dry ice engulfed the Embassy as non-stop disco played: throbbing, glistening records that compelled you to dance, to surrender to the ecstasy of the moment, even if in so many of the tunes an underlying sadness lingered, an in-built warning that the thrill was fleeting. Disco spoke to me, loud and clear. All of my favourite records had that surge of euphoria with a misty-eyed pathos complicating their abandon: Gladys Knight's 'It's A Better Than Good Time', Inner Life's 'I'm Caught Up (In A One-Night Love Affair)', the light and shade of 'Don't Leave Me This Way' (both Harold Melvin's and Thelma Houston's versions), even ABBA's 'Dancing Queen'.

Disco was suddenly everywhere. I was always listening to 'Dance Away' by Roxy Music. The lyric struck the nerve of the times. Its breezy chorus urged the listener to chase away the blues with a boogie while the verse spoke of 'Open hearts turned to stone' and revellers lit up by strobe light: 'All together, all alone'.

That was me. As I wandered through clubs I was gripped by feelings of inadequacy and a loneliness that I seldom expressed. Even on the best nights, sorrow would track me down. I would gaze at some gorgeous Adonis and hate my own bulky, podgy frame.

I felt incapable of loving anyone … or of being loved. Outwardly I was the life and soul of the party, larger than life, everyone's-best-friend Uncle Tommy. Inside, I felt tragic.

I *was* disco!

Yet even in the depths of my loneliness, I loved the music that was its soundtrack. Disco was my musical revolution, much more so than punk had ever been. It sounded like freedom and it sounded like luxury, especially in its early soul-based incarnation, which remains my favourite period.

By the end of the 1970s it was also big business: *Saturday Night Fever* had taken the world by storm and everything from Ethel Merman to the Muppets was getting a disco makeover. There was also the feeling that the world was becoming one huge omni-sexual entity. Straights and gays mixed freely at the Embassy (George and Colin had no qualms about going there).

In that last gasp of the seventies, just before AIDS struck, the world seemed like it was heading towards a bisexual culture. The mostly gay club Louise on Poland Street was a haunt of the punk Bromley contingent. Close to that was Chaguaramas on Neal Street. Neil Tennant used to go there: he nicknamed it 'Shag-o-ramas'.

But London got its first really big gay club when Bang opened in 1976 on Charing Cross Road. Over the dance floor it would project movies of old MGM musicals, inspiring many a queen to emulate those high-kick routines. Then, by 1979, there was the daddy of all gay clubs, Heaven, a reaction to the Embassy being hijacked by the straights. It played Hi-NRG through a mega-sound system.

Suddenly the influx of gay American culture was all over London. There was Adam's in Leicester Square, a heavy-duty cruise zone, a real echo of the more sexually charged American scene. The clone look came from over there, too, the ultra-butch uniform of the San Francisco scene: tight Levi 501s, white t-shirts and Village People-style handlebar moustaches.

There was obviously the leather dimension, too, with caps, chains, chaps and coded handkerchiefs denoting your sexual proclivities. Much of this scene was concentrated in Earls Court, and Paul Rodwell and I went to places like the Coleherne on Old Brompton Road.

In its own way this was as international a scene as the Embassy, bringing in everyone from Freddie Mercury to Rudolf Nureyev, Anthony Perkins and Derek Jarman. The place was charged with the threat of danger and I often felt uneasy there. The police were constantly targeting and raiding it for 'neighbourhood disturbances' and supposed indecency. It was also to become the stalking ground for three separate serial killers: Dennis Nilsen, Colin Ireland and Michael Lupo.

Yet eating out was as much a part of the gay nightlife as disco, maybe even more so. An American-style eatery in the heart of Covent Garden, Joe Allen's was the place to go. Brunches there with Paul soon became a regular ritual.

As I descended its stairs to the subterranean dining area, I felt like I was at the centre of everything. The place had a real 'New York City' feel: the exposed brick walls, crisp white tablecloths, long aprons on waiters, all of them budding actors, actresses and dancers.

Joe Allen's was full of theatre types and showbiz glitterati. You could scan the room on any given day and pick out plenty of famous faces. And the food was tasty: great steaks, ribs and the best Caesar salad in London. Back then it wasn't a city renowned for its gastronomic flair but Joe Allen's was a breath of fresh air.

Sometimes I would just sit there and gaze at the walls, adorned with theatre and musical productions. No matter how the bands that I managed might be doing, *here* was a long way from my wretched childhood, from Dad, from the tallyman.

I had finally arrived.

I loved Joe Allen's. Through Paul, I had begun moving in a far gayer crowd, all successful, creative, connected and upwardly mobile. It was exhilarating. After years of managing predominantly straight musicians, I was moving in a gay world, one with its own parlance, pithy aphorisms, withering humour and campy pop and film references. It was *my* language, and it was wonderful to be surrounded by people who spoke it, too.

Then, one day, sitting in Joe Allen's, my eyes wandered away from the table and the cackling laughter and frantic conversation. I surveyed the bustling room of diners, full of Bloody Marys. There was a feeling in the room I couldn't fathom. When my stare fixed on a man sitting at a table close to ours, I suddenly realised what was distracting me.

The dark-haired man was so handsome that his face leapt out from the fog of a crowd like an obscene word on a page. Despite all of the usual queeny cacophony flying around my table, suddenly everything was silent and in slow motion.

When I gathered my senses, I told Paul of the magnetic man I had seen. It became the talk of the table and everyone agreed I should be bold and send him my number, via the maître d'.

I suddenly realised how small the gay world could be. He was a waiter at Joe Allen's. He was also dating an actor – another fatty like me. So even though the concept of the chubby chaser was alien to me back then, I thought to myself, maybe I stand a chance with this bloke ...

I scrawled my number on a piece of paper and sent it over. When he received it, the object of my intense attraction momentarily glanced at me and his eyes burned right through me. It was a look of real confidence and authority, the steely gaze of someone who has an unwavering certainty of their allure and power over others.

I froze in my seat for what seemed like an eternity. He had only looked at me for a second.

When I got home I told my mum that a very important man had been given my contact details. If he called and I wasn't in, she was to pass on the number of where I was. Of course, this was an age long before mobile phones.

It was a nightmare. Every night I went out I had to give my mother the number of where I would be in the vain hope that he would call. Time went by and I heard nothing. I spent my days consumed by thoughts of the tall, debonair gent I had seen at Joe Allen's.

My moods fluctuated between giddy euphoria and sheer despair. I would imagine that this stranger was my romantic destiny, then a second later be thinking that he had vanished forever and slipped through my fingers like gold dust.

That all changed one night when Paul and I were visiting a friend of Paul's, a military judge named Tim. The phone rang and it was the man in Joe Allen's.

I took the call. It was one of those typical first garbled conversations with someone you have a crush on, charged with both excitement and dread. You can't quite believe you are having it and yet you can't wait for it to be over in case you say something stupid. It was a short and sweet chat and we arranged a date.

I floated out of Tim's Kensington home not quite believing my luck. Tim joked that he was going to charge me a 'fixing fee'.

I met my date outside the Kensington Roof Gardens. He was hobbling on crutches as he had sprained his ankle parachuting. It didn't diminish his suave good looks. In fact, my attraction just deepened and grew stronger every second I was with him.

The first date rushed by in a haze of small talk and feverish expectation and we swiftly went to his place in Hammersmith. We didn't hang around. Before I knew it we were an item. He said the corpulent thespian and him were over ...

Immediately I was under the spell of his public schoolboy charm and his masculine, military bearing. So caught up in the vice grip of mad love, transfixed by his good looks and grateful to have a boyfriend, I accelerated into a super-intense relationship with him. I feared that if things didn't move quickly, I would lose him and be alone forever.

This panic-stricken desire that made me rush towards him also made me totally blinkered, obstinately convinced that this was 'the one'. I catered to his every whim, moving him into my home, much to the consternation of Mum, who took an instant dislike to him. She pegged him as a gold-digger straight away.

Utterly smitten, I thought she was talking rubbish. In any case, I was paying the mortgage on the flat so I had the clout to bring him in. It was a bold move in the late seventies for a man to be moving his boyfriend into the family home.

Grudgingly, Mum tolerated it. There were withering glances and she was disgusted by our displays of affection as we cuddled on the couch. 'Tough shit!' I told her. I had earned the right, through hard graft and taking care of everyone after Dad died, to be exactly who I was.

Mum would just roll her eyes and express her perennial relief that Dad had passed on so he couldn't see what was going on. I kept a cum rag behind our door. Mum never asked what it was for – but she knew. It was a defiant symbol of our unapologetic appetites. I was in love and I simply didn't give a fuck what anyone thought.

Yet pretty soon the bubble burst and reality came intruding. He was not only a waiter at Joe Allen's but also fellow trendy restaurant Langan's Brasserie, and he was the perfect face for them. He started disappearing for long periods of time and when I asked him where he had been, he responded evasively. I got jealous, he got shifty.

We started rowing. They were hideous arguments that raged on and on, exacerbated by Mum's presence. She looked on despairingly, all her worst fears and intuitions confirmed. She even threatened to shop him to the police for his prodigious intake of marijuana, but she never did.

Then something awful happened. A plain-clothes policeman arrested him for cottaging: when he was nicked, he had had my American Express card on him. So that was it. The dream was over … or was it?

No. Love is blind, and desperate, and we stayed together.

It was torture. I would tell him to leave, knowing it was right and he was wrong. But then I would be consumed by remorse, fatalistically fretting that this was my one shot at happiness and I couldn't squander it.

Back then, there was no rulebook for men to have relationships with one another and we were making it up as we went along. We didn't have the emotional vocabulary or context to even know there was such a thing as a 'healthy' gay relationship.

We stayed together but paranoia and contempt had infected our relationship and it was doomed. I made friends with a mate of his, who spilled the beans on him, saying my lover had been seeing half a dozen blokes at once. I confronted him and phoned his friend right in front of him to get him to repeat the allegations. It was ugly.

It got so bad that I hired a private detective who found the addresses of all his flings. A member of a band I was managing called in and found him in bed with an old flame. It was so humiliating!

I took to constantly checking the mileage on the car. He told me I was pathetic and childish. I wanted a monogamous set-up and it was not to be. We went to San Francisco to see a friend of his. I found them in bed together. I was distraught.

The man I'd once seen in a soft-focus haze of romantic idealism just sighed dismissively and told me to grow up. 'That's how it is in the gay world,' he said, breezily.

I didn't know anything about that. All that I knew was that my illusions were shattered.

Before my boyfriend, all that I had known was unrequited love and squalid, brief encounters. I had thought this was the real thing. Even when the truth was screaming in my face, I couldn't bear to let this man – and the dream – go.

It took a while. Things got a lot worse. I couldn't eat or sleep and lost a ton of weight. Paul Rodwell staged an intervention and took me away to the South of France on holiday. When I came back, my boyfriend and I even moved into a basement flat in Shooter's Hill, renting it in the vain hope that a life without Mum's interference might help us sort out our problems.

We were beyond help. The fights got worse, and even turned physical. He finally left me when an even more affluent benefactor came knocking.

After he had gone, I had a breakdown. I felt beyond hope and went to absolute pieces. Everybody was worried about me, and eventually I was persuaded to go and see a therapist. He unearthed all sorts of demons that had been hidden in me for years, about my background, my weight, everything, but ultimately did me a lot of good.

After a few months, I felt ready to move on.

One thing that the therapist impressed on me was that my physical shape could help lead to depression and I should embrace exercise. Now here was a first! I began exercise classes at Pineapple Studios in my all-white kit. Unfortunately I have always suffered from irritable bowel syndrome, and an arse accident showed the entire studio what a bad choice of colour that had been.

It is a cliché that what does not kill you makes you stronger, and like most clichés it is true. Yet what doesn't kill you can make you a little stranger as well. After him, I never looked at any man quite as wide-eyed again. Even if the initial impulse was there, it quickly subsided and cynicism crept in.

I lavished gifts on potential suitors but it was more a test than a ruse to woo them. The presents and the luxuries were carrots dangled: if he took the bait, he was another gold-digger. I wasn't even aware that I was doing that but, looking back, that's what it was. Only I never left them, I just allowed each relationship to quickly descend into a loveless, calculated 'arrangement'.

When my first real boyfriend walked out of the door, a love was lost forever. It never came back.

I did get over him, eventually, but the pain ran deep, right into my very soul. For years I was processing the relationship. It seemed to me that he had ditched me for a bigger cash cow, so the only revenge I could think of wreaking on him was success. The break-up and the rejection put fire in my belly and spurred me on.

As he left my life, the eighties and the big time beckoned. The question was no longer whether I would be famous ... but when.

11

RUTHLESS FUN AND ZTT

I don't care what anyone says: the late seventies had been grim.

They were as dull as dishwater, as flat as pancakes. It was all strikes, austerity and power cuts. Musically, this was all set to a soundtrack of miserable self-important young men in raincoats, monotonously reciting sixth form poetry over sluggish post-punk. No thanks!

Punk still hung over the music scene like a big dark cloud, joyless, stifling, monochrome and devoid of sex, glamour and wit. The arbiters of good taste were the weekly music papers which exerted a Stalinist grip on what was cool and what was not.

Blah blah fucking blah.

They had never liked Giggles. Well, why would you like a band named after a chuckle when you can barely bring yourself to laugh?

As 1980 ushered in a new decade, remnants of the seventies still lingered. Watching *Top of the Pops,* you saw dreary balladeers like Johnny Rogan and grandma-friendly disco-dross ready-made for Legs & Co.

Then I saw Madness perform 'My Girl' on the show and it sounded fresh and new. Their love of dressing up and catchy, upbeat tunes was proof, along with many a floppy-fringed Bowie casualty, that pop appeal and style were coming back. Image was going to be vital. What you wore was going to be everything.

Now this was more like it!

As music changed, so did *Top of the Pops*. A new producer, Michael Hurll, bullied the audience into frenzied excitement while onscreen graphics and video screens reflected an awareness of how important the visual was in this new pop landscape. *Top of the Pops* became colourful, kaleidoscopic, frantically enthusiastic, *eighties*. It spoke volumes about the decade.

It was going to be a period of ruthless fun.

Amid all that late seventies doom and gloom, lightning flashes of colour had already started appearing. Gary Numan was a punk who had stumbled across a Moog and slapped on some white make-up. His image was crucial and his ambition was naked.

Adam Ant was another reformed punk keen to put the show back into the business. His first hit single, 'Dog Eat Dog', was a mantra for ruthless ambition and mirrored one of my own brutal mottos for the music industry: 'Kill or be killed'.

Boy George was like me, a big-boned man with a hard south-east London core, a gay man from a working-class background who was desperate to get ahead. For a while he worked in the cloakroom at Blitz club, and would hand you your coat like someone had died in it.

In fact, Blitz was like a waiting room for eighties pop stars. Steve Strange was on the door: Spandau Ballet were the house band. I found the place exciting even though I was too old and too fat to be part of the scene. I mean, nobody needed to see *me* wobbling around a club in Covent Garden trussed up like Marie Antoinette.

They called themselves the New Romantics and Bowie was their guiding influence. Of course, where Bowie was a veritable one-man academy of intellectual thought, you got the impression that some of these bright young things were a bit dim – all high style, cold blood and empty brains. Bowie's *Aladdin Sane* had been inspired by Evelyn Waugh's *Vile Bodies*. This new breed probably thought he was a female interior designer.

Human League, Heaven 17, Soft Cell ... fantastic pop stars kept coming along. All of my antics with Ice Cream and Giggles now felt like they had not been misguided, just ahead of their time.

Smash Hits magazine developed a style all of its own: innocuously gossipy, packed with trivia (what colour a pop star's socks were suddenly became vital information) and its own vernacular.

After the disaster of Grand Hotel, and then the heartbreak of my broken relationship, I felt like a life change. After Ice

Cream, Giggles and Grand Hotel, I couldn't find anyone sufficiently interesting to manage. I had a bash with a band called Portraits, but it was the same old story.

I had become weary of the whole endeavour. None of my acts had made anything like the splash that I had hoped they would. So ironically, as pop caught up with my ideas and embraced fun, flamboyance and the pop group as a total package, I went back into my first love: design.

With my background in design, my fitful but so-far-unsuccessful experiences in pop music and my love of art, my next move seemed perfectly logical. I would set up my own design studio for record sleeves and interiors.

And this time, no question, I was going to succeed.

I started out in Welbeck Street, where Paul Rodwell had his offices in a beautiful Georgian building with an incredible staircase. He asked me to redesign the interiors of his office. Lawyers were by now playing a key role in the music business. Paul even went on telly and talked about the 'quasi-managerial' role of the lawyer in the new scheme of things. I've never let him live that wanky terminology down.

Even during my band-management years, I had dabbled in design. During the last couple of years, I had done some work with Frank Sawkins of Czech & Speake, a company designing bathrooms with Art Deco fixtures and fittings.

Working with Frank, I had revisited a style I had played with a long, long time ago at Allied Breweries. It was a series of dots splattered across a background in a range of colours and it looked fantastic, like glitter scattered across a surface but classier.

Paul Rodwell loved the Czech & Speake range and he asked me to do similar things with his office. Like a kid in a toyshop, I went wild, mixing classical elements with funky touches. I bought second-hand furniture and had it enamelled bright blue. It had an impact: not garish or gauche but mesmerising and novel. Nobody who walked into a lawyer's office expected it.

I restored the original stone flooring, put in chunky sofas, covered them in grey fabric and put red leather piping on them. I took beautiful old paintings and prints and gave them contemporary frames. Everything had a twist. Archetypal classical elements were fused with forward-thinking playfulness.

I hadn't had so much fun in a creative environment for ages. It was a success, retaining the authority necessary for a lawyer's office but with a hip twist. Paul Rodwell loved it, and so did every client who walked through the door.

Enthused, we hatched a plan for me to set up my own design studio. Royston Edwards, Paul's former boyfriend and a Joe Allen's brunch buddy, came on board, too.

'Why don't you and Royston join forces? He needs a bit of a push,' Paul had said.

'There is one minor problem. I simply can't afford office rents. I want this to make me money, not cost it,' I replied.

'Well, why don't you just take my big front office upstairs, Marge?' he suggested. (Paul always called me Marge.) 'I won't charge you much. You can take care of the interior side of the business and Royston will do the other stuff.'

We had a deal! I was up and running.

Royston was working as a freelance magazine designer. He had had commissions from magazines like *Good Housekeeping* and was good at layouts and graphics. With my interest in packaging pop music, we thought it would be a great idea if we designed record sleeves. He was ideal for them. He could handle copy, illustration and graphics and was a competent illustrator with a meticulous attention to detail. But Paul was right – Royston needed pushing, professionally and creatively.

We got on famously. Royston was a true stereotype, the archetypal gay, camp but pretending to be butch, invariably decked out in checked shirts, blue Levi 501s and leather waistcoats topped off with the obligatory little moustache. He was a typical queen, hankering for rugged masculinity but too impeccably neat to be anything but pristine. I went clubbing with him to Heaven and Adam's.

Royston made me lose weight and get fit. Well, he tried!

'You're too fat, Tom,' he would tell me. 'Nobody likes a fairy that's too fat. They can't stick you on top of the Christmas tree and you take up too much space on the dance floor.'

He would deliver these merciless put-downs with the sweetest smile that made it all seem endearing rather than thorny. We made a great team. Paul's free space and cheap rent in the middle of the city was a dream come true. So we set up shop upstairs from Rodwell.

He moaned at us for not changing the light bulb in the toilet upstairs – it drove him mad! Paul was incredibly kind to me but what a mean, penny-pinching bastard he could be. I wasn't that bothered – I was getting to live my dream of running a design studio.

I named it XL. It looked great written down: simple, majestic and bold. It had a double meaning. The extra-large aspect celebrated the corpulence of the man running the show (yours truly) but it also denoted aspiration: XL meaning 'to excel'.

XL was actually the first of a series of companies over the years that I named after my hefty bulk: Massive Management, Big Features, Porky Publishing, etc. Sometimes you have to own what you've got and work it to the max: send it up before someone else ridicules you. My expanding waistline became synonymous with my expanding empire.

Business took off quickly for XL. Royston already had a roster of clients, a mainstay of his work with magazines. I had been dabbling in poster design too since the late seventies, doing gig posters for acts as famous as Blondie and paying a bloke called Terry the Pill to paste them across London (and to beat anyone up who tried putting other posters over mine).

Record-sleeve commissions soon started pouring in. Eye-catching graphic solutions (as they were yet to be called in those days) and marketing campaigns were the order of the day. It wasn't long before we were designing covers for artists, including a young duo poised to set the charts alight.

Their name was Wham!

We designed the original sleeve for their breakthrough 'Wham! Rap' single. It was a line drawing of George and Andrew in profile that I traced from the contact sheet of a photo session. Then we layered 'exotic' typography on the sleeve that looked like it had been lifted straight from a Chinese takeaway menu.

Mind you, back then Wham! were not the slick duo they quickly morphed into. George Michael and Andrew Ridgeley both had that impossibly well-coiffured hair, that perma-tan skin and those pearly white smiles, but they also had a street-tough rebel energy about them. They were like two trainee teenage hairdressers who were mad as hell and weren't going to take it any more.

I thought 'Wham! Rap' was great, a post-disco anthem to having 'soul on the dole' and living the good life courtesy of the DHSS. George was great and the song's exuberance was matched by their feral performances. George and Andrew played on their chemistry as real-life buddies, strutting their stuff like two Home Counties Tony Maneros. It was like Saturday night in a provincial disco re-imagined as pop theatre.

Their second single, 'Young Guns (Go For It)', was supposedly about George trying to lure his mate away from the fatal charms of a woman hen-pecking him into a conjugal cul-de-sac. I never bought into that! In the eighties, I would bump into him on gay nights at Heaven with a 'girlfriend'.

'Oh, I'm just here for the music,' he would tell me. 'I love the sounds in these clubs.'

Yeah, right!

George was always a bit distant, wary and distrustful. Andrew was far more fun-loving and genial and was the real-life embodiment of those songs' *joie de vivre*. George was clearly hiding something.

I guess it was fairly obvious what it was.

Between 1982 and 1983, a third member joined our team at XL. David Smart had a background in book publishing. He was gifted, secretive and could be prone to sulks, which has always been a major dislike of mine. Perhaps because I am prone to them myself and don't like being upstaged! Needless to say, we didn't get on.

Nevertheless, he was clearly talented and was conversant in great graphic artists from Russian pioneers like El Lissitzky to US masters like Paul Rand.

Smart was to prove a major asset with our next major venture, the record label with which we would forever be most closely linked – ZTT.

ZTT was the brainchild of three people: the record producer Trevor Horn and his smart wife, businesswoman Jill Sinclair, and a music journalist from the *NME* called Paul Morley. Prompted by a typically uncharitable Morley review, The Cure reworked their song 'Grinding Halt' as a 'tribute' to him for a BBC session. It was retitled 'Desperate Journalist'.

Jill and Trevor were clients of Rodwell's and had been majorly impressed with my work on his legal offices. At a Christmas party there, they told me how much they admired my interior design.

Jill and I clicked instantly. I was pushy and she was a ballsy Jewish lady. I loved her: she was by turns camp, intelligent and charming. She took no shit and was utterly dedicated to masterminding her prodigiously gifted husband's career. Jill was the embodiment of the eighties 'power-dressing' woman, an ambitious tornado with that Jewish chutzpah thrown in. Of course, it didn't hurt that she loved gay men, too. She advertised the fact, wearing a t-shirt with Friend of Dorothy emblazoned across it.

Trevor, by contrast, was an adorable space cadet. A consummate storyteller, he would regale you with the best stories, always told with the animated enthusiasm of an excited child. His enormous glasses seemed permanently fixed to his face, as if they were an actual part of it. Sometimes his eyes would glaze over until they seemed part of the spectacles.

Trevor had originally been in Buggles with Geoff Downes, who in 1979 gave Island Records its first number one single with 'Video Killed The Radio Star', which was also the first promo to be aired on MTV. As Buggles frontman, Trevor seemed a bit lost with his nerdy demeanour and giant glasses, unable to make a virtue of his gawky stage presence in the way that Elton John and Elvis Costello did.

Trevor and Downes had then joined progressive rock group Yes. Trevor became their singer and producer and carried on with Buggles, but by the early eighties he was a full-time record producer, revamping the career of tacky girl-boy duo Dollar, spinning the cruise-ship gaudiness of David Van Day and Thereza Bazar's act into pure chart gold.

Trevor was doing with sound what I would later do with image with acts like Bros. Taking raw material and moulding it into something that would be palatable to the record-buying public became my forte. You have to have an interesting core to work with. You can't make chicken soup out of chicken shit but you can take something dull and spice it up.

During 1981–2 a series of peerless Dollar singles sailed into the upper echelons of the charts: 'Mirror Mirror', 'Hand Held In Black And White', 'Videotheque' and 'Give Me Back My Heart' were all triumphs, cheesy earworms upholstered in state-of-the-art production. Trevor was able to give bland mainstream pop the frisson of something sophisticated, even arty.

Later on, David Van Day would join Bucks Fizz, long after Cheryl Baker and the sparkle had gone from the group. He then effectively cloned the group, wrestling it away from founding member Bobby G and his wife, a woman who made being in her husband's ailing pop group sound like religious vocation. There ensued a battle for the soul of Bucks Fizz, a comic power struggle by two eighties pop stars unable to accept the party was over and the dumper-shaped doldrums of the cabaret circuit were all that awaited them. There is nothing more tragic than a pop star who can't go home once the party's over and the hits have dried up.

But back then for a bit they were coming thick and fast for Dollar. And it was mostly down to Trevor's Midas touch at the mixing desk. The nagging hooks of 'Hand Held In Black And White' went on an epic journey, a cheesy melody sent skywards by dramatic glacial synthetics; the saccharine power balladry of 'Give Me Back My Heart' came housed in a production that replicated the multi-tracked vocal washes of 10cc's masterpiece 'I'm Not In Love'. He gave pop an artful edge while giving a pop accessibility to the more po-faced progressive acts, he worked with, like Yes.

Trevor also produced a Sheffield group called ABC. Enamoured with the sound of 'Hand Held In Black And White', ABC asked Trevor to work the same magic on their records. The result was 1982's pop masterpiece, *The Lexicon Of Love*.

Trevor's production was as much a talking point as the band itself but it wasn't all down to him. He had a cracking team around him of engineer Gary Langan, arranger Anne Dudley and programmer J.J. Jeczalik, who all helped build the Horn sound.

They all worked together on Malcolm McLaren's 'Buffalo Gals' hit single and *Duck Rock* album, cutting and pasting together disparate elements like a mosaic of juxtapositions. No wonder Jill and Trevor had liked my interior designs!

Yet there was a third, rogue, element to ZTT: Paul Morley.

Morley had first met Trevor in Trevor's Buggles days. He wrote a damning critique of the band in the *NME*. It was titled 'Dirty Old Men with Modern Mannerisms' and was a snide swipe at the group, mercilessly denouncing them as dinosaurs trying to be current.

Downes saw the way the interview was going and kicked Morley out before it was finished but Trevor was intrigued by Morley's intellect and his almost neurotic subjective response to pop music. You just never could tell what he was going to love or detest.

When Trevor produced ABC and Dollar's records, his admiration for Morley became a two-way process. It was just the kind of mass-market pop with a highbrow spin that pop 'intellectuals' like Morley love stroking their chins to. He even featured in ABC's video for 'The Look Of Love'.

If he had tried to plant a kiss on me, I would have been wiping my cheek for ever more. Ugh! Vile!

Morley and Trevor had a series of intense conversations about pop music that effectively gave birth to the ZTT label. Trevor wanted to make music that was current, sexy and danceable. Morley wanted to provoke, cause a sensation and stir things up.

Island Records had offered Trevor and Jill a distribution deal for the records he masterminded in his Basing Street Studio. Trevor and Jill set about devising their own label, which they wanted to call Perfect. When they got Morley involved, he quickly binned that name, saying it was too dull.

At the *NME*, Morley had been writing about the 'new pop', basically the cream of early eighties pop from the Human League to ABC. As the decade continued, Morley saw these bright minds superseded by acts he detested like Duran Duran, Spandau Ballet and Wham!

Morley once said that Simon Le Bon in his yellow Anthony Price suit looked like 'a lump in custard'. At the end of a Soft Cell review, he told them to piss off. Yes, he was a real warm, fuzzy bundle of love was Mr Morley.

Morley had a vision for a record label that was essentially a two-pronged attack on the music industry. It would have two sides and two imprints: Action, an all-out assault on the charts, and Incident for more avant-garde, left-field music.

ZTT was to be between the dance floor and Dada. One of the early Morley-penned ads proclaimed it was to be 'a radiant obstacle in the path of the obvious'. Nothing would be predictable. As another ZTT ad said, 'You can't suck on the same piece of sugar forever.'

Morley was always pilfering from highbrow sources, as all smart people in pop music do. He named ZTT after scouring the pages of Thames & Hudson's *Guide to Futurism*. In the book, noted futurist Luigi Russolo said that the movement's founder Marinetti used 'Zang Tuum Tumb' as an onomatopoeic evocation of the sound of Balkan cannons in the First World War.

Morley liked the phrase's warmongering spirit. It was perfect for his assault on the charts and got shortened to ZTT, harking back to the classicism of RCA and CBS. Morley also liked Russolo's phrase 'The Art of Noises'. He dropped the final 's' and it became the name of ZTT's first act, the, well, art-noise group made up of Trevor, Jeczalik, Langan and arranger Anne Dudley and Morley. They enjoyed a lot of success. Royston did most of their sleeves.

Critics tipped another ZTT act, German electro band Propaganda, to follow Art of Noise into the charts, but it never quite happened. They sounded great (Quincy Jones cited their album *A Secret Wish* as an influence on Michael Jackson's *Bad*), but was all too icy and remote to connect with the record-buying public. For all of Morley's babbling about how 'once something is understood, it stops being a source of energy' he often did just that with his endless notes and theorising. Marc Bolan once said that 'pop music is a spell'. Personally, I felt that Morley's intellectual clutter broke it. Or maybe I was just jealous of his breathtaking knowledge ...

Despite the success of our sleeve designs, Morley took Propaganda away from XL to the London Design Partnership, who charged crazily high fees. Morley was angry that we had worked with another German band that wanted a similar look to Propaganda, and said he felt it was 'diluting the brand'.

I think the truth was that he resented me having any input to ZTT. We just didn't get on.

Morley was by then dating Propaganda singer Claudia Brücken and was eventually to marry her. Never one to shun the limelight, Morley did a photo shoot with his future wife, styled by Iain R. Webb. Paul and Claudia dressed identically. Iain even mummified them, wrapping their heads in ties. I wished Iain had left Morley like that ...

Yet for a designer ZTT was a creative wet dream. Everything about it screamed variety and endless possibility, with multiple mixes of songs released on multiple formats with multiple sleeves promoted by multiple adverts. It was all funded with a seemingly endless budget.

Occasionally, the shrewd, sensible Jill would curb Trevor and Paul's more whimsical excesses. 'We are not the Arts Council,' she would say reproachfully when she discovered that Propaganda were making yet another video that nobody would screen. Yet ZTT's constant demand for sleeves and ads kept XL inundated with work. We even had to recruit more staff.

Morley's role at the label was essentially creative director. He was to claim that he worked in the label's 'dream department', and that he put his feet up, stared into space and daydreamed a lot. That doesn't quite match my abiding memory of him. He was, as I recall, frequently rude and a spouter of steaming heaps of pretentious bullshit (as evidenced by those infamous ZTT sleeve notes).

Morley would brief David Smart at XL. They soon struck up a close relationship. Morley would sometimes come in with his own doodles scribbled on a napkin and Smart would translate them for him. They were always in XL's studio, sniggering like sixth formers smugly in love with their own cleverness.

Smart was an ideal sounding board for Morley but Morley just wasn't a likeable chap. At least, he wasn't to me. He may well have felt threatened that I was as close to Jill as he was to Trevor. I don't know. But I'll never forget one conversation we had.

'So what's this Zang Tuum Tumb mean, Paul?' I asked him, ever eager and keen to learn.

'It's the sound the snare drum makes,' he sneered, as offhand as usual, before he and David Smart started sniggering at me.

When I realised where the phrase really came from, I felt humiliated. Only a real prick ridicules someone for asking a question, I thought to myself.

But the music business is a pissing contest between colossal, inflated egos and nobody could accuse Morley or me of having small ones. Egos that is. Coming from the *NME*, I felt Paul had a lot to prove.

Looking back, I can't help but marvel at how a journo from a weekly paper could end up masterminding a record label that was about to find itself at the top of the charts and the centre of the music business. But that was the 'go for it!' audacity of the times. I had to admire it, regardless of how objectionable the man could be.

And who knows? Maybe Zang Tuum Tumb was supposed to be like the sound of a drum machine as well. Maybe I was just being a big, petty diva ...

But if Morley wanted me to have nothing to do with ZTT, he was about to be disappointed – because Jill and Trevor gave me the job of designing their new studios, Sarm West.

12

RHYTHM AND BLUE

Sarm West in Notting Hill was a recording facility that I was already familiar with. After all, Grand Hotel had recorded their ill-fated debut there. But now it was to be radically redesigned to match ZTT's slick but arty character.

For years I had been amazed by just how drab most recording studios were. They were invariably wooden and dull. Well, no longer! Sarm West was to be a major departure from the dodgy Norwegian-wood-sauna vibe of most studio complexes. Now I would take the approach I had honed while designing Rodwell's office and spread it onto a broader canvas, helping ZTT achieve an identity as much as Morley had.

My first, main decision was that it would be blue: refreshing, aquatic and cool. It would be a shade of modern optimistic blue at the heart of London's still quite shabby W11 district, a stone's throw from Portobello Road Market. When a band recorded a session there they would feel revitalised and alert even after an eleven-hour stint, not suffocated by the beige blandness usually associated with such places.

My original Sarm West studio brochure said it all: 'Blue for function. Blue for beauty.' My trademark speckles would be splattered everywhere: across the walls, down the corridors, in the loos and all over the fake plastic ivy that I stapled onto the studio walls. I would spray dots on dots! As my plans said at the time:

'Whether it's a person's first or tenth record it will be very important to them and lots of money, time and hope will be invested in that record. So we have to make sure that they make something that is of the very best quality. We have to make sure there are no hassles, no problems, and we operate in the friendliest way. We have to help the artists and producers in every possible way – all they have to do is concentrate on being creative.'

The giant Studio One would have a sound booth with the façade of an ancient, crumbling temple stuck in front of it. Beyond this imposing Acropolis would be a wet-room studio floor. It would all look like a swimming pool, with a steel ladder, white tiles and – one final playful flourish – a flashing blue light so it looked as if a mermaid was at the bottom of swimming pool.

In the studio stood an impossibly swanky Bösendorfer imperial grand piano. Even Studio Two had a Steinway.

Next to these bastions of old-world refinement was the most innovative contemporary technology going, state-of-the-art digital equipment and the then-ubiquitous Solid State Logic mixing desk (the one that Phil Collins got those quintessentially big eighties drum sounds from).

Nobody had seen anything quite like this. Nobody had dared design a recording studio with such stylish, bold irreverence. Naturally, I met a few obstacles along the way. Jill introduced me to acoustician Sean Davies, who was working on the studio. He baulked at every idea I had – and was particularly horrified when I sprayed the wood blue.

'You can't do that!' Sean said.

'Oh yes I can!' And I did.

He wasn't the only naysayer. Word got back to Jill that some of the builders and technicians didn't like taking orders from me. Basically they didn't want a big fat poof telling them what to do. I was oblivious to their unease. I thought they just didn't like my big ideas …

It wasn't the last time I encountered homophobia. On tour with the band Electribe 101, a group I later managed, I overheard one of the road crew for Depeche Mode, the headlining act, mouthing off. He was going on about, yes, you've guessed it, that Big Fat Poof Tom Watkins.

I charged up to him, threw him against the wall and took him by the scruff of the neck.

'Don't you ever talk about me like that again, you 'ear,' dropping the h for added geezer value.

He nodded like a red-faced schoolboy who'd been shown up in front of his mates.

It's a savage world and such displays of brute force earn you respect. My bulky frame had a plus side. It intimidated plonkers like this one.

Little did he know my heart was pounding with nervous energy the whole time.

Thankfully there were no such showdowns at Sarm. If there were, it would most likely have been Jill swinging the builders around ...

As we were refurbishing the building, I took Morley to the top floor, where Jill was proposing he worked (eventually she took the office at the top of the building herself and perched up there like a queen bee). Guess what? Morley moaned about the glass blocks that I had put in to prevent the room from being too dark. Miserable bastard!

When it came to the ZTT logo, Morley had initially worked with another designer, Garry Mouat. Mouat's first draft was a Z with the two T's resembling Swiss army knives crossed like crucifixes. Morley loved it – but Jill refused to pay for it. I'm not sure why. Maybe she felt XL should do it, as we were designing the studio. Morley was flabbergasted (Mouat went on to design the Real World label for Peter Gabriel so I guess he wasn't too fussed).

Royston came up with ZTT Scrabble letters, each in its own little box, with the 10 under the Z and the 1 under the two Ts. I thought it was cute and fun, so much so that I thought it would be great to have Scrabble letters tumbling down the stairs at Sarm West.

Morley was appalled. It represented everything that was cute and cuddly to him. He hated our playful letters, said they reminded him of Hamley's toyshop and told Royston to make them more 'fascistic', which is how the slashing Z materialised.

The corridor to the canteen was covered in Coca-Cola memorabilia. At the entrance to the toilets I put 400 covers of *National Geographic* magazine with sixties ads, once again placing pop art iconography in a working environment. The toilets had funky sliding doors.

Quirky touches abounded. They made visitors look twice, not quite believing their eyes, just as they couldn't believe their ears when they heard ZTT's early recordings. A sculpture of a woman scrubbing floors stood at the edge of the stairs. Griffin gargoyles were dotted around. The reception looked like a space age counter.

The studio manager was Karin Clayton, the woman who had broken Martin Fry's heart, inspiring large chunks of *The Lexicon of Love*'s laments and even making a spoken-word cameo on 'Poison Arrow'. She later did the same on Art of Noise's records. See, even the person running the studio was a star.

The whole studio was a trip, a really special environment. Trevor and Jill loved everything, even if their mardy partner didn't. I had created an environment that matched perfectly their vanguard musical ideas for ZTT.

It was a natural habitat for Trevor. I can still picture him walking down the corridors – or, rather, his glasses floating down them, like a cartoon character with goggles hovering through space. I'd even had the idea for his trademark specs to be replicated as a giant insignia on the building's façade. Sadly, it was one of the few whims that was not indulged.

Yet I had no doubt the 'Sarmosphere', as I called it, was my greatest achievement to date. It was 1983, and from now on there would be a lot of opportunities to be made and opportunities to be taken.

Because, for me, everything was about to go whoosh!

13

FRANKIE SAYS SUCCESS

The Ship & Whale pub in Rotherhithe was one of the oldest-running gay-friendly bars in London. It had been a gay venue since the fifties and was run by 'Dockyard Doris', a publican who could have been in an Ealing comedy were it not for the fact that her establishment was serving men deemed sexually deviant by society.

Before Doris started pulling beers for queers, the Ship & Whale had been a brothel. Rotherhithe was a suitably desolate backwater for such an illicit business: an island in south-east London with derelict dockyards and savage gangsters. Even in the eighties, when I started going there, Rotherhithe was still a bit of a shithole.

The pub was a little bit sleazy, a little bit run-down … and a lot of fun. There was a black dance floor and blacked-out windows, making you feel, as so many gay establishments did, that you were partaking in some private, forbidden, exclusive ritual.

The bar was in the centre. The eyes of punters would dart restlessly from side to side, scanning the room for their next potential trick. When I first started going there, still nursing the wounds of my breakup, mine would, too.

However, on one particular night, rather than my gaze turning to the night's hopelessly out-of-reach butch number, I found myself looking at a man who was tall, preppy and handsome – but most definitely not butch. It was Gary Knibbs, who became one of my dearest friends, a colleague and a cruising, boozing and dancing partner.

Gary, it turned out, had studied at the London College of Furniture, too. It was one of a few coincidences. He also lived in the Greenwich area and loved pop music, especially the sounds that Trevor was making. He also had a great eye for design and aesthetics. He was as immaculate as Royston but in Sta-Prest trousers, Oxford button-down shirts and Bass Weejuns loafers.

I quickly took Gary on as an assistant at XL, helping me with interior design jobs I was too busy to complete on my own. He boosted my self-confidence. We partied the nights away, ably abetted by Pilsner and poppers.

The stench of amyl nitrate would fill up the cramped dance floor at the Ship & Whale as the DJ pumped out the low-self-esteem-banishing Hi-NRG soundtrack. I would forever associate that music with poppers' pungent aroma. The big song in 1984 was Hazell Dean's 'Searchin' (I Gotta Find A

Man)'. It was as camp as Christmas, throbbing with pent-up lust, in hot pursuit of some dream lover that those real nights in those real, grubby places would rarely reveal.

Or so I thought.

I would throw my head back when the rush hit me and the music pounded in my brain. In moments like those, I no longer felt like a fat man in a roomful of lithe young guys. I felt light as a feather, gliding on the wings of a cheap high and even cheaper drum machines.

Another popular song around then was 'Love Reaction' by Divine, a fat drag queen. I dressed up as her for a drag contest down the Ship & Whale. I won.

The pub stayed open until the wee small hours. It locked its doors and we carried on partying. Then Gary and I would whisk ourselves off in a cab into the heart of the city, laughing so loudly and shrieking so fiercely that the cabbies wondered what insanely camp cargo they were carrying across town.

We developed our own banter, our vernacular. We mixed a little bit of Polari, or gay slang, with references from vintage Hollywood (the entire oeuvre of, you guessed it, Bette Davis and Joan Crawford) and our own unique touches.

A sexy man walking by would elicit an exaggerated exclamation of 'Clutch your chest!' We'd show disbelief with a full-volume 'Oh puh-lease!' We addressed each other, always, as 'guurl!' We were in total flamboyant hysteria … until some hotly coveted butch number approached and we ditched the camp and tried to act all macho.

This was not easy for Gary.

Usually our cab would take us down the Strand and we'd run under the arches of Villiers Street to Heaven. There the mayhem continued until well into the next day. The dancing, drinking, drugs and ogling seemed to have no limits.

Nobody paid much attention to the bizarre death of a man called Terence Higgins who had dropped dead in that very nightspot in July 1982 of some mysterious illness. The music was too loud, the lights were too dazzling and the sweat of the bodies was too irresistible for anyone to notice.

Well, at least not yet.

It was a small miracle that Gary and I never ended up in hospital. I used to chaperone him on cottaging trips. One hotspot for toilet ducks was Crystal Palace. We ran into some queer-bashers who chased us with baseball bats.

Another time, I thought I had lost Gary. When I looked up, briefly taking a break from servicing the trick I'd pulled, there he was. Doing exactly the same thing. We were both in a graveyard. It was pure, shameless filth.

Gary moved into my flat and my mum moved in with Sally. He and I quickly became known locally as 'the gays above the car-repair shop'. Gary was always late with the rent, usually because he had spent it on yet more preppy clothing. It would all be laid out on his bed, immaculately pressed and ready to wear that night. Getting ready to go out was a supreme ritual for us, usually to the tune of ABBA's 'Dancing Queen'.

I loved Gary. Underneath my bulldozing bravado and massive ego, I was a simmering cauldron of unease about my sexuality. I was bold and brash about it on the surface but full of self-loathing and doubt underneath.

I would play the game of acting camp and outrageously flamboyant. I felt like I had to. It was what was expected of you as a gay man, in both the straight and gay worlds. It was easy but in many situations it left me feeling empty and hideous.

More than any boyfriend ever had, Gary put me at ease. Our repartee was all genuine, serious fun. People thought of us as a couple, and we were inseparable camp comrades.

Gary was also a fun addition to XL, an addition to the gay mafia. He was an antidote to David Smart's cerebral nature and more animated than the placid, unfazed Royston. Jill and Trevor adored him as well so he fitted in from the start.

One day, giving Gary and me a lift in his car, Trevor put on a track by a new act he'd been working with at Sarm West. It was the fruit of his intense labour at the mixing desk in mammoth recording sessions that had racked up £70,000 in studio time.

The players in the actual band had proved not good enough to realise Trevor's grand vision for the song. He had recruited Ian Dury's Blockheads but that had yielded nothing (except that descending bass guitar line which Trevor took from them). Eventually he had drafted in two virtuosos: guitarist Stephen Lipson and programmer/synth player Andy Richards.

Richards was working at the Royal Palace Theatre with ice-skater Robin Cousins on a show called *Electric Ice*. His job was segueing music by the likes of Mike Oldfield and Vangelis with forensic precision on the Roland MicroComposer, the sequencer used on the Human League's *Dare* album. He had also worked with Trevor in Yes – and now had helped him make this problematic recording work.

The result was the huge sound now exploding out of Trevor's car. It was a big, bulging, squelching sonic orgasm. It sounded like nothing we had ever heard but it also sounded like fantastic pop music.

It was called 'Relax' and it was the first record by a renegade bunch of Liverpudlians called Frankie Goes to Hollywood.

Trevor had first seen Frankie performing on Jools Holland and Paula Yates' edgy Channel 4 music TV show, *The Tube*. He had not been overly impressed with their song, which was at that point a bare-bones funk jingle. But the tune nagged at him. He heard it again on a Kid Jensen radio session and it dawned on him that the song was all about sex. He was intrigued.

Trevor found the Frankie's lustful aspect utterly refreshing. The Sex Pistols had belied their name by being mildly terrified by sex. 'Two minutes of squelching,' said Johnny Rotten and their songs like 'Submission' seemed to make sex sound rather unpleasant.

Not so Frankie. Frankie weren't camp like the Village People either. It was as if the Boystown Gang had been produced by Cecil B. DeMille. Imagine if they could be also managed by McLaren!

ZTT's own little McLaren, Paul Morley, was at first sceptical about Trevor's latest discovery. However, the sheer shock value of the proposition won him over and he went to town 'designing' the band as a multi-pronged assault on the media and Middle England.

XL's sleeve for 'Relax' was a collaboration between Frankie's singer, Holly Johnson, Morley, David Smart and illustrator Anne Yvonne Gilbert who provided the cover image, a drawing of a photo in the *Men Only* porno mag. It showed a tough dame in a basque back-to-back with a body builder in a foetal position.

On the reverse of the sleeve was a photo of band member Paul Rutherford's nipple ring being tugged by Iain R. Webb, who later drew a tattoo on the same man's inner thigh. Some people get all the best jobs.

Other promotional material for the single included an ad with Holly as a sex dwarf. On another ad, Paul Rutherford posed like Jack Nicholson in the film *The Last Detail* under a saucy slogan: 'All the nice boys love seamen'. It was clear that Frankie were going to be the thing the music industry needs every now and then: a big boot up the arse.

Frankie's promotional material was all one big wind-up. There was an elegant Japanese art-style ad in *The Face* for the single, bearing the immortal assurance that 'We can't all die in bed'.

Why? There just was.

Around these endless pictures, Morley went to town with his sleeve notes. He laid into pop players from Wham! to Kiss, and the sleeve to 'Relax' contained prose divided into chapters that read like an excerpt from erotic fiction. Clearly, he fancied himself as ZTT's very own Marquis de Sade.

You can't, er, always shove things down people's throats, and it took people a while to cotton on to just how perverted this all was. Then the BBC banned it, the tabloids went nuts and 'Relax' throbbed to number one.

A record wrapped in an XL design topped the charts. For five weeks. Frankie had arrived. ZTT had arrived. XL had arrived.

So what of the band themselves? What of the raw material that Trevor and Morley had sculpted into such a chiselled masterpiece of controversy and catchy tunes? Were they merely a manufactured 'boy band'? Putty in two megalomaniac's hands?

Well, yes and no. Singer Holly Johnson was nobody's puppet. He had been in bands like Big in Japan, converted warehouses into art spaces and lived in Paris. Paul Rutherford was the ultimate gay clone, like a Tom of Finland sketch come to life, and everyone loved him. He had such a sense of fun. When Frankie took off, it was clear he was enjoying the ride and there's nothing more charming than seeing a pop star enjoying being a pop star, even if (or maybe especially?) what they actually do in the band they're in is a bit unclear.

Behind them were the musicians, the straight guys who became 'the lads': Brian 'Nasher' Nash on guitar, Mark O'Toole on bass and Peter 'Pedro' Gill on drums. You wouldn't call them virtuosos but they were always up for it ... whatever 'it' was. Normally, it was getting to the bar.

Holly and Paul cultivated a gay S&M image, confrontational and shamelessly sexual in an age where we gay men had to effectively 'neuter' ourselves to gain acceptance. Frankie were like a giant pink phallus being waved in the face of the moral majority. With the three randy straight

Scallies, it was a pile-up of horny working-class hetero and homo male energy.

'Relax' deserved its success. Trevor had pored over it until it was a cutting-edge masterpiece. The groove was tighter than a gay porn star's bum. Cascading synths lit the track up like pink neon. An insistent bass guitar gave the track a bit of grit. The only sound that featured the whole band was a Fairlight sample of them all jumping in a pool.

Yet at the centre of all this hi-tech gadgetry and mucky mayhem was Holly's vocal, making it clear he was more than Trevor and Morley's puppet. It was leering; swaggering; cocksure. He had his own vision.

The lyrical content, with its sucking, chewing and coming, was clearly X-rated stuff. Yet what propelled 'Relax' to the top in the early months of 1984 was its surge of energy, its desire to 'get on top of a situation' as Holly said. It was an anthem about going for it, wrapped in leather chaps and a harness.

For the video, a straight-laced Holly was lured into a carnival of vice, replete with cages and fetish-clad sex people. By the end of the video he was corrupted and riding a slave. The dirty deeds were surveyed by a huge corpulent Roman emperor, a Nero-like monstrosity who, the editing implies, urinates over the crowd from his theatre box at the song's climactic 'come'.

I was pencilled in to play Nero but came down with a chronic case of irritable bowel syndrome. Inevitably, the video got banned and a cleaner one, with laser beams and Holly in white gloves, was aired instead.

Frankie were an overnight sensation. Soon another XL ad featured a photo of the band triumphantly coming off the stage at the Camden Palace where they had launched 'Relax'. Holly hid behind cool Ray-Bans and pointed a gun at the camera. The rest of the band swirled around him, caught up in the frenzy of their rising stardom.

The caption said it all: 'Big, Banned & Beautiful'.

Not everyone was enthralled. In 1984, Boy George wrote an open letter to *Record Mirror* denouncing Frankie. He said the 'Relax' video presented a 'Hilda Ogden' view of homosexuality. Maybe he should have been focusing on his music rather than picking fights with other poofter pop stars. But George always loved a rumble. Around the same time he said that Soft Cell was music for people that wore black and hated their parents.

XL went into overdrive. We had so much work that we had to move away from Welbeck Street and relocate in Poland Street, right in the heart of seedy Soho. Naturally, I made the office another post-modern playroom: more crumbling classical ruins and blue speckles.

At one point we felt like we were just the Frankie Goes to Hollywood image-making machine. ZTT wanted something new every week – in fact, it was more like every day. We would design separate ads for *Smash Hits*, the *NME*, *Blitz*, *i-D*, everybody. It was wild.

Morley produced Frankie t-shirts mischievously aping Katherine Hamnett's agit-prop attire. They were everywhere: FRANKIE SAYS RELAX. FRANKIE SAYS WAR! HIDE YOURSELF. FRANKIE SAYS ARM THE UNEMPLOYED.

Eventually cheapo rip-off t-shirts came back at us: WHO GIVES A FUCK WHAT FRANKIE SAYS?

Well, people did. Trevor worked hours on their second single, 'Two Tribes', layering, scrapping versions and throwing everything but the kitchen sink at it until he'd made another masterpiece. It was Hi-NRG, funk, metal, Wagnerian pomp and Russian folk music all packed into a record that DJ Roger Scott called 'the sound of the end of the world'.

Trevor turned it all into musical disco theatre, adrenalised and overblown, and Patrick Allen did a voiceover of his chilling 'Protect and Survive' monologue. For XL, it meant more sleeves; more ads; more promo posters to design. Happy days.

It was around this time that Trevor introduced me to the new format that would take the eighties by storm: the compact disc. He excitedly showed me the small silvery object (containing the sounds of Buggles, if my memory serves me). He then proceeded to smear strawberry jam all over it.

'Trevor, what the bloody hell you doing with that? You'll ruin it,' I said, laughing. He can't be so out of his gourd that he thinks it's a slice of toast, I thought to myself. Can he?

'No, Tom, I won't. They're indestructible. You can do what you want with them. Use them as a Frisbee, ashtray, give them a wipe and they'll still play,' he replied, beaming like a kid with a new toy.

He wasn't completely right, as evidenced by my collection of scratched CDs languishing in the garage. But the days of crackling, jumping vinyl were numbered. Or so we thought.

How wrong we were.

ZTT hit pay dirt again. 'Two Tribes' hit number one and stayed there for nine weeks. Nine weeks! Meanwhile, 'Relax' sailed back up to number two. The *Sun* camped outside the Liverpool home of Holly's parents, hassling them about their gay son. Holly ripped up a copy of the rag on *Top of the Pops*.

My old acquaintance Neil Tennant interviewed Frankie for an April *Smash Hits* cover story. Neil was disarmed by Frankie's niceness, anticipating a lascivious gang of hoodlums rather than the charming, genial fellows he actually encountered. He asked the band about the discrepancy between the image and the reality.

Holly sighed. Some of the controversy, he explained, was about other people's ideas. It was just a hint that the band weren't going to be prepared to play ball forever with Trevor and Morley.

Unbeknown to everyone, the man who was interviewing Frankie was to be a big part of pop's future. That same month, April 1984, Neil's own band, the Pet Shop Boys, released their first single, 'West End Girls'.

The man from Marvel Comics who had chastised me for the state of the Spiderman costume during Giggles' day had walked into the XL offices, and back into my life, to ask me to design their sleeve. We did: a swirl of black and white with a small photo of Neil and his bandmate, Chris Lowe, silhouetted with their eyes lit up.

The song was great. Later on, it would be re-recorded and it would be even better. Unbeknown to me, the Pet Shop Boys were going to be a big part of my future.

XL was becoming a revolving door of young, fresh talent. That year a young man call Lo Cole brought his portfolio into the studio. He'd been working at *City Limits* and Royston had done a few magazine jobs with him. He was cute and he fancied himself as a pop star.

This was not to be but he was a great artist. I made sure everybody at XL/ZTT knew about his work, which I proceeded to buy up in large quantities. Even Paul Morley was impressed with Lo, although he had been a discovery of mine. Before he knew it, he had commissioned him to paint the deluxe sleeve for Frankie's lavish debut double-album, *Welcome To The Pleasuredome*.

It was a grand folly, a sprawling two-record set made by a band that barely had enough songs for one. Morley said there was something 'beautifully absurd' in a pop group behaving like a dinosaur like Led Zeppelin. With his prog rock roots, Trevor was a willing accomplice.

Lo's artwork was suitably excessive, erotic and exquisite. He worked frantically, having only a week to complete it. He used pencil and ink for the line drawing, wax crayons and watercolour on paper for the colour.

The finished result was staggering. A whole cornucopia of animals performing unspeakably depraved acts on one another was the original front. It was demanded that the offending acts and genitalia be covered with the modesty of green fig leaves. They spoilt the fun but added another bit of colour.

Yet after much ZTT in-house discussion, the animal orgy got put on the reverse sleeve instead. The front was a Lo Cole

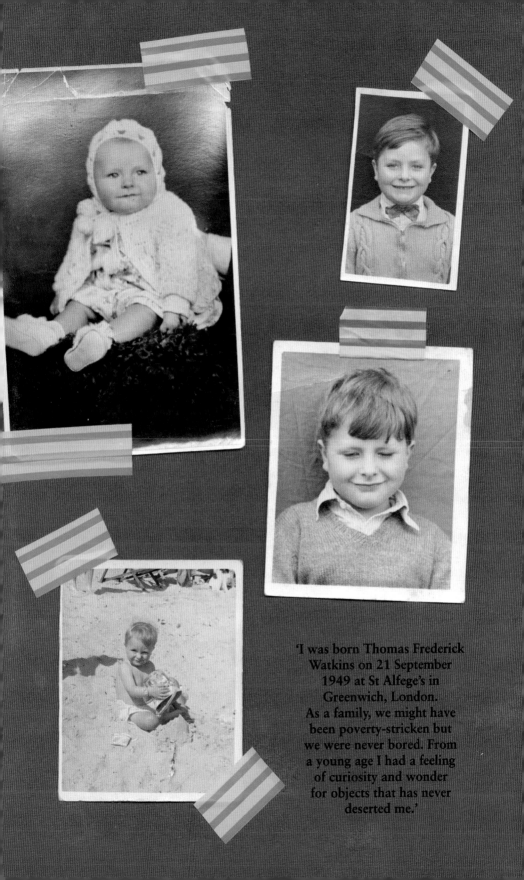

'I was born Thomas Frederick Watkins on 21 September 1949 at St Alfege's in Greenwich, London. As a family, we might have been poverty-stricken but we were never bored. From a young age I had a feeling of curiosity and wonder for objects that has never deserted me.'

'My mum, Patricia Daphne Diet. She had a magnetic personality – something I probably inherited from her.'

'Me and my American mom, Betsy Morgan.'

FRAG

'Dear old Aunt Joyce. She was a far better formative influence than either of my parents, and shaped so much of what I came to be.'

'Sometimes being a big fat poof paid off. Me, advertising a masterclass for JWT.'

Meet the man who gave birth to Bros, the Pet Shop Boys and East 17.

Meet Tom Watkins. Armed with just a fertile imagination he's brought into the world some of the most successful bands of their generation.

See what you can learn from his experiences at the rebirth of the JWT Masterclass on Wednesday 17th Jan. At 5pm.

Come along to The Commodore and listen to his delivery.

The JWT Masterclass

'I often felt like I was banging my fist on desks trying to get advertising and marketing campaigns signed off. But here I am literally banging my fists for an advert to promote my Radio 1 show in *Music Week* magazine.'

'Janet Street-Porter: a journalist,
motormouth, outspoken B-lister and, back
then, the queen bee of 'yoof' television.'

'Janet was a professional friend. She was a real mover
and shaker: fun, smart and mouthy. She pursued Neil
Tennant just as she pursued me. I loved her.'

'Mark Farrow with another guy from the XL office. A sexy, sarky northerner and the mastermind behind *Please*'s sleeve design.'

'Paul Rodwell (my best friend) and Jim Mackay. Paul and I shared a sense of humour that had us giggling like schoolkids from day one.'

'John Buckland and Sally Shiers. John was one of Bros's long-suffering minders. He was an efficient, sharp professional, a real salt-of-the-earth bloke.'

'My 40th birthday, with the manageress in Madame Jojo's, Soho.'

'Probably dozing while listening to the 100th tape of the day sent in by an aspiring pop star. Or Bros's second album.'

'Even my early flats were design projects, full of Mickey Mouse and Coca-cola. Nowadays I suppose it would be dubbed "kitsch", but in those days it felt like a breath of fresh air.'

CLOCKWISE FROM TOP LEFT: 'Gary Knibbs, Paul Rodwell, Mike Dawson and Sally Wickens.'

'Bros playing Wembley Stadium, 19 August 1989. I hung out in the VIP box with Kylie Minogue and promoter Harvey Goldsmith, and as the crowd gathered, I surveyed the sight with real pride.'

'Me with my friend and business partner Royston Edwards. He was a typical queen, hankering for rugged masculinity but too impeccably neat to be anything but pristine.'

'Richard Stannard and I. "Biff" Stannard was the executive producer of East 17's debut album *Walthamstow*.'

'Tony Mortimer, a lithe lad from Walthamstow and a shrewd little songwriting spitfire. Along with John Hendy, Terry Coldwell, Brian Harvey and Robbie Craig, he made up East 17.'

'Neil Tennant and I messing about.'

'My first step out of London life: an Art Deco marvel in Fairlight, the White House was built from a design by Wells Coates. It was once the home of Agatha Christie.'

'My Georgian town house in Maida Vale. I renovated the place, installing a basement swimming pool and adorning the walls with pop art. Mickey Mouse, of course, was everywhere.'

'The library in the home that I built: the Big White House, a Bauhaus-derived beauty. I often get asked if the Pet Shop Boys live in my house.'

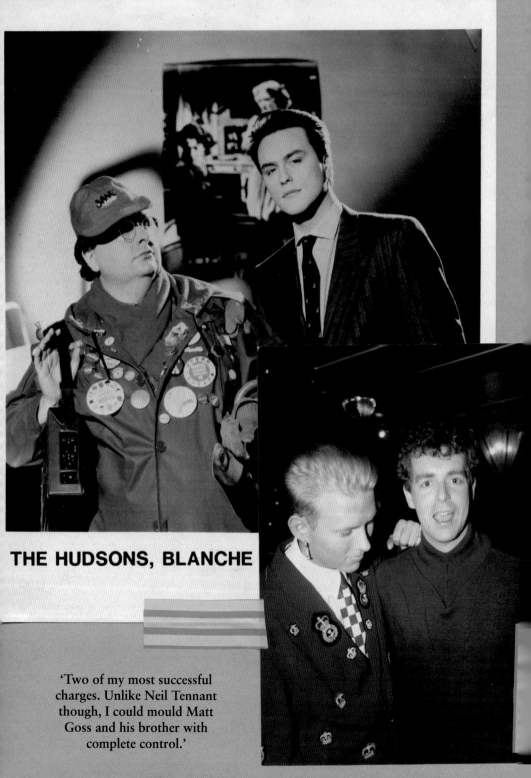

'Gary Knibbs and I formed our own little pop duo, the Hudsons, a short-lived outfit that was inspired by watching *Baby Jane* one too many times.'

THE HUDSONS, BLANCHE

'Two of my most successful charges. Unlike Neil Tennant though, I could mould Matt Goss and his brother with complete control.'

'Giggles were natural entertainers and I envisaged them as more than just a pop group. However EMI seemed to do nothing to help their cause, and my relations with the label grew increasingly strained.'

'Me with Faith Hope & Charity, a three-girl, pretty, feisty group: Dani Behr, Sally Ann Marsh and Diana Barrand. Their debut single "Battle Of The Sexes" went down the dumper.'

'Me trying to give Matt Goss some advice. Underneath Bros's layers of crap clothing and even crapper hairstyles I immediately saw a possible teen sensation.'

Tom
Remember always,
my River runs deep
for you!
My Warmest Regards,
Bruce

'Over brunch at the Chateau Marmont, Bruce
Springsteen came over to our table. He was polite and
charming, and happily signed this photo for me. Life
didn't get much better than this.'

'With Liza Minelli, everything was "Oh darling!" and "Wonderful!"; she was so affable and warm.'

Love Liza

'The Pet Shop Boys in LA [left] and Japan [right]. Neil was lively, funny and erudite, but he had a brittle mask that he had fashioned to face and conquer the world with. Chris was trickier. He was nearly always remote and aloof and fiercely guarded. Yet he was also loyal, protective and loving.'

'Sooner or later, life becomes about more than shopping, sex and three minutes of music. But I have had a good life. I got away from the tallyman and built some perfect pop groups. And I got laid more times than anyone with a big gut and a lifelong aversion to exercise has any right to expect.'

portrait of the Frankie gang, shirts off, raving and waving, like a Picasso painting in a gay club.

Inside the gatefold sleeve was a tableaux of a troupe of creatures entering a giant phallus; Noah's Ark for the sexually perverted. For me, Lo's artwork for the *Pleasuredome* album was the greatest achievement of the whole XL era.

The advance orders were staggering and *Pleasuredome* became the fastest-selling debut of all time. It rocketed to number one. It took a while for people to realise that as great as parts of the record were, the impeccable style outweighed the substance.

If early eighties pop albums like *Dare* and *The Lexicon Of Love* had songs the equal of their shiny surfaces, now it looked like the wrapping was getting better than the present. The singles teased a brilliance that could not be sustained.

For Frankie's third single and third number one, 'The Power Of Love', the packaging was again a lavish affair. Smart had seen a Titian in the Basilica dei Frari on a trip to Venice and we worked it into the sleeve. One 12-inch featured all five Frankies praying. Another comprised white cardboard squares with pink crucifixes and pink envelopes to send to a loved one.

But the real revelation was the song itself. It was another grand, epic statement but also heartfelt and haunted with something impossibly sad and unbearably tender. Even the lads played on the song. Maybe they did have a bit of talent between them after all.

Yet Holly's vocal was the real showstopper: impassioned, yearning, controlled and stately. He harkened back to a golden era of golden voices, the world of Johnny Ray, even Roy Orbison. And Trevor made 'The Power Of Love' sound like it was booming out of the world's biggest, grandest cathedral. The Godley and Creme-directed video recreated the birth of Christ just in time to cash in on the Christmas market.

Yet the single was dislodged from the top spot by the record that would be 1984's seasonal top seller, Band Aid's 'Do They Know It's Christmas?'. This was also recorded at Sarm West and produced by Trevor, topping off 1984, an incredible whirlwind of a year.

All that I remember about Band Aid is a lot of pop stars arriving at Sarm. I remember a lot of hair, a lot of big coats, and a brief moment when every eighties diva's ego was checked in at the door to help the starving children of Ethiopia.

Frankie were in their imperial period, but obviously it couldn't last. The next year, their fourth single, the *Pleasuredome* title track, missed the top spot, even though the XL ads featuring a pegboard background were great.

Holly met his lover and manager, fellow art connoisseur Wolfgang Kuhle, and began to distance himself from ZTT. He felt that the contract Frankie had signed was a bit shoddy, with meagre advances and pitiful royalties.

The band wanted to distance themselves from the very architects of their momentous success and found themselves cut adrift, a shadow of a band whose sound other people's mixing-desk magic had created, and whose vision had been dreamed up by somebody else.

Pop music is all about the sound and the vision, and that belonged to Trevor and Morley. They had known how to do it. Package up sex, controversy and sentimentality and make it sell, sell, sell. Whip up frenzy, create a sensation, take the money and run!

A little bit can go all the way to the top when it's wrapped up right. All the way through the Frankie palaver, I was watching and taking notes. I used them. So did everybody else.

Can you imagine anything like that happening now? Can you imagine a manufactured band having a debut double album wrapped in obscene art? Can you imagine One Direction issuing an ad with the instruction 'Lick that shit off my shoes?' No, nor can I …

But as one star falls, another rises. That's pop music. And back in 1984, as one door closed on Frankie, I imagined that I could create, shape and market a band that would leave even ZTT floundering in my wake.

Sadly, it didn't work out quite like that.

14

SPELT LIKE HITS!/SPELT LIKE SHIT!

In November 1984, a journalist called Noreen Taylor interviewed me for the *Daily Mirror*. There I sat, cross-legged with my curly locks and cheeky grin, telling Noreen all about XL's role as 'image-makers' in a new pop era where 'a star is no longer born, but styled, packaged and ruthlessly sold'.

Noreen told her readers how I 'arranged my large bulk' on the office sofa to tell her all about it. Cheeky cow! The headline dubbed me 'Mr Big' (so I got there first, *Sex and the City*) and the article's headings buzzed with words like 'idols', 'money' and 'macho'.

You'd have thought my life was a Jackie Collins novel. If only!

The more I talked to the press in those days, the more I bullshitted. I told a TV crew it was 'an absolute fallacy that we tell people what to wear and do'. Guess what? I lied. That was exactly what we did.

Pretty soon I was telling lies in everyday life as well. On my way home to Blackheath, an old lady stopped me as I got on a bus.

''Ere, dear, how do you get your hair so lovely and brown and curly?' she asked. 'It is really beautiful, like a Roman emperor's. You look just like Peter Ustinov in *Spartacus*.'

'Teabags,' I told her. 'Used teabags. I put teabags in my hair.'

The old lady beamed, ecstatic to know the secrets of my impeccably coiffured hair. Well, who wants to know the mundane truth?

With our roster of stylists like Iain R. Webb, XL was fast becoming the company that pop stars and record labels came to for help with styling. An image overhaul was becoming as crucial to a pop star's continued success as keeping their sound fresh and exciting.

Sometimes it worked, sometimes it didn't. We softened Wham!'s bleached streaks, solarium tans and flashy jewellery with a softer, more elegant pop-star glamour. Soon, Andrew and George were looking pretty chic. At some point, George became indistinguishable from Princess Di.

MCA approached us to help Kim Wilde with her look. She'd enjoyed huge success with 'Kids In America' in 1981 and was instantly appealing. She was glamorous enough to be a pop star but also 'girl next door' enough, with her self-styled Oxfam clothing, to talk to pop kids. She was a smash, a Brit-born Debbie Harry for the *Saturday Superstore* generation.

Kim was an independent soul and she knew how she wanted to look: black and white stripy t-shirts, jeans and her dad's jackets, a bit tomboy, a bit girly, but mostly just Kim Wilde. Like Frankie, Kim was manufactured and self-styled all at once, the perfect little pop star.

The trouble was her last album at her previous label, RAK, had flopped. Now she had a new label and she needed a new vision to go with her new sounds on her album, *Teases and Dares*. MCA sent her to us, XL, to help her devise an image.

The album had added a harder electro-edge to Kim's sound, especially on its first single, 'The Second Time'. It was smothered in synthetic brass and was all about going out to get a man who would 'Go for it!' and 'Do it!' with her, again and again. Hands clapped ferociously, like a row of bottoms being spanked. By robots.

Kim was initially open-minded and wanted someone to 'look objectively' at her image. She came into XL and we talked excitedly about the 'Kim Wilde reinvention'. She was lovely, sweet, intelligent and grounded and liked a cocktail or two, particularly Sex on the Beach. We got a bit carried away. Well, MCA had put up £10,000 and we were drinking Sex on the Beach, so why wouldn't we? The hairspray cans came out in full force. We made leather dresses. Suddenly Kim Wilde, the poster-pretty innocent of 'Kids In America', was a *Barbarella*-style supervixen. It wasn't so much girl-next-door as Wonder Woman crashing into Ann Summers.

The single's video recast the battle of the sexes as a wrestling match, pitting Kim against her male opponent in a ring. Hunky blokes in black sleeveless tops looked on, spurring them on with chants of 'Go!' It had lots of slo-mo shots of Kim in combat with her lover-foe. When she pushed him over, it was as erotic as a health and safety warning video.

In the vid, Kim sauntered into a cheap motel in one of the new black-leather dresses like a pouty vamp with a briefcase. Something blew through the window. Things crashed through a wall while Kim held on to it. A bed exploded. Kim sat in a chair looking slightly demented – and not at all comfortable.

According to the *Daily Mirror*, XL had rescued Kim from her 'denim-clad doldrums' and turned her into a 'leather-clad Batwoman'. But Kim wasn't happy and it showed. One person's sexy makeover is somebody else's ill-advised image change.

The leather dress looked like a bin liner, with a belt wrapped around the middle. All the excited talk and spraying of hair had resulted in something awkward and overblown. It was like watching a young girl wobble down the high street in her big sister's shoes.

Nobody forced Kim into these clothes. It was only supposed to be a one-off sex-up for this particular single anyway. It was all a bit like a drunken one-night stand. And now she'd woken up and come to her senses. It just wasn't 'her'.

The problem was the record company had forked out for this vampy revamp and they were going to milk it. To her dismay, a shot from the single became the cover of the *Teases and Dares* album. The 'Second Time' single limped to number twenty-nine.

The album didn't fare much better. Kim's instincts were right and her audience were as confused as she looked in these images. Another single, 'The Touch', dragged Kim into the realms of camp, playing Cinderella stuck at home doing the housework while her two transvestite ugly sisters hit the town.

Her fairy godmother appeared and all manner of magic and mayhem unfolded. The broom turned into a sparkling new hoover, ducks flew out of a toaster and onto walls, and when Kim opened the washing machine a head popped out.

A disco ball appeared and Kim, in a black dress, partook in some truly unremarkable choreography with two hunky back-up dancers. At the end, Cinders rode off into the night in the back seat of a fancy car with her Prince Charming, who looked suspiciously like one of the ugly sisters out of drag.

Kim should have looked ecstatic at her video's happy ending but she just looked plain drained. And confused. Poor Kim. It was another flop.

The moral of the tale? Sometimes all of the inspired ideas and the ludicrous excesses result in a great pop moment. Other times you jump the shark. Kim's time with XL didn't work out and she was gone by the end of the year.

Nik Kershaw came from Ipswich. He'd been in a band called Fusion. He'd been unemployed. While he was on the dole, he honed his songwriting craft and placed an ad in *Melody Maker* looking for management. One of the responses was from a character called Micky Modern. They secured a deal with MCA, the label Kim had been signed to.

After 'I Won't Let The Sun Go Down On Me' flopped on its initial release, 'Wouldn't It Be Good' hit number four. His debut single was rereleased and got to number two. Suddenly Nik was massive.

He looked like the bloke down the pub trapped inside the quintessential mid-eighties pop star. A bit Kajagoogoo, a bit *Miami Vice*, a lot slightly bewildered bloke from Ipswich. A bit too sane, a bit too stable to truly embrace the whirlwind success he was enjoying. An interviewer told him he had sexual charisma. Nik asked him what that was.

His two singles were the sound of the mid-eighties charts distilled, rock guitars and synths sitting happily side by side in slick productions, neither one getting in the way of cleaver-sized hooks that made both songs staples on the radio. They sounded bright and perky enough. 'I Won't Let The Sun Go Down On Me' was a slice of new wave reggae as jaunty as the previous year's 'Break My Stride' by Matthew Wilder. You got the catchy chorus in your head, you heard the Day-Glo synths and you thought it was all about an eternal summer, or something. Wrong. It was originally conceived as a folk protest song. Nik sung about pushing blue or red buttons. Like the same year's 'Two Tribes', 'I Won't Let The Sun Go Down On Me' was all about the nuclear threat, the Cold War.

'Wouldn't It Be Good' was equally infectious, wrapped in an MTV-ready video that turned the white-suited Nik into a miracle of Chroma Key, using state-of-the art editing technology to turn his outfit into a backdrop for myriad projections. Pretty flashy. By the end of the video Nik turned into a blur of static. The song kept saying he didn't 'want to be here no more' and that his spirit was 'frozen to the core'. What seemed like ruthlessly commercial mid-eighties rock-pop was actually as morbid as a suicide note. It all sounded like he was beating a retreat from pop stardom just as soon it was happening.

The accolades kept flying in. Elton John praised him as a fine songwriter and he turned up on 'Nikita', Reg's smoochy ballad, a soft-focus attempt to ease Russian–West relations. Not that Nik was a diva like his collaborator. He walked down a corridor backstage at a TV show and saw sushi flying out of Elton's room. Probably nothing unusual for Elton in his booze period. It wasn't the sort of thing Nik would do. He played Live Aid. He found it terrifying. After one more hit album in 1985, *The Riddle*, he disappeared. When he re-emerged in 1989 with 'Radio Musicola', the critics applauded; the charts barely noticed. You can imagine he breathed a heavy sigh of relief when all those teen posters came down.

Tellingly, around this time I also got back into artist management.

Russell Mackenzie, who had been the bellboy cover star of Grand Hotel's album and played bass in Portraits, came back onto my radar once more. He was now in a seven-piece soul/Motown band called the Motivations who were a bit like Dexy's.

The Motivations had a singer and guitarist called Alin Karna, a musician from an earlier age whose striking dark looks contrasted perfectly with Russell's blond features. Like

Hendrix, he played guitar left-handed and could play it upside down. Unlike Hendrix, he was about to find himself in a Tom Watkins boy band.

I yanked Russell and Alin out of the Motivations and put them in a trio with a bloke called Gary (I think that was his name). Immediately I saw this as my chance to 'do a Frankie'.

The pop world had caught up with all my promotional and packaging capers and now was my chance to cash in. This was going to be a manufactured act like Frankie but with all the scary shock value removed so that all the suburban Colins and Ednas wouldn't be frightened away. Frankie Goes to Huddersfield?

I started writing with Russell. We wrote big, catchy songs, majestic anthems that I was certain would become permanent fixtures on daytime radio: 'Larger Than Lions', 'Stop This Rumour', 'Contract Of The Heart'. I supplied the words and some of the hooks and Russell wrote the music.

I was convinced this trio would be high-concept, streamlined and beautifully packaged. I would use all of my XL experience to market the ultimate mid-eighties pop band. I even came up with a name that could be used as a promotional gimmick: Spelt Like This, a punchy, Scrabble-inspired moniker. It could be jumbled up into anagrams to circulate to the press to generate the maximum buzz.

Before I knew it, I was negotiating a deal at EMI for them with Dave Ambrose, a music industry legend who had played in bands with Rod Stewart, Mick Fleetwood, Brian Auger and Julie Driscoll and been in heavyweight prog-rockers King Crimson before getting into A&R and music publishing. He looked like a hippy but he had been shrewd and savvy enough to sign the Sex Pistols to EMI, and had struck gold when he signed Duran Duran.

It was Ambrose who had said of Giggles, years earlier, 'There isn't anything wrong with them. But there's not a lot *right* with them either.' However, I convinced him and EMI that, after Frankie, Spelt Like This were going to be the next big thing. I think my proximity to Frankie definitely helped.

We struck a great deal. The marketing campaign was going to be monumental and the records were to be produced by Stock Aitken Waterman, three men with a poptastic master plan.

SAW took the sound of the clubs, the Hi-NRG and disco, and wed it to simple songs of good times. They were easy on the ear but with thunderously cheesy dancefloor-ready productions. They made choons for ordinary people with Woolworth's ears.

The lyrics were simple and the tunes uncomplicated. SAW once gave *Smash Hits* readers a songwriting masterclass: 'If the song is called "Blue Eyes", stick to blue eyes. Don't start getting complicated and talking about her blonde hair.' Eat your heart out, Bob Dylan.

SAW enjoyed a slew of mega-hits, with Bananarama, Mel & Kim and Rick Astley. But where Trevor Horn worked to craft a production, SAW churned them out like a factory production line. The rhythms were credited bluntly to the drum machine that supplied them, a Linn. There was a lot of chirpy synth brass. But the hits kept coming.

So in 1984, Stock Aitken Waterman were working on Dead Or Alive's *Youthquake* album, convinced that 'You Spin Me Round' could be a big hit. Their Woolworth's ears were clearly in good order. They were also working on Spelt Like This's debut. It was not going well.

SAW declared that the songs we had written were substandard and the band lacked talent (this from the people who would later give the world the Reynolds Girls). At the time, they were relocating from Soho to Borough.

Pete insisted on hiring the most expensive equipment, the latest Neumann microphones as I recall. Amazing, isn't it, that it took so much money to make records that sounded so wonderfully cheap ...

After its difficult birth, I gave a huge sigh of relief once the Spelt Like This album was done and dusted. I was eager to package and present the group to the public. First I sent the anagrams to Fleet Street. The tabloids' pop columns wrote about them.

This was going to be sensational – I could feel it!

Their first single was 'Contract Of The Heart' which I envisaged as the 'All You Need Is Love' for the MTV generation. Where Frankie had brought discord with 'Two Tribes', surely Spelt Like This would now spread harmony. I knew it would sound great on the radio.

No expense was spared for the video. The whole world became a stage for Spelt Like This to lip-synch on. There were representatives from all nations; archive footage of cataclysmic political events; zany animation; twirling ballerinas. The boys learned their dance routine and mimed their hearts out.

The single sleeve was another budget-busting affair, stylish and striking. Inside this designer dream, the inner sleeve was a shot of a torso from the belly button to pubic hair: female on one side, male on the other. It looked great. In March 1985, 'Contract Of The Heart' hit the shops.

And then it hit the charts. It went straight in at … number ninety-one. It was a totally dismal placing. I was gutted.

The press got nasty. It's a fine line between a carefully put together pop package and a manufactured hype, and everyone decided that Spelt Like This was the latter. Even bloody *Smash Hits* sneered. It was probably them who decided that the most fitting rearrangement of the Scrabble letters was Spelt Like Shit.

The follow-up single also tanked, the record never made it onto the shelves and the group split. Alin went to Hollywood, took bit parts in movies and continued to make music. Russell soldiered on and was soon to be behind the mixing desk for my one foray into music making.

I've got no idea what happened to the other bloke. Sorry.

So Spelt Like This, my return to the world of managing acts, had gone straight down the dumper, another Tom Watkins flop act. Everyone could smell a hype. But I could only sniff the sweet smell of success getting stronger and stronger all the time.

Spelt Like This felt like one step closer. It had been another building block towards building the perfect boy band. The wrapping had been right: the present just hadn't lived up to expectations.

Next time it will be a different story, I thought.

And it was.

15

TWO IN A MILLION

Let's backtrack a little.

During the summer of 1981, the eyes of the world were on London. Charles and Di's marriage had caused a right royal frenzy. The temperature rose to a balmy 23°C; not too hot, not too cold: perfect. As the couple's 29 July wedding at St Paul's Cathedral approached, revellers up and down the nation poured out into the streets, basking in the English sunshine to toast the Queen's jug-eared eldest and the impossibly elegant Sloane Ranger, Diana. Shops everywhere flogged memorabilia emblazoned with the couple's faces; cups, tins, tea-towels. I didn't see any bog roll featuring the dynamic duo, but you never know …

Waves of Union Jack flags swept through crowds. Occasionally news cameras would zoom in on a real devout

Brit who, overcome by a surge of national pride, had actually painted the flag on their face. They weren't alone. That summer everywhere was recast in red, white and blue. When you walked through London, it glistened in the golden summer light.

It was one big knees-up.

Ian Botham had beaten the Aussies at cricket (149 not out!), Sebastian Coe had broken track records. Cinemas were filled with people watching *Chariots of Fire*, a movie of English triumph, in sport and beyond. That April, we even won the Eurovision Song Contest thanks to the sparkling foursome Bucks Fizz and their equally effervescent ditty, 'Making Your Mind Up'. It seemed England was working again.

And winning.

On the day of the wedding, crowds of dedicated spectators slept outside Buckingham Palace to witness events and a whopping 750 million watched the marriage on television sets across the world. As Di emerged from her carriage at St Paul's, a large per cent of the world population gasped in awe at the sight. Elizabeth and David Emanuel's ivory silk taffeta, lace-festooned gown was a dazzling confection with a 25-foot (!) train, straight out of the illustrated pages of a fairy tale. When Di emerged from the car, the train had been all crumpled up. Panic ensued and disaster quickly averted as it was straightened out ...

Cameras snapped relentlessly, champagne corks popped and fizz flowed like one big jubilant British river. It was all too perfect. Trouble was, unbeknown to anybody, the Spencer family tiara atop Di's head was giving the new

Princess of Wales a terrible headache. If you were one of those goons who likes to read meaning into everything, you'd see it as a tiny but significant sign, one that suggested the ending of this fairy-tale wedding might not be such a happy one after all.

And there were far more glaring examples of discontent that year than the royal burden of ill-fitting tiaras. Just before the pomp and circumstance of the Charles and Di wedding, a series of riots had kicked off in England. In Toxteth, Southall, Moss Side and Brixton, the dam burst on simmering racial tensions and social division.

Thatcher had just brought in Stop and Search, allowing police officers to do just that to anyone they regarded with suspicion. That meant an awful lot of black youths got harassed, often for no good reason. Violence erupted.

On a weekend in April 1981, Brixton, once a quaint Victorian suburb, was ravaged by its worst attack since the Second World War. The place was ablaze, petrol bombs flew, police cars and buildings were all on fire. Stores on the high street were looted, a man pushed a whole clothes horse of leather jackets down the road, trying them on as he went along.

One lady told of how her wedding reception had to be unceremoniously abandoned as the building was burning down. When she returned a few days later to salvage what she could from the carnage, all the food from the celebratory spread had gone stale. It was quite a different wedding scene from the one that was to grip the world two months later. And you didn't have to be one of those over-analytical goons to see it as a sign of a divided nation.

Amid the royal blue optimism, the Eurovision victory, the swells of the national anthem, discordant notes were ringing louder and louder. Unemployment rose to 2.5 million. And just a month before Charles and Di had tied the knot, six blanks had been fired at the Queen during the Trooping the Colour ceremony by an unemployed Royal Marines reject called Marcus Sarjeant.

And it was the best of times and the worst of times (them again!) in the pop charts, too. In mood and quality. The Specials' eerie masterpiece, the chart-topping 'Ghost Town', had wafted across the airwaves like a phantom, a memento mori to all the towns decimated by the Thatcher regime. The ersatz *Hooked on Classics* and *Stars on 45* were even grimmer. And then there was Shakin' Stevens' reheated rock 'n' roll, a microwave jobbie compared to the sizzling original fifties sound. His 'Green Door' topped the charts for four weeks, catchy as the common cold and ten times worse.

Album buyers were also just as likely to go for the sublime (Adam Ant's *Kings of the Wild Frontier*) as they were the ridiculous (more *Stars on 45*, Cliff Richard's *Love Songs* and the BBC's documentary of the royal wedding). But elsewhere, the sound of a bright, synthetic future flickered through the hit parade. Depeche Mode promised a perky 'New Life' that summer and the Human League's 'Love Action' wed unwavering amorous conviction to obscenely alluring electronics.

But the biggest synth pop triumph that summer was a cover version of 'Tainted Love', an old Northern Soul floor-filler, penned by Ed Cobb and originally performed by Marc Bolan's girlfriend, Gloria Jones. But it was another dynamic duo, Southport's Marc Almond and Blackpool's David Ball, that had taken the song's scorching soul and chilled it with an icy, wholly synthetic surface.

Between its 7 July release and its ascent to the top of the charts on 5 September, one day in August, the 19th to be precise, two men walked into a hi-fi shop on London's King's Road. One of them, Neil Tennant, was buying a lead for his newly acquired synthesiser. The other one, Chris Lowe, started talking to him about music.

As they got chatting, the pair sized each other up. What were their first impressions? Chris thought that the bespectacled, mop-haired Neil was brainy. He was impeccable with his words and claimed that he liked all that literate, serious rock music. Stuff like Elvis Costello.

For his part, Neil thought maybe Chris was a bit mad. He chuckled like Muttley from *Wacky Races* and, worse, he said he liked 'Body Talk' by Imagination, a steamy soft-porn slice of funk-soul that Neil disapproved of but real-world record buyers loved.

Nevertheless, despite their differences, the pair kept chitchatting. After all, they both liked David Bowie. Neil said that he worked in publishing but wrote songs. They agreed to meet up again.

Chris said that he would pop around to Neil's nearby flat soon, to hear some of his works in progress and tinkle on that synth that Neil had just bought a lead for. As the two men walked out onto the King's Road and went their separate ways, they both felt charged with an awkward, tentative excitement.

It was the kind of energy that you usually get from an unexpected, promising encounter. But it was more than that. They didn't know it but they had come face to face with the other half of a partnership that would change both of their lives and the face of pop music.

Neil got back to his flat with his lead. The small, cheap apartment was above a shoe shop called R Soles (arseholes, geddit?). Across the street, a storefront flashed words that spelt out Neil's future with the nonchalant character he'd just met.

It said: BOY LONDON.

Neil Tennant had always been a bit on the uppity side. As a kid, he nurtured a cut-glass accent despite growing up in Gosforth, near Newcastle. The other kids at school called him 'poshy'. His school reports said this:

'Neil attends when he chooses to and writes what he wishes— on what does he base his claim to superiority?'

Inveterately arty, he loved pop from an early age – Cilla Black, Dusty Springfield – as well as the drama of Noël Coward. By his teens, he was watching trains pulling out of Newcastle Grand Station bound for London's King's Cross and wishing he was on them.

Neil had formed a folky Incredible String Band-type group with a friend from a theatre group in his adolescent years, but glam rock was his epiphany. He was steeped in Bowie and Bolan, Liza Minnelli and musical soundtracks.

Moving to London in 1972 to study history at North London Poly, he was ensconced at Marvel Comics by the time I met him in 1975. Inspired to write songs by the punk explosion of 1976, he entered what he was to call his 'Billy Bragg period' and even put adverts in music papers for other musicians.

He had moved into publishing and was working for ITV Books – and about to decamp to *Smash Hits* – by the time he met Chris Lowe in 1981. Chris had had a rather different journey.

Growing up in Blackpool, he had even worked on the Big Wheel on the Pleasure Beach one summer. In fact, I always thought I could see both sides of the Pleasure Beach – the thrill of adventure and the melancholy when the lights go out – in Chris, the introspective party animal.

He came from a musical family, playing piano in a jazz band in his early teens and even briefly joining a heavy rock group with the appropriately virile name of Stallion. He hadn't cared much for pop until disco got him with the Bee Gees' soundtrack to *Saturday Night Fever*.

After studying architecture at Liverpool University, Chris had moved to London in 1981 and begun working in an architect's practice. When he strolled into the hi-fi shop that fateful day, he was living in Ealing.

His flatmates were all boys. They lived above a pet shop.

Before long, Chris was popping over to Neil's flat on a fairly regular basis. He liked some bits of the songs Neil played him and they would drink in the nearby Chelsea Potter and talk about music. They began to write songs, initially as a little hobby, without any clear direction or grand plan.

Their songs were all spritely, skimpy synths and arch words with a bit of melancholy. One early offering that I heard years later, called 'Bupadum' was very Depeche Mode, except for Neil drolly reciting the title like a funny monk running through a tunnel.

They also later played me something called 'Oh Dear', about meeting a man on the street. Chris noodled away on a synth like he was still on the Pleasure Beach and it made me think of 'Ghost Town' sung by Noël Coward. Only not as good. Chris said his flatmates liked it, mind you.

But they clearly had something, and struck gold when Chris went up to Blackpool and wrote a song on the family piano. Back in London, Neil wrote some lyrics for it and they called it 'Jealousy'. Now this was more like it.

If I can get poncy for a minute, if Edward Hopper had written songs instead of painting pictures, they would have sounded like 'Jealousy'. It was all sweeping grandeur and street-level grit. Later, Neil told me that it was written about a friend that resented the time he was now spending with Chris.

I didn't really care about that. What was more important to me was that Neil Tennant and Chris Lowe had written their first masterpiece. And Neil was just about to get into the pop world properly. He was about to join *Smash Hits*.

16

NEW YORK, NEW YORK

Neil Tennant actually got into *Smash Hits* via his book job. While he was working at ITV Books, *Smash Hits* editor David Hepworth asked him for help to publish a Madness book. He liked Neil a lot and in June 1982 he offered him a job.

Neil's brain was arguably too big to be immersed so deeply in the trivia of pop. But as his hero Noël Coward once said: 'Extraordinary how potent cheap music is.'

Even to an outsider like me at the time – running XL, but also reading *Smash Hits* avidly every week – it was clear that Neil was the heart and soul of the magazine. With his nerdy, encyclopaedic knowledge of the world of pop and ready wit, he coined his own language that came to dominate the magazine.

Artists that were doing well were 'on the giddy carousel of pop'. Bands that were struggling were 'down the dumper'. And anybody who was enjoying a comeback was 'Back! Back! Back!'

Neil's arch tongue – or pen – could get him into trouble. After he slagged off a Culture Club gig, he bumped into Boy George, who called him 'pathetic'. Neil feared that George and drummer Jon Moss were going to rough him up.

Let's just call him Neil Coward.

He was still writing songs with Chris and was keen to push them. When *Smash Hits* gave away Panini stickers of pop stars and took out radio adverts to publicise them, the promotional jingle – 'Six little stickers!' it went – was a Tennant/Lowe composition. They were paid a princely £500.

They had even come up with a name for themselves: West End. It was a bit naff, but they figured they would change it further down the line.

Renting out a cheap studio, they wrote a big churchy piece of music called 'It's A Sin'. It was all about guilt and shame. They were a funny, prickly pair.

Neil told me a story I've never forgotten about just what they were like in those early days. They went to a café for a cup of coffee and, on the way in, Neil absent-mindedly tried to push open a door that had to be pulled. When they got in, Chris stood aghast and horrified.

'What's wrong?' Neil asked him.

'You've shamed us,' whispered Chris. 'We have to go.'

They turned on their heels and promptly exited, despite the fact that nobody in the café had even noticed their incredibly minor faux pas. What a pair of twits.

Chris loved 12-inch singles and was a real vinyl hound. One day in early 1983 he stumbled across a single called 'Passion' by a female trio called the Flirts. But they were just window dressing. The song was by a New Yorker called Bobby Orlando who went as Bobby O.

When Chris played 'Passion' to Neil they both loved this slab of NY gay disco and Neil took to pulling Bobby O records out of the 'down the dumper box' at *Smash Hits* as well as buying his import singles and charging them to expenses. Before long, the mag was making Bobby O its 'Single of the Week'.

Their own winsome material started getting a harder edge, especially a new song they had written called 'Opportunities (Let's Make Lots Of Money)'. While I was having the time of my life at XL and designing Sarm West, Neil and Chris were going Bobby O-mad – and then Neil got a chance to meet him.

Sent to New York by *Smash Hits* to interview the Police, Neil figured it was his chance to track down Bobby O in person. Neil got on very well with Sting, a fellow snooty Geordie who had even been to the same school. When he wrote the feature, he called the Police front man 'a bronzed Adonis'.

Well, let's face it, Sting's ego could do with a bit of a boost, eh?

Bizarrely, the New York office where Neil interviewed Sting was in the same block as Bobby Orlando's HQ. Bobby O was happy to go to a diner with Neil, impressed by the Brit's knowledge of, and love for, his music, and readily agreed to make a record with him.

Shortly afterwards, Neil and Chris headed to New York and started recording with Bobby at his own studio on Broadway. Just before they left London, they came up with a song called 'West End Girls'. Neil had got the inspiration from an old James Cagney movie.

So I guess we were lucky he didn't call it 'You Dirty Rat'.

In New York, Bobby O liked Neil and Chris. He was surprised by how neat and tidy they were. They reminded him of a cartoon couple from his childhood, Peabody and Sherman.

The recording sessions went well. Between times, Bobby and Neil walked and talked through New York. It was an exciting time in the city. Hip-hop was breaking out. Afrika Bambataa had made *Planet Rock* with Arthur Baker. Madonna had just released her debut album. Neil and Chris took note of them all.

For the next year Neil and Chris went back and forth across the Atlantic, writing and recording songs like 'I Want A Lover' and 'Rent' with Bobby Orlando. They signed a production deal with him and licensed their recordings to his Bobcat label.

They also tried hard to think of a band name. West End didn't cut it. Altar Boys was considered and rejected. Eventually they settled on Chris's nickname for himself and his housemates back in Ealing. The Pet Shop Boys it was.

Neil recruited an old mate and fellow Geordie, photographer Eric Watson, to take some photos. He shot Chris holding a tennis racket and wearing sunglasses and both of them in sporty, preppy attire. To me, they looked like a dour Wham!

Back in the *Smash Hits* office, Neil finally found the courage to play his colleagues some music he had been making with Bobby Orlando. But he didn't play them the one song where he – sort of – rapped. He was still a bit embarrassed about 'West End Girls'.

He didn't need to be. Bobcat Records put out the song in the US and it came to the ears of Gordon Charlton, a London A&R man at Epic Records. Gordon loved it, and in no time Pet Shop Boys were signed to Epic and planning the release of 'West End Girls'.

They needed a single sleeve. Gordon Charlton suggested that Neil and Chris get in touch with XL Designs and Tom Watkins. A bell rang in Neil's head. Wasn't Tom Watkins that funny, fat, loudmouth who always used to return the Superman costume reeking of BO?

Oh no! Not him!

17

BOY LONDON

Neil Tennant might have had misgivings about me, but he was also a keen student of pop trends and he knew that XL had been slipping Frankie Goes to Hollywood's records into some pretty wild, crazy and inventive sleeves. He made a call and pretty soon he and Chris were chatting to me in our Poland Street offices.

It was like I had seen him just yesterday. Neil was his usually chatty self, full of funny things to say and carefully considered theories about the current pop climate. As ever, the withering put-downs spouted from him like a fountain.

I had never met Chris before and he was a lot more inscrutable. I couldn't work him out. One minute he seemed dead surly, the next he'd break out in a smile like a cheeky schoolboy. Instantly, I got the sense they lived in their own closed world, privately sharing their own jokes, amused and bemused by everything that was going on around them.

XL did a great job on the 'West End Girls' sleeve. The typography contorted the letters of their name into different shapes and sizes. It was the nearest thing they ever had to a band logo and I hear Chris still signs their name in the same way even today.

On the eve of the record's release, the *Evening Standard* commented that Pet Shop Boys was a ridiculous name. Worried, they toyed with the idea of dropping it. Of course, years later people were to suggest that Pet Shop Boys was the name given to those prone to sticking hamsters up their bums for sexual purposes.

Neil was still balancing being a wannabe pop star with being a pop scribe, of course. On a trip to Miami to interview Wham! for *Smash Hits*, he slipped their manager, Simon Napier-Bell, a Pet Shop Boys cassette. It contained 'West End Girls', 'Opportunities (Let's Make Lots Of Money)' and 'It's A Sin'. Napier-Bell was irritated that a mere journo should be so presumptuous and never listened to it. Good. His loss was to be my gain.

During an interview with Eurythmics, he told Annie Lennox about his plans for musical glory. The reliably serious Annie thought hard about her years of struggle and told him that, no, no, he had to pay his dues. He had – he'd been determinedly building his plan for most of his life.

Neil and Chris were growing further apart from Bobby Orlando. Not only was he across the ocean, he was thinking of scaling down to an eight-track recording studio. They were grateful for all Bobby O had done for them but they wanted bigger and better things.

Their fortunes took a bit of a hit. 'West End Girls' failed to set the chart alight, or even get anywhere near it, and Epic dropped them. What were they to do now?

Neil and Chris realised that they needed someone to bang a fist on the record company table for them. They needed a spiel merchant who could extract money from record companies to fund their growing ambitions.

And they decided I was the man for the job.

I could see their reasoning, of course. I was close to the Frankie Goes to Hollywood phenomenon. They both loved the huge, orchestral dance records that Trevor Horn was making at Sarm West with Art of Noise. They were probably even impressed by the size of the deal I had negotiated for the arguably somewhat ropey Spelt Like This.

Yes, Tom Watkins was the mean (if hardly lean) bullshit machine that the Pet Shop Boys needed if they were going to break through, get a decent deal and get into the charts where they belonged. Towards the end of 1984, I became their manager.

Naturally, I told them straightaway that they needed an image overhaul. I told everyone that. I can't remember the details, but I am sure that I initially suggested something that they would have baulked at. That was how things normally started.

I wouldn't have suggested that Neil and Chris raided the superhero wardrobe like Giggles or got trussed up in leather chaps like Frankie's Paul Rutherford, but I definitely told them that they should 'sex it up' a bit. Well, there was no point. Very early on, I realised that trying to get the Pet Shop Boys to do anything they weren't sure about was futile.

Still, they definitely needed guidance and were a bit unsure of how to present themselves. I sent them shopping with Iain R. Webb on the King's Road, a wad of cash in their hands. They picked up some clothes at Boy London (across the street from Neil's gaff): caps and t-shirts boldly emblazoned with the label's name in capitals.

That stuff was perfect. It was vaguely homoerotic, close enough to their name to imply it but not so blatant that it became tacky self-promotion. Of course, the cap was to become synonymous with Chris, but back then both of them wore one.

Neil picked out some checked shirts and trousers. Iain suggested that they blended up-to-date apparel with vintage clothing. All that Chris was really interested in was accessories, such as an expensive gold watch or a gold chain.

Wearing their new outfits, they did some low-key live performances. Just after they hired me as their manager, they did a short PA set at the Fridge in Brixton. They were both petrified but they took a deep breath and got through it. It was OK: no better, no worse.

We went to Luxembourg where Neil and Chris were expecting just to do a couple of songs on a radio show. When we arrived, they were led into a concert hall with a crowd waiting for them. I guess it was what Annie Lennox would call paying their dues.

To say the least, they were finding their feet. As they ran through 'West End Girls' in Luxembourg, Neil made valiant efforts to be a pop star. His curtains of hair made him look like Oscar Wilde and he even pulled *that face*, as if he had smelled something awful. He swayed his mic from hand to hand like Bowie and at one point made a strange, crazy gesture as if he was shooing away an invisible pest. Let's just say he didn't look comfy.

Meanwhile, Chris gyrated, smiled and looked as if he was actually having a good time. His pelvic thrusts into the synthesiser were so forceful that I wondered if he might mount and hump the keyboard. It was a long way from the two imperious, motionless statues that they were to develop into.

As I began managing them, I naturally got to know them a lot better. From the start, I liked Neil a lot. His outward demeanour always gave the impression of supreme confidence, as if he was calm, unruffled and shrewdly aware.

Neil seemed permanently switched on, the wheels in his brain constantly turning and absorbing everything, from recent current affairs to a movie, a photograph, a book or an obscure dance track. His composure and slightly prickly, quick wit made him good company, especially as he softened it with sweetness, a self-deprecating humour that stopped him seeming too pompous.

Yet he could be a dreadful snob. I always suspected that I had committed some dreadful faux pas when I was around Neil. He would get icy – or, even worse, his nose would tilt towards the heavens as if he could smell that used Spiderman costume all over again.

Maybe because I was similar, I recognised that underneath his calm exterior was a real vulnerability, a mass of insecurities. Sometimes, late at night, my phone would ring. It would be Neil, his voice quieter and even softer than usual.

He was on his own, and sad. We would sit and talk for a while and then he'd hang up. And the next time that I saw him he would be lively, funny, erudite Neil. It was the brittle mask that he had fashioned to face and conquer the world with.

Of course, being the big, brash, loudmouth 'fat poof' that I styled myself as, stricken with body issues and self-loathing yet on the surface all hail-fellow-well-met, I could totally relate to this. And I think it was these contradictions – calm and unease, romantic longing and chilly cynicism – that fed into Pet Shop Boys' songs.

Chris was trickier. He was nearly always remote and aloof and fiercely guarded. Yet when I saw him around people he had 'let in' beneath his guard, he was loyal, protective and loving. I saw it with his constant companion, Pete Andreas, and his family.

Chris had as many ideas as Neil; he just wasn't as loquacious, which, as time went by, made people unaware of how much he contributed to the Pet Shop Boys. But he simply did what he wanted to do. He would never stoop to the usual pop malarkey of feigning excitement in photos or promotion. They were a chore that Chris found boring and he made sure that the world knew it. If there was an appearance scheduled and Chris didn't want to do it, it didn't happen.

Neil was naturally cagey. When Pet Shop Boys signed to Massive, my management company, he initially still kept the day job at *Smash Hits*. He went off on the road with Depeche Mode and even used his knowledge of the book world to hawk his journalistic colleague Dave Rimmer's book about Culture Club around publishers.

They settled on Faber & Faber, whose music side was run by the Who's Pete Townshend. At the book's launch party, Neil got into a fracas with none other than a belligerent Paul Morley. Neil got so pissed off with my old bête noire that he gave Morley a kick in the shins. Now *that* I would have paid good money to see!

Signing with Massive meant I had to extricate them from their deal with Bobby Orlando. Bobby O was a tough negotiator and drove a hard bargain. When we had finished, he walked away with a points deal giving him royalties on Pet Shop Boys' subsequent three albums.

It would make him a millionaire.

18

OPPORTUNITIES

We had some killer songs. We had a look (or, at least, a work in progress). Now all that we needed was a record deal.

Everybody loved the three-track tape that was being circulated – including David Munns and Dave Ambrose at EMI. Given that Spelt Like Shit, sorry, This, were fast heading down the dumper, you would have thought the last thing they would be interested in was another Tom Watkins act.

But the Pet Shop Boys had 'West End Girls' and I still had the gift of the gab.

Before they knew it, Neil and Chris were driving around in Dave Ambrose's car, playing him a couple of new songs they'd written. Dave liked 'Beautiful Beast', a campy travesty that the world was never to hear.

Neil was quietly dismayed. The A&R man had barely noticed 'Love Comes Quickly', the beautiful mid-tempo electro ballad that they had proudly played him. But for now, it didn't matter: Ambrose had already decided that he was going to sign them.

Neil and Chris got out of his car and Dave drove away into the London night. For what it was worth, he was going to meet a man who wanted to put his beloved Duran Duran on postage stamps in Latin America.

Pet Shop Boys signed their deal with EMI subsidiary Parlophone in March 1985. Neil had told me that he was keeping his day job until a pop star salary could match it (they were paying him a princely £12,000). Well, once the advance came through, Neil finally quit *Smash Hits*.

One of his last assignments for the magazine was a report on the star-studded Brit Awards of 1985. The main attraction that year was Prince's appearance. He had come to accept two awards, accompanied by burly bodyguards and a furry stole draped over his shoulder that looked like a dead Fraggle.

Pandemonium ensued. People cheered and cameras flashed as everyone tried to catch a glimpse of the tiny purple genius. Holly Johnson presented Prince with the award live on TV, sharing the stage with a nervous-looking Noel Edmonds, clearly apprehensive that the Frankie singer might pull an X-rated stunt. He wasn't wrong. Holly, in bow tie and a big puffy leather jacket, told Great Britain that he had had sex with Prince on the phone.

When the barely audible Prince accepted the award, he mumbled something about how nice it was to be loved by somebody from far away. Presumably he meant the appreciative music fans of the UK, and not international phone sex with Holly Johnson.

Neil was stuck with all the other press in the upper balcony of the Grosvenor House Hotel. All the journos had been shoved upstairs well away from the main A-list action downstairs. He gazed down on his old mucker Sting looking 'gaunt and glamorous' with a new hairdo.

After the ceremony, Neil slipped downstairs. He bumped into Frankie, 'who were all pissed'. He said hello to George Michael and asked Elaine Paige if she had heard what Prince had mumbled onstage. Like a good hack, he even tracked down the group that had shared a table with the Purple One, Strawberry Switchblade.

He would never be stuck up in the Grosvenor Park Hotel balcony ever again. Soon he'd be down on the floor with the A-listers. Yet being a journalist never quite left him. In future, his feet would be down on the pop stars' floor but, in a funny way, his eyes would remain forever staring out from that balcony.

Smash Hits threw a party for the departing Neil at a little club off Carnaby Street, presenting him with a mock issue that featured him as the cover star, as they did whenever one of their hacks moved on. Across the fake copy was a suitably irreverent headline:

NEIL TENNANT: 'HOW I LEFT BRITAIN'S BRIGHTEST MAGAZINE TO FORM MY TRAGIC POP GROUP, WENT DOWN THE DUMPER AND ASKED FOR MY JOB BACK'

They were only half joking. Everybody knew somebody who had tried to cross over to the other side of the pop fence. Most had failed. They would miss Neil, his sense of humour, his erudite take on pop music, and his pithy banter. He had been earmarked as a future editor.

Nobody believed that within nine months of leaving *Smash Hits* he would be smiling from the magazine's cover. And this time it would not be a mock-up.

The hardest bit is always telling your parents. I remembered that from my dad. Neil phoned his mum and told her he had signed a deal with Parlophone Records, the same EMI imprint that the Beatles had been on.

'That's great news, Neil,' she said. 'But you aren't going to leave your job, are you?'

'I already have,' he told her.

As I could tell from the late-night phone calls I started getting, Neil spent quite a bit of time worrying about the decision that he had made. He feared he had been reckless in giving up a steady job to attempt to leap onto the 'giddy carousel of pop'. He would miss the free records and the flowing conversations about all things pop. Yet there is no doubt his time at *Smash Hits* and the *knowingness* he picked up there always informed Pet Shop Boys.

Yet as Neil and Chris's ideas on their image evolved it soon became clear to me that they would be subverting this 'giddy carousel' as much as they were riding it. Neil's photographer mate Eric Watson started feeding loads of enigmatic monochrome images of Neil and Chris to magazines like *Blitz*, *i-D* and *The Face*.

Like one-time Frankie lensman John Stoddart, Eric had been looking at legendary US fashion and portrait photographer Richard Avedon's shots, particularly the portraits of elderly composer Igor Stravinsky and the poet Ezra Pound. These sombre black and white shots gave their subjects a craggy, almost religious intensity, as if they were ascetic saints.

Eric's photos of Neil and Chris portrayed the pair in an equally unvarnished light, with their stubble visible and lines and shadows across their faces. I quickly began referring to them as 'the ugly pictures'.

The point was that magazine readers flicked the pages of their style bibles and wondered what these photos were all about. At that point they weren't promoting anything specifically. It got people thinking and scratching their heads, as they had done when XL/ZTT adverts had appeared for Frankie records that hadn't been finished yet.

And what they were thinking was: *Who are those dour, miserable bastards?* There was a distinct absence of peroxide, tans, make-up or zany smiles. Neil and Chris didn't seem to be trying to make anyone like them. In fact, in one image Neil looked clean away from the camera, refusing to pander to it.

It hadn't been my idea and initially I was bloody horrified. This wasn't what I was used to at all! I had spent my whole career trying to get my acts to entertain, to slap on the lipstick and mascara and please the punters.

However, Neil may not have been older than me but he was wiser. He and Chris realised that they couldn't play the pop game straight if they tried. They weren't 100 per cent sure what they were yet, but they knew what they *weren't*. They would not be following in the footsteps of Spandau Ballet, Duran Duran or Wham!

For me, there was also something distinctively *northern* about their contrariness. I soon twigged that everything in the Pet Shop Boys' world was about putting opposites together, creating a tension, cancelling itself out and producing what a pompous pseud (who could I have in mind?) might call a 'dialectic'.

East/west. Posh/rough. Irony/sincerity. Pop/anti-pop. The list was endless. It made the band an enigma, constantly reacting against itself but also impossible to pinpoint. In an odd way, it occurred to me in one of my more lucid moments, Neil and Chris were a bit like Arthur Seaton, the angry young man of classic British movie *Saturday Night and Sunday Morning,* obstinately refusing to be defined by anyone else's perception of him:

'Whatever people say I am, that's what I'm not.'

Yet not all of their ideas were impeccable. Most of them were, but a few were horribly pretentious. When we signed our management deal, they put out a press release with a manifesto of sorts, listing all of the things they weren't. It was very Neil and Chris; very Pet Shop Boys. They wanted to call the document 'Two in a Million'.

Fair enough: I've always loved a big gesture. But they wanted this bold stroke of hubris to be in Italian. *Italian!* Sure, they liked Italy and they wanted to be big there, but what a load of pretentious bollocks! I winced, rolled my eyes and said

I thought it was a horrendous idea. For once, just *once*, they listened as I lectured them.

'We want to sell records and get in the hit parade, right?' I asked them. 'This will just scare the record-buying public off!' I paused, and hit them with the question that I used so much that it became a bit of a catchphrase: 'What would Edna from Huddersfield think?'

As time went on, and their ideas got grander and artier, I would pose this question many, many times. Ah, good old Edna. She has served me well.

The great thing was that the songs kept coming, showing increasing confidence and ever grander ambitions. After the exquisite 'Love Comes Quickly' came 'I'm Not Scared', which initially had the crap punning title 'A Roma'. Both of them showed a debt to the elegant, sophisticated side of Italian disco. They were love songs but they were devoid of sappy sentimentality.

After we got the Parlophone deal, Pet Shop Boys went into Terminal Studios in Elephant and Castle and in a single day knocked out first drafts of 'Suburbia' and 'Tonight Is Forever'. Not a bad day's work! I rubbed my hands. They both sounded like hits.

So, still, did 'Opportunities (Let's Make Lots Of Money)'. It was decided that it would be their first EMI single. We hired the Art of Noise's J.J. Jeczalik and Nicholas Froome for production duties. Neil and Chris loved the ZTT records that J.J. had worked wonders on, and Jeczalik and Froome had been responsible for that year's hit rerecording of 'Kiss Me' by Stephen 'Tin Tin' Duffy. Neil liked it and wanted to work with them.

J.J. also knew his way around a Fairlight, which excited Chris. By the time Neil and Chris got to Terminal, J.J. had already constructed a rhythm track for 'Opportunities' on the sampling synthesiser. It immediately gave the song a harder edge than the Bobby O original.

The 'Opportunities' sessions stretched out for three weeks. No expense was spared. It cost £40,000. We threw a party at Sarm East in Brick Lane so that we could record it for the song's middle section. It got edited out of the final cut. Yet when we had finished, nobody was that happy with the result.

Neil and Chris flew to New York to work with Ron Dean Miller, who had recorded dance tracks they loved, including Nuance's 'Love Ride'. He did a terrific remix of 'Opportunities', running the oomph of the chorus drums through the whole track and giving it more punch. Then they recorded another track with him, 'Why Don't We Live Together'.

With me on board to keep on EMI's case and strong-arm them into spending money, the budgets were flowing and our every whim was indulged. One of Neil's catchphrases at *Smash Hits* (after a reliably grumpy Paul Weller had said it to him in an interview) was, 'It's like punk never happened.'

It certainly felt like that now.

Neil and Chris met Blue Weaver, a keyboard player who had worked on Chris's beloved *Saturday Night Fever*. Blue was also a very proud owner of a Fairlight. Bored of the never-ending 'Opportunities' sessions, Chris wrote some music on it that became the record's B-side, 'In The Night'.

'In The Night' had a Hi-NRG feel, like a cross between 'You Spin Me Round' and 'Blue Monday', but the words were all about the *zazous*, a bunch of French hedonists who defied the Nazis during the occupation but were more concerned with partying than joining the French Resistance.

Ever the bookworm, Neil used the lyric to detail actual locales that the *zazous* frequented such as Select and Le Colisée. Yes, while other eighties pop musicians were snorting cocaine off supermodels' arses, Neil Tennant was burning the midnight oil brushing up on modern history.

I suggested they cut it with Phil Harding, the engineer at PWL who had been such a lifesaver during the torturous Spelt Like This sessions. In no time, 'In The Night' was in the can. It was terrific, dead smart and danceable, Hi-NRJ and novel all at once. What was more, Neil and Chris had just recorded the future theme for Jeff Banks' *The Clothes Show* without knowing it.

With the single's two sides recorded, we set about getting the sleeve designed and filming the Pet Shop Boys' first video. Eric Watson directed the clip with Andy Morahan, a gifted young promo maker who was to go on to big things working with Guns N' Roses.

Eric had seen *Wise Blood*, the 1979 John Huston film about a con artist who preached the gospel and swindled cash, and thought Neil should model himself on the character. He stuck him in a garage pit with a hat and glasses on. However, when certain members of EMI's staff saw it, they disapproved. They thought Neil looked like a Hasidic Jew singing a song about making lots of money.

Oops! But it was purely unintentional. Behind him in the video, a car was parked. Neil's image twitched with fancy editing and eventually crumpled into dust as the car drove off, leaving the song's gloomy final words to be accompanied by smoke-filled space. And Chris.

Chris hung about the shoot wishing that he was somewhere else (he'd had to postpone a dental appointment and was none too pleased). He drifted through the clip like a bit-part soap opera actor, maybe a car mechanic extra on *EastEnders*. The on-site catering company, who didn't know who he was, also refused to serve him.

On the record's sleeve, Neil stared out the camera, his hair tousled and his coat lapel decorated with a dollar-sign brooch, a cheeky nod to the song's sending up of aspiring yuppies, of money culture in the era of Thatcher. It was another 'wind up'. Or was it? Neil was ambitious with a real need to get ahead. The dollar sign was a tiny emblem of his own drive, one that he was too cool to ever really show but one he undoubtedly possessed. On the back of the sleeve, Chris pouted in a peaked cap and leather jacket, looking like a vintage American biker, a bit Brando, a bit Kenneth Anger.

After all the time and money spent on 'Opportunities', we eagerly awaited its release. We were sitting in my office when it got its first play on Radio 1 and all huddled around the speakers.

On the air, Neil breathed the last few lines of the song: 'The love we had, the love that we hide, who will bury us when die?' The notes faded away. 'Huh, that was a bit pretentious, wasn't it?' commented the DJ.

He might as well have blown a raspberry. I wondered if Edna from Huddersfield would have been nodding in agreement. Awkwardness filled the room, so I set about offering words of reassurance.

'Oh well, what do DJs know about these things? Mike Read hated "Relax" and look at how well that did.'

'Opportunities' came out. It stalled at number 116.

So, £40,000 spunked away in three weeks, flights to New York to work with remixers, and all for a record that charted twenty-five places lower than Spelt Like This's turkey 'Contract Of The Heart'. I had one thought: *Here we fucking go again.*

The irony that this dumper-bound ditty was about making lots of money did not escape me. Neil had said that the song was about two losers who weren't going to make it. I wondered if he thought life was imitating art.

Because I certainly did.

Still, we soldiered on. The EMI deal was for an album and so that was what we had to deliver. We brought in producer Stephen Hague to work on the record. He had made 'Madam Butterfly' with Malcolm McLaren, and 'Hey! DJ' by The World's Famous Supreme Team, the rapping duo who had worked with Trevor Horn and McLaren on *Duck Rock*. Hague's productions sounded 'grandiose and street' at the same time, which was perfect for the Pet Shop Boys.

The first job was to rerecord 'West End Girls'. The original was now nearly two years old, an eternity in the ever-moving world of pop. Bobby O's production was rooted in the early eighties and New York. Stephen Hague, Neil and Chris worked on it diligently for five days.

They added sampled noises of street sounds and traffic, making it feel cinematic and 'giving it three dimensions', as Neil said. In came a trumpet solo, or, rather, a fake one on an Emulator, giving the song a jazzy feel somewhere between a film noir soundtrack and a yuppy wine bar – the kind of place we hoped 'West End Girls' would soon be pumping out of.

It was slowed down and sounded moodier, even gothic, and more soulful all at once. Backing singer Helena Springs added her vocal presence, sounding a bit like Grace Jones, majestic and mournful, like a statue weeping.

It sounded great. Surely this time it would work? It had to. We were in the last-chance saloon.

Eric and Andy again shot the video. I told them that it had to be 'a travelogue around London' and their cameras followed Neil and Chris around the capital, from the East End in the early hours to Waterloo Station and the Embankment. A tramp followed them down the street.

At Eric's suggestion, Neil wore a £400 Stephen Linnard overcoat. He was so taken with the garment he got EMI to buy him his own. It was money well spent. This overcoat became a vital part of Neil's early image: part costume to suit his metropolitan, urbane image, and part protective armour for when he faced the public in performance.

On this 'West End Girls' video shoot, Chris Lowe truly became *Pet Shop Boys Chris*. There he was, insouciantly walking two steps behind Neil, looking bored, looking away from the camera, occasionally glancing at it. There were no keyboards in the video, just the footage of their journey through the 'bright lights and grim lives' of the capital, interspersed with aerial shots of the city.

On 28 October 1985, EMI released the rerecorded 'West End Girls'. It charted at an inauspicious number eighty. *Here we go again ...*

But then it rose steadily. Word of mouth spread. Radio 1 kept playing it, with Gary Davies particularly partial. It seemed to me that whenever it came on the airwaves it stopped people dead in their tracks, just like Kate Bush had done with 'Wuthering Heights'. It was exciting and original and people were genuinely startled by it.

In fact, Dusty Springfield was later to tell me that when 'West End Girls' hit American radio, she was so awestruck when she first heard it that she swerved across the freeway and nearly crashed her car. This was quite a coincidence – as Neil and Chris had already written a song that they wanted her to sing.

I was looking after Allee Willis, a songwriter behind hits like Earth, Wind & Fire's 'Boogie Wonderland' and the Pointer Sisters' 'Neutron Dance' (and a woman with seriously crazy hair, which blocked up the plughole of the shower in my flat) and I suggested that she write a song with Neil and Chris.

The three of them came up with a purpose-built duet between a male and female voice. A lifelong fan, Neil wanted Dusty to take the female part. But we couldn't track her down and the song – called 'What Have I Done To Deserve This?' – was temporarily shelved.

Meanwhile, 'West End Girls' kept crawling up the charts. Neil and Chris did promotion to try to help it on its way. On their first *Top of the Pops* performance they were introduced as 'an odd couple'; a pair of strange men with a strange record.

On *TOTP*, Chris mimed the bass line on the keyboards while Neil stood stock-still as if rooted to the floor, authoritatively gesturing with his hand, his fingers curled, as if pointing to a holy revelation in a Renaissance painting. Or, more likely, it was something a lazy bastard who can't dance does when he wants to look important.

I watched the broadcast with a vague sense of horror. *They don't do anything,* I thought to myself. *How are people going to go for this?*

Yet they did. I had spent so many years putting red-hot pokers up performers' arses (figuratively speaking, of course) to get them to work to win over a crowd and my big break had come with two men who barely broke sweat. I could certainly see the irony of this.

What was funny was that, away from the cameras, Chris loved to dance. Every now and then he would excite Pet Shop Boys audiences by unexpectedly showing his fancy footwork. It was like watching a mannequin come to life.

Neil and Chris got interviewed for Neil's old alma mater, *Smash Hits*. The pair slagged off everybody else's records: Paul McCartney, Tina Turner, Starship. It was no surprise that they could be awfully bitchy, and *Smash Hits* happily dubbed them 'the rudest men in pop'.

Talking to the mag, Neil declared that he only really liked pop stars once they had hit the dumper, like Gary Numan or

Culture Club. This was a remarkable claim, especially since he might still be heading there himself.

Ever a promotional natural, Chris told *Smash Hits* that he channelled Tchaikovsky when he composed, then a few days later, after a long night, he dozed off on breakfast TV while Selina Scott was interviewing them. It was a shame Tchaikovsky couldn't keep him awake.

By Christmas 1985, 'West End Girls' was safely nestled in the top ten. It was a fantastic present for all of us. Everybody was ecstatic. Finally, the Pet Shop Boys had a hit. Even more amazingly, finally a Tom Watkins act had a hit.

When the best acts hit the top, they keep climbing. In the first singles chart of 1986, 'West End Girls' hit number one. *Number fucking one!* I danced around the office, as the phones just never stopped ringing. Dreary post-Christmas blues? Forget it! I was on Cloud Nine.

Pet Shop Boys had wrestled the top spot away from Shakin' bloody Stevens and his 'Merry Christmas Everyone' travesty and it was utterly glorious. The stars were aligned, fireworks exploded in my head and trumpets sounded in my heart.

Well, that was me. What was Neil Tennant's reaction? He airily told the press that being number one 'feels like vaguely nothing – like having a cup of tea'.

Oh puh-leaase!

Nevertheless, it was interesting that he equated being number one with a cup of tea – the same analogy that Boy George had used to pretend he wasn't interested in sex. Clearly Boy George was bonking, and clearly Neil Tennant loved being number one.

There again, if I have learned one thing in this life it is that pop stars are full of shit.

Neil was completely over the moon but he wasn't going to show it. Nor was Chris. Years later, Neil was to tell journalists that coming to pop music later in life meant that he never had to worry about being cool.

This was complete contradiction. Neil and Chris were obsessed with being cool. They were like teenagers, pouting rather than beaming enthusiastically. In fact, at the start of their chart-topping *Top of the Pops* performance, Chris leaned forward for a quiet word with Neil.

'Don't look triumphant.'

Again ... oh puh-leaase!

'West End Girls' was number one for two weeks and outside Britain it was a global smash. It topped the charts in Norway, New Zealand, Israel, Hong Kong, Finland and Ireland and made the top ten almost everywhere. It was number one in America.

Number one in America!

For me, the years of Ice Cream, of support slots with Leo Sayer, of never getting a hit with Giggles, of the false start of Portraits, all evaporated overnight. All of my 'dodgy acts' (yes, thank you, Neil) faded from memory.

The Pet Shop Boys were now firmly installed on the 'giddy carousel of pop' and I fully intended to keep them there. Ever a retiring soul, I also intended to climb on there myself, as long as there was a seat big enough for my fat arse.

As 'West End Girls' continued to hang around the top of the charts, Neil and Chris continued to record their debut album at Advision Studios with Stephen Hague. Hague proved to be an inspired choice. He made the songs bigger and bolder than the Bobby O originals while retaining their hard, electro edge, and worked endlessly on the backing tracks.

On 'Opportunities', he took elements of J.J. Jeczalik's take and brought in parts of the Ron Dean Miller version, creating a dynamic hybrid of the two that finally got it right. Now it packed an industrial wallop. If it *was* a swipe at Thatcherite values, it was a neat trick to get yuppies grooving even while they were being cleverly mocked. Talk about having it both ways!

Stephen also knew how to record Neil's singing. It could sound weak and thin in the cold light of day but became a fantastic pop voice on record, especially when double-tracked. It was a voice you wanted to hear. Credit to Neil, he had also taken a few lessons.

After the album sessions, Neil, Chris and Stephen would drink some Retsina and head off to a nearby kebab joint on the Edgware Road. Yes, believe me, Neil Tennant and a doner may sound an unlikely match, but he got through a few of them.

Some guests dropped in. Andy Mackay from Roxy Music stopped by to blow some sax on 'Love Comes Quickly'. His then wife, Jane, was in tow and chatted endlessly with Neil. I was excited, but Andy's contribution was buried in the song's mix.

'Love Comes Quickly' became my favourite Pet Shop Boys song (and still is). It was gorgeous, a vintage love song set to the breezy sound of Italian disco at its most sophisticated.

Here was all the agony and ecstasy of falling in love … in a pop song. Wonderful!

Around then, I showed the Pet Shops my mock-ups for their album's sleeve design. I was eager to get their feedback. I thought my sleeve concept was a great idea: a big fold-out lattice-work cover, opening out into a crucifix that contained all the mean and moody images they had created over the last couple of years. I excitedly folded the cardboard out in front of them, knowing they were going to just love it.

An awkward silence ensued. Neil and Chris mumbled a few words with an overwhelming air of indifference. Perturbed looks flashed across their faces. They didn't like it.

I didn't show it but I was mortified. They were able to make me feel like the most gauche, tasteless vulgarian in all the cosmos – even if they didn't mean to. I left the studio feeling like a pile of poo.

Even so, I still knew that my fold-out sleeve was a great idea. *Fuck them*, I thought. *I'll use it myself at a later date. It's a better bloody idea than 'Two in a Million' in sodding Italian!*

In actual fact, when the album, *Please*, emerged in March 1986, its sleeve could not have been more different from my original concept. It was a huge white space with a postage stamp-sized photo of Neil and Chris at the centre with white towels draped around their necks.

The fact that the images were so tiny made them enigmatic. It made anybody who saw them wonder: *What have these two shifty blokes been up to? Have they been enjoying a game of tennis? Have they been relaxing at a health club? Or been naughty at a steamy sauna?*

You just didn't know. That was the whole point.

However, the real mastermind behind *Please*'s sleeve design was one Mark Farrow, who was a fairly recent heterosexual addition to the XL team. He was a sexy, sarky northerner to whom Neil and Chris had gravitated towards instantly.

This was despite Farrow announcing to them that he 'loathed and detested' the sleeve for 'West End Girls'. He hated everything: the design; the lettering; the feel. *Christ*, I thought, *this man takes record covers very seriously.*

Farrow didn't hold back and his lack of tact made him unpopular in the XL office. He definitely ruffled a few lily-livered southerners' feathers, including David Smart's. Yet Neil and Chris loved him: like them, he was northern, assertive, funny and sarcastic, a dead cocky character. And, more than that, he had a singular eye for design.

He showed this when asked to design a sleeve for a 'Mastermix' 12-inch remix of 'West End Girls'. It was, frankly, a work of art. All excess imagery and uneven lettering was removed and he added bold blocks of red and blue, with a yellow circle at the centre like a record label.

Neil Tennant had apparently cried with admiration and jealousy when he saw the sleeve to New Order's 'Blue Monday'. He must have been a blubbering wreck when he saw his own sleeve housed in such a similarly modern, vibrant and elegant sleeve. It was Bauhaus. It was Memphis. It was fucking genius. From that moment on, Mark Farrow was a vital part of Pet Shop Boys' team.

Farrow did an equally great job with the sleeve to the follow-up single, 'Love Comes Quickly'. He just used Eric Watson's brilliant photograph of Chris with no busy, distracting typography, as if the 'Boy' cap alone was enough to identify the artists (the philistines at the American record company didn't agree and added the band's name and the song title).

Yet despite the cool sleeve and the calibre of the song, 'Love Comes Quickly' failed to emulate the meteoric rise of 'West End Girls' and stalled at a disappointing number nineteen. Maybe it was more like a third or fourth single than a follow-up to an epoch-defining chart-topper.

Neil, of course, pretended not to be at all concerned. After all, when 'West End Girls' hit number one, he had fallen back on his *Smash Hits* parlance to assure journalists that 'if our next single flops, I won't slash my wrists – we'll [just] be down the dumper'.

Neil didn't do anything as horribly dramatic as slashing his wrists but for a few weeks tetchy unease filled Pet Shop Boys' camp. It dispersed when *Please* hit the shops and sailed to number three in the album chart. Crisis averted, brow wiped of sweat, dumper nimbly avoided.

Like the title-free 'Love Comes Quickly', Farrow's cover for *Please* was an alluring artefact that didn't do anything as gauche as trying to persuade customers to buy it. I believe they call it 'reverse' or 'anti' marketing? Whatever. Thankfully, it worked.

Farrow's stylish, gnomic shrunken images and absence of descriptive typography betrayed his earlier years crafting post-modernist japes at Manchester's Factory Records. He had loved their sleeves for Joy Division and dropped out of college and networked frantically to get a foot in the door at Factory.

Crucially, he saw himself as a graphic designer who happened to work in sleeve design for music rather than as a mere record-sleeve designer. He was drawn to music but brought something outside pop into it. It all made him the perfect designer for Neil and Chris.

Farrow was, over the years, to win many awards for his work with Pet Shop Boys, including for his sleeve for the 'Suburbia' single from *Please*. It was another masterpiece of design: an anti-pop sleeve. Its inner sleeve carried a blurred pic of Chris throttling Neil, which was a real luxury for a single.

His sleeve for the rerelease of 'Opportunities' was equally audacious. There was no band pic, just computerised lettering coldly spelling out the song and band name all in silver and gold, the colour of money. For 1986, it was incredibly ahead of its time.

The 'Opportunities' rerelease and 'Suburbia' both fared far better than 'Love Comes Quickly' had done. Not as well as we would have liked, but perfectly respectable.

The video for 'Suburbia' was also a triumph. Eric Watson's film cut between suburban England (Kingston upon Thames) and Los Angeles (north of Pasadena) and featured Neil and Chris in suits on a sofa, watching themselves on TV. Neil got up to spray away pesky flies and Chris wielded a baseball bat. Then they walked through America with Neil in, of all things, a cowboy hat.

He started wearing this hat all the time, even to 1987's Brit Awards. Of course, by now he was firmly on the main floor, well away from the lowly journos on the balcony.

Neil was there to receive the best single award for 'West End Girls' from a ropey-looking Boy George, who made a joke about punching a journo who had compared his voice to Japan's David Sylvian. As he handed the trophy to Neil, he resisted the chance to take a hit at the smarmy former *Smash Hits* writer he had once called 'pathetic'.

After all, Neil Tennant was a proper pop star now. And Boy George really liked 'West End Girls'.

And where was Chris Lowe? He stayed home, ate his dinner on a tray and watched the Brit Awards on the telly. Well, of course he did.

19

DROSS. GLOSS. CAVIAR!

Just as the Pet Shop Boys' career took off, disaster ensued for me.

XL Design went bankrupt.

We had always had plenty of work – how had this happened? Well, none of us were exactly skilled accountants, and the ever-increasing deluge of invoices coming into the office proved to be impossible for a bunch of scatty queens to deal with. So now what did we do?

I brought in my old friend Mick Newton, who had been bass player in one of my old 'dodgy acts', Burglar Bill. Mick had retrained and was by then a virtuoso accountant. He set about helping me to sort out the whole mess.

It was a right old palaver. For a start, I had to 'buy back' the Pet Shop Boys' contract from the liquidator. That cleaned me out. We also had to vacate the Poland Street offices. David and Royston promptly went off to form Accident, another design group. I took Mark Farrow with me and went into business with Mick Newton.

I retained the Massive Management name but we also formed a new company, Three Associates, which we shortened to 3a. Another new name was Freestyle. After all, the more names you use, the bigger your empire looks.

In reality, I moved back into the old, cheap rent space upstairs from Paul Rodwell's lawyer's offices on Welbeck Street.

Mark Farrow, Gary Knibbs and me were all crammed into two small rooms with a draughtsman's table and all the things you needed for design and graphics before computers became commonplace. Then there was my PA, Nikki Slight, who I had poached from Lynne Franks.

Lynne was the PR titan who became the inspiration for Edwina in *Absolutely Fabulous*. Lynne was always on a fad diet: mustard and cabbage, cashew nut and celery, you name it. She did our PR at XL for a while and I thanked her by luring Nikki away.

Luckily, there was no time to lick my wounds from XL's financial meltdown. The Pet Shop Boys were exploding. Their schedule was so hectic and demanding that we needed a new recruit to help deal with the demands.

Enter Rob Holden. Rob walked into the offices in his dad's Tonic suit, with a shaved head and a black eye (courtesy of a disgruntled musician he was looking after). Naturally, I hired him on the spot.

Rob was a real grafter. He had been working for Hayzi Fantayzee and Boy George's mate Marilyn in some vague capacity, and was also supposedly setting up a small record label with a friend while on the Enterprise Allowance, basically a scheme to reduce the unemployment figures. You got your rent paid and £50 a week if you came up with a business plan and had a bank account.

Rob needed somewhere he could use the phones for free and a mutual friend told him that I might need some help with Pet Shop Boys. He made an appointment with me and found out what he could about the Pet Shops.

I was very upfront and asked questions like 'Do you do drugs?' to see if it fazed him. I knew everything was about to go supernova and I needed someone I could rely on. He plainly had an entrepreneurial streak, which endeared him to me. He was a go-getter.

Rob met Neil and Chris a couple of days later at *The Old Grey Whistle Test*, which they were filming. Andy Kershaw introduced them and they sang a couple of numbers from *Please* with a bank of TV sets behind them. It was evident that Neil was terrified of singing live and it showed in his shaky vocal performance. He certainly felt nowhere near ready to tour.

The day after *The Old Grey Whistle Test*, Rob accompanied Neil and Chris to Manchester for a kids' TV show and then went straight to Italy to do TV there. It was a baptism of fire for the new boy.

There again, doing promotion with the Pet Shop Boys was easy (even given the fact that Chris hated it). There were only two of them and all they needed were a couple of keyboards and a microphone. You could send them off around the world with very little equipment and minimal entourage.

I went with them on some great promotional trips to the States. I remember checking out of the Mondrian Hotel in Los Angeles, only to return because the hotel we decamped to wasn't half as nice. We bumped into Bananarama there, who entertained us with impressions of Beverly, the gin-soaked housewife in Mike Leigh's *Abigail's Party*. What a hoot!

The time came around to start gathering ideas for the follow-up album to *Please*. We demoed tracks at a studio in Wandsworth. Neil and Chris were on a roll. Not only were they coming up with new songs all the time, but they still had a vast backlog of tunes from their early days that they could cherry-pick material from.

One of my first major tasks for the second album was to get Dusty Springfield for the duet 'What Have I Done To Deserve This?' At this point, Dusty was pretty washed up. After a series of flop albums she had retreated to LA, living above Sunset Strip in a house with coyotes and raccoons, and was pumped full of Mandrax, cocaine and booze like a cross between Little Edie from *Grey Gardens* and a hapless protagonist from *Valley of the Dolls*. Unsurprisingly, her confidence was at an all-time low.

Yet as I said, Dusty had loved 'West End Girls' so it wasn't that hard to persuade her. Everybody agreed it was a terrific song, a winning combo of eighties electro, Neil's white-boy rapping and classic sixties pop.

The song was really stitched together from disparate pieces, with Neil, Chris and Allee Willis all contributing a section. They worried that it wouldn't come together but the end result was perfect, a timeless pop song for star-crossed lovers who were both licking their post-split wounds. It was totally of its time: they were clearly yuppies in crisis.

Allee's bridge, a throwback to the kind of evergreens Dusty sang in her heyday, was the best bit of the song. I was there when Neil and Dusty first met to discuss the track.

'How do you want me to sound?' asked Dusty, anxiously.

'Like you,' replied Neil, succinctly.

Neil and Chris had to be away doing interviews when she laid down a classic Dusty vocal, but Stephen Hague coaxed a great performance out of her.

I have to admit, weirdly, I was a bit unsure about the song when they first played it to me. What a fool I am ...

At times. But at others, I see a potential diamond where everybody else just sees a rotten heap of coal.

In the middle of 1986, three teenagers from Camberley walked into my Welbeck Street office. Two of them were twins, Matt and Luke Goss; the other one was their mate, Craig Logan, whom the brothers had met in the lunch queue at Collingwood High School. My old A&R and producer mate Nicky Graham had suggested me to them as they had formed a band that was then being looked after by a bloke called Bob Herbert (who would later briefly look after the Spice Girls).

The trio were frustrated with how slowly their career seemed to be progressing and Nicky told them I could be the shot in the arm they needed. So they shuffled into my office, sheepishly looking at me from the other side of my desk.

My first impression: they looked fucking dreadful. They were an eyesore of mullets, earrings and ruffled attire like a trio of poodles dressed up like New Romantics and primped and preened at the doggie parlour. In the office, my sophisticated London staff all rolled their eyes in disbelief. What was I thinking?

No question, these kids from Camberley were unspeakably naff. The two twins, singer Matt and drummer Luke, looked like the offspring of some grim union between Radio 1 DJ Pat Sharp and an Essex girl. The brown-haired, bass-playing one, Craig, looked like a spotty oik from *Grange Hill,* dressed up like William of Orange.

It was surely a case of DOA – Dumper on Arrival.

Don't ask me why, but underneath their layers of crap clothing and even crapper hairstyles I immediately saw a possible teen sensation. *They could be the three musketeers of pop*, I thought to myself. And when I heard their music, dire as it was, it didn't hurt that the singer sounded like Michael Jackson.

Mentally, I rubbed my hands gleefully, sensing that they were putty in them. Unlike Neil and Chris, I could mould this lot with complete control.

The Goss twins had been encased in the womb with synchronised heartbeats so their parents hadn't expected twins right up until the second one – Matt – popped out. After their dad, Alan, moved out, their mum, Carol, had met a new man,

Tony, who moved the family down to Somerset, apparently inspired by *The Good Life*.

Matt and Luke hadn't taken to their yokel life, the move hadn't worked out and they moved to Camberley, even living in a caravan for a while. Their dad had tried to get custody but they had remained loyal to their mum.

Music had been an escape from this tumult. Tony bought Luke a set of electronic drums and a sax for Matt, although he could barely play 'Baa Baa Black Sheep' on it. Matt loved Stevie Wonder and Michael Jackson: Luke was more into Phil Collins.

Once they went to Collingwood School, they had joined up with Craig Logan, who was posher than the Goss twins and came from a stable family. Their first band was called Caviar. They didn't know it was fish eggs. They just though it sounded dead sophisticated.

All three loved dressing up and going out. Carol would help the boys with their outfits, stitching together ruffles for their shirts and helping them dress like Duran Duran. They once went to see Divine at the Lyceum. Su Pollard from *Hi-De-Hi!* was sitting next to them and ran her fingers through Matt's hair.

After Caviar, the band went through a bunch of duff names such as Hypnotized and, er, Goss. They played working men's clubs to utterly indifference audiences. Then Bob Herbert came along.

Luke briefly dated Bob's daughter, Nicky, and they began rehearsing in Bob's summer house (cue a burst of inspiration that caused them to change their name for a short time to Summerhouse). At Bob's suggestion they recorded a song called 'Mystery Lady'. In the video, Bob could be accidentally glimpsed working the smoke machine. It wasn't the slickest showcase for the trio's considerable talents.

Still, Bob at least introduced them to Nicky Graham, who pointed them in my direction. I saw diamonds in the rough. The photogenic potential alone of two blond twins offset by the brown-haired mate was great. This was the kind of malleable material I liked to play with.

Also, after being so excluded from the Pet Shop Boys' creative process by the ever-picky Neil and Chris, I fancied a challenge. Making these guys look stylish was certainly going to be that.

It was obvious when I first introduced them to Rob Holden, Mark Farrow and Gary Knibbs that they all had the same thought: *WTF?* A glance at those curly-permed mullets made them think that I had finally lost it big time!

Who were these children who had been driven up to London from Camberley in a knackered old VW Golf? What was I thinking?

What I was thinking was that they were great. *Potentially*.

As ever, we started off with a brainstorming session to try to come up with a decent name. Somewhere I had seen a picture of a lorry that said 'Thompson Bros' on the side. For some reason it had caught my eye in a pop art way.

With Luke and Matt being twins, the name Bros seemed totally appropriate. I sketched a little draft logo and got Mark Farrow to refine it.

Next, they were in chronic need of a major image overhaul. I sent them to get their offensively long hair chopped off at Cuts in Soho. Instantly they looked the business: sharp, clean-cut and pin-up good-looking.

This was going to work! I just knew it.

Problem was, this control freakery was spilling out into my personal life. I had met a man through an ad in a contact magazine. He was a lovely man, on reflection, he was devoted to me, although back then I was too self-loathing deep down to realise it. We were together throughout the mid to late eighties. The last I heard he was a pop star's gardener ...

After our first meeting, I told him to get a haircut. Just like I told Bros. The lines were blurring between boy bands and boyfriends ...

Initially, it was hard to tell Bros what to wear. A long process began of initiating the boys into what was cool and stylish. Firstly, I paid two hip girls, Toula Mavridou and Jane Goldman (who was later to marry Jonathan Ross), to take them out on the town. Jane and Toula were club-savvy kids and knew all about the latest street clobber.

The twins and Craig quickly became more open to their clothes ideas – and they looked good in them. When we suggested Doc Martens they initially rejected them as 'fucking monster boots!' but they were to become a major part of their image – especially after Matt started putting Grolsch bottle-tops on them.

We kitted them out in Harrington jackets, ripped Levi 501s, natty American Classics attire, plain white t-shirts and red handkerchiefs. It was a real James Dean goes eighties image: *Rebel Without a Cause* meets hard times. Suddenly, all of the

XL in-house naysayers started to realise that maybe I was on to something.

We shot some promotional photos to circulate and create a buzz. They looked terrific: two blond, chiselled twins and their handsome brown-haired mate. The pictures said it all.

Bros were going to be mega! I could feel it!

Now we had to work on that infernal, necessary evil in the pop game – the songs. At first I wasn't involved in the songwriting process, but I didn't like what I was hearing. It was dross; sub-Jacko bilge.

Sick of my bitching about the songs, one day Nicky Graham asked me, 'Well, Tom, do you think you could do better?'

'Yeah, I think I could as it happens!' I told him, as bolshie as ever.

Thus began a very short-lived Graham/Watkins songwriting partnership. We knew we had to do something. Bros were proving to be a hard sell. Record labels just didn't seem to think they were going to be successful.

However, Muff Winwood was still in A&R at CBS, who had signed up Grand Hotel all those years ago, and he bought into my enthusiasm and gave us a deal. Now all that we had to do was write and record an album.

Nicky wrote the music and I penned the lyrics. I got ideas from everywhere. I revisiting my penurious childhood on a song called 'Ten Out Of Ten', which took me all the way back to the horror days of the tallyman and our curtains of 'fabric so limp the night can see through'.

I also settled some scores with past romances. 'I Owe You Nothing' stuck two fingers up at my former beau from Joe

Allen's. On a more serious tip, 'Shocked' addressed the then-all-dominating AIDS epidemic.

I targeted some of the other songs very directly, thinking about those that would resonate with a teen pop audience. An example was 'Drop The Boy', a song all about growing pains and a youth demanding to be taken seriously as a young adult.

I always made sure that the song titles and lyrics stood out loud and clear and punchy like the headlines in a tabloid. There was 'I Quit', for instance.

Oh, and another song called 'When Will I be Famous?'

'When Will I Be Famous?' had originally been intended for another project rather nearer to home. Gary Knibbs and I had formed our own little pop duo, the Hudsons, a short-lived outfit that was arguably inspired by watching *Baby Jane* one too many times.

For shits and giggles, we made an outrageously camp dance number called 'One Man's Meat Is Another Man's Poison', produced by Russell Mackenzie from Spelt Like This. It was a hoot. Eric Watson took the sleeve pics of Gary and me, which came out on the tastefully titled Wheelchair Records, courtesy of EMI's money.

We wrote our own sleeve notes: a bunch of Morley-baiting bullshit. On the track itself, we introduced our musical alter egos over some pumping music:

'Blanche and Jane ... the Hudsons ... '

It even got played on the radio when Gary was working for Jill and Trevor at ZTT. Jill looked up from her desk to ask: 'Is that you and Tom?'

'Yes, yes it is,' Gary replied, awkwardly.

Without comment, Jill returned to her paperwork. The song even made the dance charts, rising to the giddy heights of number thirteen.

The Hudsons had other song ideas. The Pet Shop Boys had written some music for a song idea that I had had about a guy leaving his boyfriend for a woman. But I was too busy to do anything with it and the three-chord wonder became the mighty 'Paninaro', a paean to sharp-dressing, pop-loving Italian youth cult that was the B-side to 'Suburbia' here and a single in its own right in Italy.

The Hudsons' eventual follow-up to 'One Man's Meat ... ' was going to be 'When Will I Be Famous?' In its original incarnation, it was much more homo than the song the world finally heard. In fact, I think there were a few rent boy references in there.

Its title was actually inspired by Cliff Richard's 1976 comeback album, *I'm Nearly Famous*. However, it was ultimately a comment on the ever-increasing *Hello!* magazine cult of celebrity. It was written as a duet between two queens: a desperate young wannabe and an older, wiser figure. It was more camp and outrageous than its predecessor.

The trouble was when Gary went to record his part he couldn't sing it at the mic. This record-making business had suddenly become a bit too serious for him. Yet it was catchy as hell and was a real chant of an earworm. What would we do with it?

Nicky Graham and I realised that the song could be toned down and made into a perfect pop song – a dialogue between a man and an aspiring starlet. We decided to give it to Bros.

Like every good idea we had for them, Matt and Luke baulked at it initially. Its Hi-NRG feel put them off. *It was too dance; too club; too damn gay.* Yet there is nothing like the promise of success to twist a pop star's arm and make them compromise all that so-called 'artistic integrity'.

'So what about "When Will I Be Famous?" Have you given it any more thought?' I asked Matt one day.

'Nah, Tom,' he said. 'It's just not for us.'

'But the American record company have heard the demo,' I shot back. 'They think it's a transatlantic smash!'

'Oh, really? Well, I suppose we could give it a go,' Matt quickly reconsidered.

Naturally, the American record company *hadn't* heard it. It was total bullshit. But who cared? It coaxed Bros into recording what was to be their most famous song. It was also proof that pop stars could have zero commercial instinct for what made good pop.

We recorded it at Nicky Graham's Hot Nights Studio in Fulham. It was a tiny place, small but effective, rather like its owner. I had channelled all my frustrations and ferocious ambition into the words and Matt did them justice with an almost feral delivery.

He was a terrific singer. To give him credit, Matt worked tirelessly on his vocals, injecting an Olympian vigour into his takes. He sounded like a young man on a mission, eager to scale the heights of his hero, Michael Jackson. And, occasionally, he sounded like a man with ants in his pants.

CBS thought the material was a bit 'hard' for an act aimed at the teen market, so we came up with 'Cat Among The Pigeons' to show a softer side. The words were inspired by someone I used to know and their need to fill the void left by their dad's premature death with turbulent love affairs, affairs that failed to live up to their impulsive desires ('patiently waiting for love at first sight').

There again, that could just as easily have been said about me.

Even Neil Tennant liked my lyric to 'Cat Among The Pigeons', singling out the chorus as particularly good. The music was soft-focus and dreamy, the perfect respite from the hormonal, adrenalised funky pop on the rest of Bros's debut album.

Dee and Shirley Lewis and Pet Shop Boys favourite Helena Springs did the backing vocals. Matt had a little fling with Helena and Luke began an enduring relationship with Shirley. In fact, trying to foster the illusion that the boys were free and single caused a bit of a clash.

Fostering the illusion that a boy-band member is somehow available is essential to their appeal. The female fan must feel that he could potentially be theirs, no matter how remote that chance may be. Wives and girlfriends ruin that. Yet Matt and Luke were smitten and my advice fell on deaf ears.

Dee actually sang the title in the chorus of 'When Will I Be Famous?', effectively playing the girl role, but Matt mimed her words when they did it live. Dee was to tell a tabloid that Bros was a fake entity just because she had sung those lines! Matt and Luke fretted about their 'artistic integrity' – but I knew that all publicity is good publicity and artistic integrity doesn't pay the bloody rent.

Later on, Matt felt that his vocal inflections, like those highly charged ooh-ahs on 'I Owe You Nothing', should have earned him publishing money. It might have been a good move politically (and songwriting credits are notoriously political) but a few 'ooh-ahs' do not make a song. If they did, every vocalist or backing vocalist that ad-libbed would want a cut.

Luke was also dead peeved that his drums were largely omitted on Bros records, supplanted by programmed rhythms. Well, boo hoo! Nobody wanted to hear pure pop with 'real' drums! This was Bros, not Phil Collins!

But the twins just didn't get it. Luke was especially stubborn. They desperately wanted to be seen as a credible act, not manufactured puppets.

Indeed, ultimately that would prove their downfall. Drum machines and glossy pictures are what propelled Bros to stardom, not Luke's drumming prowess, as good as he was and proved to be on their live shows. But the awful truth was, some of the time he might as well have sat on those sticks.

A few years later, I would have shoved them up his ungrateful arse myself.

We launched Bros properly in mid-1987 with 'I Owe You Nothing'. The video was your average eighties extravaganza with ropes, a scantily clad, furiously choreographed dance troupe and Craig bouncing off a wall.

It stalled at number eighty. *We've been here before*, I thought to myself. *Don't panic.* The album was going to be called *Push*, and that was all we had to do: push harder.

In any case, a lot of signs were incredibly positive. There was ample evidence, even on that first flop, that Bros were set to be scream-inducing, hysteria-making pop stars.

I have a very clear memory of the moment I realised it was all going to kick off. Rob was up in Newcastle with the band to film the pop show *The Roxy*, an ITV alternative to *Top of the Pops* presented by Kid Jensen. Bros were on it when it looked like the first single might just make the top forty.

No one in the audience knew who they were. The audience were basically kids who were drafted in after school, mainly girls. Bros did their first run-through, and within thirty seconds the crowd went from ambivalence to a wild frenzy. It was just crazy.

Rob called me from a payphone. 'Don't worry,' he said. 'It's going to happen.'

He didn't even know what 'it' was. But he knew that he was right.

20

HIT MUSIC

For the Pet Shop Boys' second album, everything was conceived to be bigger, grander and more ambitious than its predecessor.

Stephen Hague produced a couple of tracks but Neil and Chris also worked with Julian Mendelsohn and New York DJ Shep Pettibone, among others. Mendelsohn turned 'It's A Sin' into a lavish slice of gaudy, Catholic euro-disco during some entertainingly barmy sessions.

They went to the Brompton Oratory to record the ambience for the 'Father, forgive me ... ' section of the song and recorded a preacher and a choir at Westminster Abbey. Neil even recited the Confiteor, a Catholic prayer, in Latin.

They slowed down 'Rent', an urbane love song for a money-obsessed decade. It presented a relationship between a prostitute and her rich lover, one not without tenderness but which is ultimately a business transaction: 'I love you, you pay my rent'.

The hook of 'Shopping' was dreamed up as Neil and Chris did exactly that on Oxford Street but really it was about Margaret Thatcher's privatisation plans and the selling off of national industries. It was Neil getting all political, in sneaky ways.

'Hit Music' was an ode to the joys of chart pop and dance music, the banal, trite confections that actually have a far greater impact on the average listener's life than does any serious rock music. It even nodded to the Stock Aitken Waterman sound that ruled the airwaves in the second half of the eighties.

'Hit Music' sounded like the 'desperate hit music' it both celebrated and gently mocked. Yet because this was Pet Shop Boys they inserted a few interesting lyrics like the references to Kensington and Spanish Harlem, a surprise tempo shift and lines about living and dying and wanting a friend 'at the journey's end'. Behind the cheesy insistency it was another song about AIDS.

It was my job to indulge the pair's every whim. Neil and Chris asked me to get Ennio Morricone to score the string parts for 'Jealousy'. That didn't happen but they ended up writing a song around a piece of music that he supplied, a stately comment on the escalating AIDS crisis called 'It Couldn't Happen Here'. It reminded me of 'Air on a G String' (the famous classical tune, not a lament for a stripper).

When it came to arrange the tune, they enlisted Angelo Badalamenti, David Lynch's musical partner. This was how fancy they were getting: Morricone for the music and Badalamenti for the arrangement! Yet when they needed to perform the song, Stephen Hague hadn't hired the required orchestra. After a bit of grumbling, they created the sound of the orchestra via samples.

They had written 'Heart' to give to Madonna, then to Hazell Dean, but ended up keeping it for themselves. It was an irresistible tune, one of their most straightforward to date, a late eighties disco love song propelled by a hypnotic synth line imitating a human voice.

The closing track, 'King's Cross', was one of Pet Shop Boys' finest: majestic, haunting and full of atmosphere. King's Cross Station is where hopeful north-easterners arrive in London in pursuit of a better life but the song didn't yield it.

The austerity of Thatcherism and the threat of AIDS hung like a black cloud over the song. It felt an almost mystical dream vision of grim reality. It ended the album with a very dignified, elegant kind of sadness.

The called the album *Actually* and I still think it might be Neil and Chris's finest hour. It was timeless pop that also took a snapshot of the world at that time but did so without hitting you over the head with politicking. It managed to capture all the Pet Shop Boys' contradictions perfectly. I thought that it was a better record than *Please* on just about every level, and I was dead chuffed.

'Heart' was intended as the first single: a safe choice, they thought. It carried a picture of them smiling, a reaction to their moody bastard reputation. However, EMI demurred and thought that 'It's A Sin' was the obvious contender.

Neil and Chris were doing interviews in France when I phoned to tell them this news. They capitulated with surprising ease. They were proud of 'It's A Sin' and felt its maximal production would be a great taster for the album. Initially they wanted just to use the mooted 'Heart' sleeve for 'It's A Sin'.

Jill Carrington, who worked in marketing at EMI, disagreed. She felt that the song was so dramatic that it needed its own sleeve. She was right, and Neil and Chris knew it. They took note of her impeccable judgement. It was to rebound on me.

Eric Watson shot the 'It's A Sin' cover photo at Nicholas Hawksmoor's early eighteenth-century Christ Church Spitalfields. It cost an arm and a leg to hire but they made good use of the grimy old disused sacristy. A shot of Neil leaning on a table as Chris stood like a statue became the single's inner sleeve. The title was framed in inverted commas, a distancing effect and protective veil from the sadness and guilt at the song's heart.

The video was similarly grandiose. The iconoclastic gay filmmaker Derek Jarman shot it: he had made *Sebastiane*, punk movie *Jubilee* and most recently *Caravaggio*, which Neil particularly liked. In the vid, various actors played the seven deadly sins, Chris was a jailer and Neil played the persecuted sinner. Given his monkish, guilt-ridden nature, it was type-casting.

'It's A Sin' was a huge hit, a number one in Britain and top ten in the US. Then professional loudmouth Jonathan King started a campaign against it, claiming that it ripped off Cat

Stevens' 'Wild World'. He even recorded a version of 'Wild World' arranged like 'It's A Sin' to highlight the supposed similarity.

His campaign was a flop and, when the Pet Shop Boys sued King, the court found in their favour. They donated their damages to charity.

Even more bizarre was a Catholic magazine contacting us to say they were grateful to Pet Shop Boys for reintroducing the concept of sin into society! They asked Neil to appear on the cover of the mag. He politely declined, explaining that he wasn't a practising Catholic.

Next up was the Dusty duet, 'What Have I Done To Deserve This?' It hit number two in both the UK and the US, in a sleeve that featured Neil and Chris posing on a motorbike in front of a giant vintage 1964 pic of Dusty.

Mark Farrow thought that the bike was a useless prop and Neil and Chris should have just flanked the iconic image in their customary deadpan manner. For my part, I liked it: it gave the Warhol-like pop art image retro cool and silver-screen glamour. Mind you, you would be stretching it to say that Neil and Chris resembled Brando and Dean!

The Eric Watson video was even more showbiz, albeit in that slightly distant, arch Pet Shop Boys way. Neil and Chris dressed up in tuxedos and surrounded themselves with a troupe of showgirls, one of them wearing specs. Very droll!

Chris got his trombone out and mimed the synth brass. He did a spot of dancing, spinning around like a little boy in his own little world, simultaneously fun-loving and sulky. We even managed to coax Dusty out of her dressing room and into the video.

During the shoot, photographer Cindy Palmano took some snaps of Neil and Chris in their tuxedos, sitting at a reflective surface. They were going to use them for a *Smash Hits* cover. They were to be rather more than that.

Fancy as ever, the pair wanted Alison Watt, the Glaswegian winner of the National Portrait Gallery's Portrait Award, to paint their picture for the album's sleeve. Alison wanted them to sit for three weeks but their hectic schedule made that impossible. She worked from a photo instead, but the results looked quaint, stuffy and just un-pop.

Eric Watson shot a session with Neil seated, Chris standing and an imposing brick wall behind them. It was a good image, full of their trademark weird mix of decay, austerity and glamour. Yet it just wasn't a cover. It did for the inner sleeve.

Then Mark Farrow had one of his blinding bursts of inspiration. He took one of the Cindy Palmano pics that showed Neil yawning, tired from the hard day's video shoot. Farrow cropped the image so that it isolated Neil and Chris and placed it on a white background.

It was a cut-and-paste job that was clearly inspired by a 1985 XL design for Grace Jones' 'Slave To The Rhythm' and it was a stroke of genius. Here was an instantly iconic piece of record art: a crisp, clean white space, Neil and Chris in tuxedos and Neil indifferently yawning, as if to say, 'I don't give a damn whether you buy this or not – but you will, because it's great.'

All Chris could say was that he hated his hair in the photograph. He got it cropped shortly after. As for *Smash Hits*, they had to make do with a hastily snapped pic of Neil and Chris with Chris looking every bit a Kenneth Anger/ Robert Mapplethorpe leather-clad bit of rough trade.

Critics loved *Actually* when it was released in September 1987 and, more importantly, so did pop fans, who fired it to number two. 'Rent' finally came out as a single with a great video featuring the actress Margi Clarke. Neil played a chauffeur and Chris starred as a rough trade hustler. He threw a strop on the set. They seemed to get more frequent.

The hits just kept coming. They were so thick and fast that Phil Oakey was jealous. One of the Human League girls told Neil so. I was tickled pink. The Human League were jealous of one of my acts!

The Pet Shop Boys entered what Neil, always one for a bit of la-di-da pop commentary, called their 'imperial phase': the time when a band can do no wrong artistically or commercially. Fittingly, 1987 ended with the ultimate triumph, the best end to their best year – a Christmas number one single.

Central TV were shooting *Love Me Tender*, a tribute to Elvis on the tenth anniversary of the King's death. They asked the Pet Shop Boys to perform a song and Rob gave them a bunch of cassettes to sift through. They loved 'Always On My Mind'.

I could see why. It was so sentimental, so syrupy and unabashedly romantic. It was an irresistible choice, appealing to both their twisted sense of irony and their love of genuinely heartfelt pop music.

So Neil and Chris appeared on *Love Me Tender*, walking down a deserted railway track clad in full leather miming to their version of 'Always On My Mind'. At one point, a seated Neil started rubbing his knees like someone's randy uncle. Or maybe he just liked the feel of leather. Either way the record sounded great.

Originally it was just going to be the B-side of 'Rent', but again Jill Carrington at EMI was having none of it. She said 'Always On My Mind' was potentially massive and should be a single in its own right. Again, she was spot-on.

It came out in November 1987 and its sleeve was once again a mass of white with a tiny still from the specially shot Joss Ackland-starring video in the corner. Yet wilfully perverse, arty high jinks could not prevent the single's inexorable rise.

Gary and I were in my car as we listened to the chart rundown that would determine who would occupy the festive top spot. There it was! *Number one: Pet Shop Boys with 'Always On My Mind'!*

I stopped the car, jumped out, turned up the volume full blast and Gary and I had a boogie around the car. Those two moody bastards, the sulky sods that *Number One* magazine had dubbed 'the obsessive spinsters of pop', had done it again!

It was their peak, and, like so many golden moments in pop that bring an exultant full stop to a great period, things would never be quite the same again. At least not between Neil, Chris and me.

During their golden year, they had been plotting and filming the ultimate artistic folly: the pop movie. 'Always On My

Mind' had been hastily incorporated into the film they had been shooting with Jack Bond, a director who had worked with Salvador Dalí and on a Roald Dahl *South Bank Show* documentary Neil had liked.

Originally they had just planned to make a video album of *Actually* but *that* turned into *this*. Three weeks in Clacton-on-Sea and various bits of London with various stars such as Barbara Windsor.

I just didn't get it. The Pet Shop Boys had hardly put a foot wrong since 'West End Girls' and I thought this was a great big boot stomp in the wrong direction. It was total pretentious crap.

But you can't tell pop stars anything, especially when they are riding high on the crest of a wave of success. This was going to be an arty, audacious monument to the Pet Shop Boys' imperial phase. It was also going to be a colossal turd. I just knew it.

They decided to call it *It Couldn't Happen Here*. And it *shouldn't* have happened – here, there or bloody anywhere.

Around this time, French and Saunders' sidekicks Raw Sex, aka Simon Brint and Roland Rivron, spoofed Neil and Chris on TV. It was a hilarious parody based on 'Rent'. Brint got Neil bang on as Rivron stood behind a keyboard looking bored, picking his nose.

Their song went: *'You're good at standing still/I'm quite good at singing.'*

I'm not at all sure that Neil and Chris appreciated the skit, but I couldn't stop laughing when I saw it.

Meanwhile, as Pet Shop Boys busied themselves with their ludicrous movie, I was concentrating on relaunching Bros after their first single had stiffed.

We continued to refine their look. I knew we couldn't afford to be subtle. We stuck socks down their Levis to enlarge their packages.

When your first single flops there's only one thing for it: make the bulge bigger. It was not a tactic that I could ever have envisaged Neil and Chris adopting. But with Bros, it worked.

Matt and Luke got in bed with presenter Emma Freud for a 'pillow talk' TV interview over Christmas. I thought she was insufferably patronising to the twins in that insidious, snooty English way, making it clear that she was doubtful they would succeed.

She was about to be proved wrong.

Bros's second single was 'When Will I Be Famous?' We shot a video with the boys wandering the streets of Soho, interspersed with shots of Matt spinning around crazily, mostly after every time he yelled 'Woo!' It was great.

It broke the top forty and started climbing in the early months of 1988. Eventually it peaked at number two. In an audacious move, we fired the internal marketing division at CBS and took charge of things ourselves.

The album was still going to be called *Push*. We made little promo items like stickers bearing the album's title to be stuck on record-store doors, making it both a Bros advert and a useful instruction.

Stickers and socks ... if you ask me, it's what pop music is really all about.

Matt and Luke's mum, Carol, had moved into London to live in Peckham. Even before Bros broke, big, ferocious fans began gathering around the property, desperate to catch a glimpse of their idols. This was to go on for years.

Some of the girls were sweet, some of them were scary and some of them were certifiable. For every wide-eyed, smiling fan there would be a total nutter proffering a half-frozen turkey for a gift or arguing with Carol about the circumstances of the birth of her own sons. At one meeting in the house, I turned towards the window to see a Bros fan hanging upside-down.

After 'When Will I Be Famous?' catapulted Bros into the stratosphere, Craig stayed grounded. I always liked him: he was smart, down-to-earth and free of the gargantuan ego you expect with an 'overnight' teen sensation. People started calling him 'Ken'.

However, the Goss twins fully embraced stardom and the fan frenzy that went from 0 to 60 overnight. They would whisper sweet nothings in girls' ears as they fell to the floor, fainting with uncontrollable excitement.

As hyperventilating girls swarmed around their chauffeur-driven limos, Matt and Luke would wave, beam and do nothing to quell the insanity. 'Love ya, babes!' became their stock greeting for these mobs of fans. Once, screaming girls pulled a door clean off a limo.

Meanwhile, Neil and Chris were still using public transport.

In March 1988, we followed up 'When Will I be Famous?' with 'Drop the Boy'. At a record-signing session at HMV Oxford Circus, the traffic was gridlocked owing to the multitudes flocking to meet Bros. It was bedlam. The Crown Prosecution Services threatened us with charges for disrupting the streets of London.

It was total pandemonium and I loved it. We relocated the office to Neal Street, where I would stand at the office window and just watch the faithful down below begging to see Bros.

When Neil arrived one day, he was asked for his autograph by a Bros fan. She said it was for her mum.

As 'Drop The Boy' hit the shelves, so did the Pet Shop Boys' 'Heart', the final single from *Actually*. It came with another striking video, directed by Jack Bond, and starring the venerable Ian McKellen as Dracula and a Tiffany lookalike as Neil's bride.

Chris played a chauffeur who drove the newly married couple to the vampire's castle, where the Count lured the bride away from Neil and claimed her as his latest victim. The combo of straightforward pop song and oddball video proved as winning a formula as Neil had predicted it would.

In April 1988, 'Heart' became the Pet Shop Boys' fourth number one single. Hot on its heels was 'Drop The Boy' by Bros. As a pop manager it doesn't get any better than having your two top acts occupying the two top spots in the charts.

Mick Newton and I presented Bros with some congratulatory Rolex watches. It was to start a deluge of profligate spending that would soar to comical levels even for a flash shopaholic bastard like myself. Chris Lowe's close friend, Pete Andreas, had a word with me.

'Neil and Chris are dead upset, you know.'

'Why?'

'You bought Rolexes for Bros and Neil and Chris got nothing. They are the ones at number one. It isn't fair, Tom!'

Hell's bells! Bloody pop stars, eh? Even the ones that come across as loftily above the narcissistic diva behaviour of their peers are just pretending. They are big kids who must be pampered.

I went out and got Chris a Porsche watch and Neil a Jaeger-LeCoultre one. Egos stroked. Problems solved. Children!

There again, Matt and Luke didn't wait for presents to be bought for them. They had absolutely no trouble buying their own. The twins had no apparent understanding of money and seemed to have little interest in developing any.

Their spending quickly became an issue and I remember one meeting in the boardroom at Neal Street to try to get them to slow down a bit. Mick Newton gave his helpful, thoughtful analysis of their financial affairs and how they had to rein it in a little. The Goss twins were so upset that Luke bought a Porsche on the way home to cheer himself up.

Matt and Luke needed twenty-four-hour security, drivers and the whole pop-star package. Everybody would give them stupid amounts of credit and then bill the office. If one of the brothers bought a leather jacket for £2,000, the other had to get one that was at least as expensive. They would be worn once and then discarded.

The Goss tastes quickly outgrew those Levis and white tees. Before I knew it, it was goodbye Red or Dead and American

Classics: hello Comme Des Garçons! Poor old Ken, I mean Craig, he got to pick through what they didn't want.

We gave them a personal stylist, Al Berlin, who customised their clothes for them. He was the dictionary definition of long-suffering. And any time that one of Matt and Luke's crew or entourage got pissed off, they gave them a Rolex. They dished out these watches worth thousands of pounds as if they were boxes of frigging Milk Tray.

Luckily, *Push* sold bucketloads. It needed to, to keep them in Rolexes and designer clothes. It was only kept off the top spot by a *Now That's What I Call Music!* compilation.

But, nothing could stop 'I Owe You Nothing' from hitting the number one position when it was reissued as a single again. When they featured on an accompanying *Smash Hits* cover in July 1988, it was one of the mag's best-selling issues. Bros were now firmly installed as star attractions on the giddy carousel of pop.

The *Big Push* tour took them up and down the country for a series of sell-out shows, including Matt's favourite venue, the Hammersmith Apollo. The stage shows became increasingly bombastic. Soon they were being catapulted onto the stage in harnesses, somersaulting towards their screaming audience like superheroes. Craig and Luke would flank Matt, elbows bent, fists clenched by their sides, like supermen. Matt and Luke took this business hugely seriously. Craig looked vaguely embarrassed.

To work the crowd into a huge frenzy before the shows we made an overture, sprinkled with motifs from their songs. The audiences grew more and more mental as they waited. Talk about Pavlov's dogs!

Even I got affected. One night I stood and watched by the stage then turned to the guy who ran the Bros fan club, Mike Hrano.

'I think I'm having an orgasm!' I told him.

In fact, 1988 had felt just like that. It had been one big pop orgasm. Well, 1989 would have its own share of climaxes, but it would end badly – like a ham-fisted wank.

21

A HARD DAY'S NIGHT IN HELL

I have always loved being in the limelight, just as much as the acts I have managed (in fact, probably more than Neil and Chris). So, naturally, I got well into schmoozing and hobnobbing with the celebs and media figures that I ran into.

One of the people I got close to during the Bros and Pet Shop Boys golden years was Janet Street-Porter: a journalist, motormouth, outspoken B-lister and, back then, the queen bee of 'yoof' television. She masterminded Channel 4's *Network 7*, a pretty edgy show that made *The Tube* look safe in comparison.

I went on *Network 7* and reviewed Bill Drummond's manual on how to have a number one single. I reviewed it in the bath. Fully clothed. I liked the show and also got pretty chummy with its presenter, the infamous Magenta Devine with her glass eye.

Janet was a force to be reckoned with. Maurice Oberstein told me that if you ever get asked to an event you should always go, but only for five minutes. Just work the room, say hi and leave.

Not so Janet! With her big teeth, big specs, outré (i.e. dodgy) fashion sense and her severely straight hair, she looked like a cross between Deirdre Barlow from *Coronation Street* and a Manhattan art dealer. Janet got everywhere. And she never shut her mouth.

I loved her.

Initially, she pursued me. She did it in the same way she had pursued Elton, Neil Tennant, even Sigue Sigue Sputnik's Tony James (whom she dated). When I first became friends with her, Lynne Franks rolled her eyes at me and said, 'Oh, so you're this week's friend, are you?'

That was Janet: the professional friend. And what a laugh she was. She introduced me to people as disparate as Alan Yentob and Ruby Wax. She was a real mover and shaker: fun, smart and mouthy.

She was always fun to be with. Once we were having dinner in a snazzy London restaurant when across the dining room she spotted a columnist who had penned an unfavourable news item on her.

Before I had a chance to blink, Janet made a beeline for the journo. *Wallop!* Her Chanel handbag had crashed into the tabloid hack's face.

'That's the closest you'll ever come to class, bitch!' Janet informed her, as she returned to her seat.

She got herself tied up in all kinds of sticky situations. Unbelievably, she persuaded me to go hiking with her in Yorkshire (she had a home in the idyllic Dales). Our walking expeditions were a hoot.

Janet would drag me out of bed in the early hours, assemble the boots, maps and anoraks, and off we'd go. I think she was even the head of the bleeding Ramblers' Association or something daft like that.

We would trail up and down hills and around giant reservoirs. Janet would sally forth like a pioneer woman with me trailing behind her, hardly enthralled by an activity requiring physical exercise.

It wasn't easy going, and I have to admit that I would dip into my little dispenser to have a toot of coke or two. It was just to keep me going, of course. They don't call it Bolivian marching powder for nothing.

Once, in the arse-end of nowhere, we saw a hiker approaching in the distance. As the woman grew closer, she looked excited and obviously wanted to talk to the celeb she had happened across in the wilds of the Yorkshire Dales.

'Oh gawd, that's the last thing I need,' said Janet to me, *sotto voce*. 'Getting hounded by some bumpkin and I have nowhere to run to!'

The hiker reached us, stopped dead, ignored Janet and stared straight at me.

'Aren't you that Tom Watkins?' she asked. 'That bloke off the telly that looks after all the pop bands?'

'Well, yes, I am, actually,' I replied, doing an unconscious lofty Neil impersonation.

'How bizarre to come across a celebrity here, of all places!' the woman mused aloud before wandering off.

The rest of that walk with Janet passed in uncharacteristic and very uneasy silence. The hiker recognising me and not her had pissed her right off!

On another trip to Yorkshire, Janet ran over a pheasant. I was gobsmacked when she stopped, picked it up and put it in the car. 'Right, we'll hang that in the larder and have it for dinner later,' she declaimed.

Even my usually accommodating stomach suddenly turned over at the prospect of eating Janet's roadkill cuisine. Thankfully I never sampled it.

Then there were the shopping trips. Janet loved to shop as much as I did. Again in Yorkshire, we went to an old antiques shop, a real picture book store, decrepit and quaint. It was one of those places where you had to ring the bell to get the old woman in the store to grant you entry.

Within a few seconds, Janet had swooped down on several vintage handbags from the thirties. She bought them. And in her blinkered acquisition of accessories, she had completely missed the really valuable items in the shop. On the top shelf was some Wedgwood by Keith Murray. There was a very rare, extremely beautiful black vase. I bought it: a snip at £60. While Janet was ogling bags, I found the real goodies.

Naturally, she was hopping mad that she had missed out.

'Shit! You are buying lunch, Watkins!'

Janet, I thought to myself, *I never even imagined for one second that you would fucking buy it!*

I also had in mind acquisitions rather more significant than desirable Wedgwood vases. Around this time I bought my own country home, a refuge from the Big Smoke and the pretentious bubble of the pop machine.

My old friend Frank Sawkins had moved to Rye in Sussex and I started visiting him and his family at weekends. I quickly fell in love with the tranquillity, the clean air and the proximity to the sea. Rye was serene, pretty and everything London wasn't.

The only problem was I hated all the twee cottages that everyone lived in down there. Those genteel olde worlde properties make me feel claustrophobic just looking at them.

Then, one night, Frank's wife Frances called me up.

'Tom, I have found the most perfect getaway for you!' she enthused.

Oh Lord, I thought to myself. *I bet it's some kind of horrible Anne Hathaway's Cottage-type monstrosity. No thanks, Frances!*

I could not have been more wrong. It wasn't. It was an elegant, Art Deco marvel in a village called Fairlight, just down the coast. It was known as the White House and had been built from a design by Wells Coates, the same trail-blazing modernist architect who had created the Lawn Road apartments in Belsize Park. This ocean liner-style block had once been the home of Agatha Christie, who had noted that the resemblance to a ship was so uncanny that 'it ought to have funnels'.

The White House had been built from Coates' template, designs for which were produced for the 1936 *Daily Mail*

Ideal Home Exhibition. It would have been one of the first modernist homes in the UK. And although he didn't oversee this building's construction himself, it was one of the few Wells Coates houses still surviving.

It was everything I adored about architecture. It was ultra-modern, with a structure clearly informed by the villas of Le Corbusier. It was minimal and magnificent, free from gaudy decorative features but with striking balconies. It looked like a sculpture, a work of modern art amid the grassy landscape, overlooking the sea.

The views were spectacular. I had to have it. Plus, it was funny to me that the village it was in went by the same name as the synthesiser that everybody I knew was currently using!

A previous owner had carried out an ugly garage extension in the seventies that was wholly incongruous and not harmonious. I got rid of that and added a far more suitable semi-circular sunroom at the building's rear with materials faithful to the original design. It was an addition borrowed from Coates' ideas for larger homes.

It wasn't my first step into property owning. Back in London, I had already bought a Georgian town house in Gladstone Street in Southwark. But the White House was a thing of real beauty – and my first step out of London life.

I entertained there frequently. Neil Tennant would come over for brunch. He was often popping down to Rye with his friend, the journalist and author Jon Savage.

In nearby Dungeness, Derek Jarman dwelt in a small cottage, living out an arty East Sussex equivalent of Thoreau's *Walden*.

No doubt my proximity to such eminent company appealed to Neil and Jon.

Ever since the sixties, rock stars had been moving out to the country 'to get their heads together'. The trouble was, when you were in the company of these two you'd be unlikely to think of their heads being anywhere else but being stuck up their highbrow rectums.

They were definitely engaged in some tacit competition as to who was the best pop scholar. Jon had trained to be a lawyer but he saw the Sex Pistols and became a music journalist, swapping one ignoble profession for another.

He became the pre-eminent intellectual heavyweight on punk, going on to write the seminal tome on the subject, *England's Dreaming*. And he could be dead snooty about those beneath him.

Back in the golden age of punk, Savage had slagged off the Stranglers, a critical dressing down that got him well acquainted with bass player J.J. Burnel's fist. I'm entirely sure that J.J.'s knuckles were also acting on behalf of countless others.

Neil and Jon would sit in my living room, sipping tea from bone china cups and exchanging bon mots like two queens out of *The Portrait of Dorian* bloody *Gray*. I would sit there wondering how I could possibly interject into their witty, pithy dialogue. For once, my big mouth was shut. Then I was addressed.

'So, Tom,' Jon said, teacup in hand, nose tilting skywards. 'Is this the house that Neil and Chris bought you?'

Needless to say, Mr Savage never got another invitation to tea at the White House ever again.

There again, Neil wasn't invincible, as was proved when the Pet Shop Boys' disastrous movie *It Couldn't Happen Here* finally appeared.

They held an exclusive preview at a 'top-secret cinema location'. I can't even remember where it was. The film was an oddball romp through Neil and Chris's skewed universe. Neil thought it should have been called *Escape from Suburbia*. I wouldn't have minded a quick escape from that pile of drivel!

I squirmed in my cinema seat as I watched the film, which seemed to last an eternity. I winced as Neil recited the words to 'It's A Sin' as a spoken poem. Neil and Chris's thespian skills were about as three-dimensional as the cut-out figures that Mark Farrow had pasted onto the cover of *Actually*. This wasn't going to give Bobby De Niro and Al Pacino any sleepless nights.

It went on and on. A zebra was escorted off some train tracks. A man spontaneously combusted in suburbia. My fat bum moved restlessly around my uncomfortable cinema seat. Finally it was over.

Muted, obligatory applause filled the auditorium. Everyone gathered around Neil and Chris and tried to change the subject quickly. Even their trusty PR man, Murray Chalmers, started to talk about where we were heading for dinner, eager to circumvent the celluloid car crash he had just been witness to.

It Couldn't Happen Here won an award in Houston! Whatever drugs the panel were on must have been pretty strong. Everywhere else it lived up to its name. It didn't happen.

Neil vaingloriously attempted to defend the film, stubbornly detailing its scant merits. Sometimes even the most knowing pop stars have gigantic egos. He just couldn't admit that the film was an almighty balls-up from start to finish.

The film was the first real setback for the Pet Shop Boys since the disappointing chart performance of 'Love Comes Quickly'. But they speedily busied themselves with getting back to doing what they did best: making great, intelligent pop records with sexy, stylish sleeves.

Their next album was going to be a dance-oriented collection where the extended versions were the definitive album cut rather than merely a special 12-inch 'extra'. I thought this was a great idea, a nod to the continual, ever-growing importance of dance culture in pop music.

Chris and Pete Andreas had been enjoying the burgeoning acid house scene and going to parties and raves. The Pet Shop Boys had already released a remix album called *Disco*, and now this was going to be a new album in the same vein.

Except that the cheeky bastards only wrote two new songs for the album, which was to be called *Introspective*. It was six songs long and contained a reworking of the B-side of 'Rent', 'I Want A Dog'; their own version of 'I'm Not Scared', a song they had written for Patsy Kensit's Eighth Wonder; an overhaul of 'Always On My Mind', with a funny Neil rap in the middle; and a cover of Sterling Void's 'It's Alright', a Chicago House track.

So, two covers, one already released B-side and an old song written for another artist. What an almighty swizz! Yet somehow, despite this shameless recycling of borrowed, old and used material, *Introspective* proved to be a great record.

This was largely because the two news songs were fantastic. For a while they'd been toying with the idea of making a Latin-inspired pop record. Finally they got to do one, and they got to record it with the Florida-based DJ, producer and songwriter Lewis Martineé. This meant they had to jet off to Miami to work on it.

Bummer. It was like punk never happened, as Neil used to say in his *Smash Hits* days.

That song was 'Domino Dancing', a title inspired by Chris reproaching Pete for his self-congratulatory boogie every time he won at dominos on holiday in Antigua. It was gorgeous. They employed real local Latin musicians to provide authentic instrumentation to the track amid all the electronics.

I wasn't there, but I was told that one of the trumpet players gave Neil a hug at the end. I would love to have seen Neil awkwardly receiving that tactile embrace. I bet he was stiff as wood. Due to the discomfort, of course …

I loved the song. The music was sunny and danceable, but over the breezy summer sound Neil sang a sad song of unfaithful lovers, full of torrid passions and hurt feelings, neatly conjured by the lyric's references to burning suns and red skies, thunder and storms.

Here was another Neil Tennant lyric that the tunesmiths of Tin Pan Alley would have been proud of. It was like 'Smoke Gets In Your Eyes' meets 'La Isla Bonita'. The minute I heard it, that shitty film was forgiven and forgotten.

The spectre of AIDS again hung heavy over the song, intentionally or not. Neil compared it to Soft Cell's 'Numbers', an ode to endless cruising. On 'Domino Dancing', all the lovers were falling down. You couldn't help but hear a warning amidst the sun-kissed trumpets, ripples of acoustic guitar and programming.

The single came out with a super-cool, lo-fi sleeve. It was a Polaroid taken by Chris's friend Pete of Neil and Chris out on the Miami beach by a Latin American Party van with a wonky skyline.

The video was rather more lavish. It was yet another Eric Watson-directed extravaganza starring a woman and two young, bronzed Latin hunks supposedly slo-mo wrestling in the waves to gain her affections. But, really, they were clearly into each other.

I half expected them to get the KY jelly and condoms out and start bumming each other by the end of it. It was like a *Bel Ami* porn film with a dame, Neil and Chris bizarrely spliced into the middle of it.

Again, I wondered: what was Edna from Huddersfield going to think?

Or, indeed, America. The 'Domino Dancing' video is widely credited as being the culprit that contributed to the Pet Shop Boys being relegated to cult status over there, its overtly homoerotic content being too much for the notoriously conservative mainstream American market. Was it? Who knows? Their move into more full-on dance-oriented records probably had something to do with it, too.

Neil always claimed the gay bent, if you'll pardon the expression, was wholly unintentional. Yeah, sure, Neil! And there is no such thing as 'gay music', he added. All this from a man who was later to cover 'Go West' by the Village People ... doubtless while still claiming there was no such thing as 'gay music'.

The other original track on *Introspective*, 'Left To My Own Devices', was one of their very best. It was a big, grandiose dance number, augmented by an opera singer and an orchestra. It also marked the first collaboration between the Pet Shop Boys and Trevor Horn.

Trevor had made a remark about trying to do the whole thing live, orchestra, singer and programming, all in one wild session. Nice idea. It didn't quite work out like that, though. It ended up taking six months.

Yet 'Left To My Own Devices' was fabulous, a magical and mundane day in the life of someone who sounded a lot like Neil Tennant. He bashed the lyric out on a typewriter, after Trevor heard the demo and wanted full words for it.

And what words they were. The song followed a character through dull daily routines: drinking tea, shopping, watching telly, while his wild, exciting, interior life unfolded as the song progressed.

As I say, there was more than a bit of autobiography in there. Neil was most definitely the kid in the garden, lost in an imaginary world and later on facing a choice between whether to 'write a book or take to the stage'.

The party animal was apparently Jon Savage. Ahem. Neil being ironic again, surely?

But the best line came courtesy of Trevor.

'I've always wanted to put Debussy to a disco beat,' the producer mused in the studio.

'Ooh, Trevor, that's a great line!' said Neil. 'Can I use it?'

Trevor gave his blessing and Neil took Debussy, roughed him up with Che Guevara and a bit of revolutionary history he had been into since he was fourteen, and then put it all to a disco beat.

When first I heard it, for the nth time I thought, *What a pretentious show-off*. Yet I was dead impressed. It was a wonderful line, the kind you'd never hear in a pop song these days. 'Left To My Own Devices' was a masterpiece. Initially Neil and Chris were unsure about the opulent orchestration, but they eventually came around to it.

'Domino Dancing' entered the charts at number nine, peaking two places higher. It was perfectly respectable, but as Neil drove back to London from my place in Rye as the new entries were announced, he sensed that the Pet Shop Boys' sequence of uber-hits had been broken.

Sadly, he was kind of right.

Despite this, *Introspective* was Neil and Chris's biggest-selling album to date. They joked that it was so popular with punters because it didn't have their faces on the cover: it boasted a fantastic Mark Farrow abstract design that made me think of the old TV test card.

Yet when you pulled out the inner sleeve, there they were, one on either side, both holding Booblies, a friend's Yorkshire terrier. Booblies was a de facto third Pet Shop Boy for a brief time until an unfortunate incident on *Going Live*, when he attacked Gordon the Gopher.

Meanwhile, in Bros-land, I thought it would be a great idea for the band to live together. It would foster the ultimate image of the band as a brotherly gang: three eligible heartthrobs in a bachelor pad.

Obviously, it was all a myth (Luke was already attached to Shirley at this point) but the fans would love it. It was a throwback to the days of the Monkees, or even the Beatles movie *Help!* where they all lived in what looked like separate houses until you went through the door and each house had no walls.

Actually, for a while living together became standard procedure for manufactured pop groups, from 5ive to the early days of the Spice Girls. It would bring Bros closer together.

Or so I thought.

I found them a flat in Clive Court in Maida Vale, a very swanky part of London. The interior designer in me got to work on the pad, kitting it out with the latest furnishings and gadgets. It had remote-controlled mobile lights, Venetian blinds instead of wardrobe doors, and luxury Japanese carpets. It was a sleek, modern apartment.

Unfortunately, Bros were profoundly unimpressed. Luke preferred more traditional interiors and in any case wanted to be with Shirley. Craig had started seeing Kim Appleby, one half of the Stock Aitken Waterman sister duo, Mel & Kim, and wanted to be with her. Pretty soon, Matt was the flat's sole occupant.

It made no difference. Brosmania erupted. The band were greeted by screaming fans when they got off the plane in Australia, where *Push* was massive. Everywhere they went was a cacophony. They needed constant supervision, bodyguards and minders.

I found one of their minders at a Shirley Bassey concert at the Royal Albert Hall. John Buckland was an efficient, sharp professional, a real salt-of-the-earth bloke. Bros gave him no end of grief.

John had to liquidise Luke's food, because by now the drummer was declaring himself too tired to do anything as strenuous as actually chewing when he came off stage. He also had to listen to the twins' constant whining, which got worse as their workload increased.

The Gosses repaid him with puerile pranks such as putting laxatives in his chocolate mousse and applying Deep Heat to his phones. To the twins these pranks were a real laugh. To everybody else, the Bros twins were starting to resemble, well, a pair of blond brats.

Had the same jokes been played on them, they would have sulked for an eternity.

Within the band, problems started arising between the twins and Craig. Craig was never allowed to dress as well as the other two. Matt and Luke would scoop up the latest designer clobber eagerly. Whatever was left would do just fine for Craig.

As Bros toured the world, the gulf between the twins and Craig grew wider. With no brotherly bond of his own for support, he missed his new girlfriend. Craig became tired, ill and developed ME, or chronic fatigue syndrome. The twins were unsupportive; they were too young, too hungry for fame and too in thrall to the juggernaut they were on to really get their heads around Craig's illness. To be fair to them, there was a lot of ignorance around ME which persists to this day. I myself could have been more understanding.

Soon Craig had to sit in a wheelchair onstage. This prevented the twins from making their pole-vaulting entrance in the harnesses, which made them resent Craig even more.

To be fair to Matt and Luke, they were young, and the glory and celebrity of being big pop stars was something I'd encouraged. But I started to feel as if I were Dr Frankenstein and I had created a pair of twin monsters.

Things got physical. Luke had to be restrained by his own bodyguards when he attacked Craig, while Craig was sitting in his wheelchair. Matt then leapt in to defend his brother from the bodyguard. Not a pretty scene.

The pressures and joys of megastardom had turned them into a deadly dose of double diva. Poor, professional, publicity-shy Craig was stuck right in the middle.

In the beginning, Bros were the three musketeers but Craig became the twins' whipping boy and that took its toll. It became bonkers. Before a show in Germany, one of the twins ran off into the Black Forest.

Meanwhile, being pushed to the side of the stage in his wheelchair every night, Craig was basically having a breakdown. They were too young to deal with it all – and, if I am honest, I was too busy and too distracted to handle it properly.

Craig left the tour. He briefly returned to the fold to accept the best British newcomer prize at the February 1989 Brit Awards, but after that he was gone. I can't say that I blamed him.

And then there were two. Without Craig, Matt and Luke would get even more demanding. Forget monomaniacal. This was duo mania.

Lying in bed in the Lister Hospital in London, Craig was visited by Mel and Kim, the former now stricken with the cancer that would ultimately take her life at a tragically young age. He saw Mel's fortitude in the face of her illness and felt galvanised to get better. Craig bounced back and won six court cases against Bros. In the future, the one they had mocked as 'Ken' was to manage Sade, Tina Turner and Pink, work with Robbie Williams and became a major player in the global music business.

Yet now I was left to deal with the terror twins. There was a second Bros album to be made and megastardom to maintain. Bros were about to perform one of their biggest gigs ever but their egos were swelling to the point where they were on a fast track to losing all touch with reality.

There is a reason why there's only one letter differentiating pop from poo.

22

NO DOUBLE VISION

For me, 1989 was destined to be the year of the diva. The Pet Shop Boys were to work with both Dusty and Liza Minnelli. Bros just started acting like a pair.

Luckily, I just remained my usual shy, retiring, unassuming self.

Neil had bought a house in Rye. Gary and I helped him with the interiors. We got him Arts & Crafts antiques, found the appropriate fixtures and furnishings. I even acquired some Solomon Joseph Solomon paintings for him.

Neil liked his Rye getaway, and so did Janet Street-Porter. By now, she was moving closer to Neil and Chris. An off-the-cuff comment about her own power dressing would provide them with the title of one of their next projects – the legendary Liza Minnelli album.

While I was on a business trip to New York, an A&R man at Epic asked me if Neil and Chris were receptive to working with other artists. I said that would depend entirely on the artist.

'Liza Minnelli,' he said.

I told him that I thought they'd be very interested. Immediately, I got a mental image of Neil doing high kicks to the *Cabaret* soundtrack.

As I expected, Neil was ecstatic and Chris was his usual nonchalant self. Bizarrely, Liza's manager at the time was Gene Simmons, the Kiss founder and leader. He was a loudmouth Jewish American rock idol. Unsurprisingly, we got on.

I discussed the project with Gene. First we met in London and then I flew to LA and stayed at my favourite hotel there, the Mondrian. Gene and I talked about the prospective Liza and Pet Shop Boys collaboration over brunch at the Chateau Marmont.

So there I was, talking to the man with the longest tongue in rock about the Pet Shop Boys making a record with Judy Garland's daughter, the Oscar-winning actress, Broadway song-and-dance queen and showbiz sensation Liza Minnelli. What a surreal and fabulous life I was living ...

And then Bruce Springsteen came over to our table. As I tucked into my eggs Benedict and slurped on my Mimosa cocktail (or two), The Boss hovered above me. I couldn't believe it. I nearly spewed my food out all over Gene's leathery face.

Thankfully I didn't, and Bruce sat down and chatted. He was polite and charming, happily signing a photo for me that

I've kept to this day. The Liza–Pet Shop Boys deal got sealed and I got a signed picture of The Boss. Life didn't get much better than this.

Liza flew to London to begin work on the album in the spring of 1989. She stayed at the Savoy, naturally. Liza connected with Neil and Chris immediately. When she arrived, we had dinner at Orso's, a top-notch Italian in Covent Garden that Neil was particularly fond of.

We were escorted downstairs to a screen. Behind the screen, there sat Liza Minnelli … with rollers in her hair. This showbiz icon sat at the dinner table like Hilda Ogden. Nevertheless, she exuded total star power: loud, bubbly, gushing, with an almost clichéd charisma that it was hard not to be utterly seduced by. It was infectious.

Everything was 'Oh, darling!' and 'Wonderful!' and before you knew it you were talking like it, too. But she was so affable and warm that Neil and Chris, as star-struck as they undoubtedly were, felt totally comfortable in her company.

Inevitably, the record company wanted something 'contemporary' but also 'quintessentially Liza'. The boys had some strong ideas. Neil suggested updating Stephen Sondheim's 1971 song 'Losing My Mind' from the musical *Follies*, giving it a Hi-NRG Pet Shop Boys oomph. It was a stroke of genius, a high-camp ode to romantic obsession set to a throbbing beat.

Naturally, Liza threw herself into the project like the trouper she is. They dusted off 'Rent' and 'Tonight Is Forever' from the Pet Shops' back catalogue and an ancient song called 'I Can't Say Goodnight', a tune written all those years ago when the duo drank in the Chelsea Potter and Neil lived above R Soles.

One of the new songs written for the album was 'So Sorry, I Said', an unbearably poignant, characteristically Pet Shop Boys melody sung by the most theatrical woman on the planet. It was a marriage made in gay heaven (although there is no such thing as 'gay music', eh, Neil?).

David LaChapelle took the classy photo of Liza for the album cover. As I mentioned earlier, the record's title, *Results*, came from a slightly less classy source – my dear old mate, Janet.

Janet always referred to a certain kind of outfit as her 'results wear' as she claimed those clothes 'always got me results'. Considering some of the get-ups that woman went out in, I'm surprised they yielded any bloody results at all apart from outright horror!

Neil, Chris and Liza all went on *Wogan* to promote the album and the single from it, 'Losing My Mind'. Inevitably it was a major luvvie love-in. They even gave me a mention for a change, which pleased me no end. The three of them performed the single, with Neil and Chris playing keyboards and Liza serenading them.

No wonder Janet was losing her bloody mind! She was definitely not going to get any 'results' trying to woo those two ...

As a thank-you for putting the whole project together, Liza sent me a whole load of Calvin Klein briefs, all gorgeously rolled and presented to look like a display of rosettes. I gazed at them admiringly. Not only were they quite a display: the woman who played Sally Bowles in *Cabaret* had sent them to me.

Liza with a Z! What a tremendous superstar she was!

And what a lovely lady!

But how the fuck did she expect me to stuff my fat arse into those skimpy pants?

The album did respectable business in the UK, hitting number six. In America it was a different story, coming in at an abysmal number 128. Stateside, the Pet Shop Boys seemed to be becoming box office poison.

Neil and Chris had also been busy writing another song for Dusty Springfield to sing. They had penned 'Nothing Has Been Proved', the theme for the film *Scandal*, the story of the sixties Profumo scandal involving spies, prostitutes and the government.

The Pet Shop Boys had totally rehabilitated Dusty. Where she had been firmly down the dumper, 'What Have I Done To Deserve This?' had rescued her from obscurity, a follow-up greatest hits album had sold well, and by now she was getting the credit she truly deserved as one of the great soul singers.

'Nothing Has Been Proved' continued this progress. It was a work of art, and a testament to Neil and Chris's generosity that they gave the composition away. But then when I heard Neil singing the demo, it was clear it required a proper singer to do it justice.

As was her wont, Dusty approached the song like a method actor. She sang one line at a time, agonising over every one in painstaking detail, subtly modifying verses and injecting them with nuances before building to the big Dusty climax, where all the song's pent-up emotions explode in soulful catharsis.

Even for me, just sitting watching, it was an exhausting session that nevertheless produced a stunning performance. Neil compared it to a painter with a canvas. Her technique would inform and improve his later singing style. But the poor engineer, spending the day watching Dusty utter a single syllable and then stop, probably went home and had a nervous breakdown.

Everything about the performance was essence of Dusty distilled. It was maddening and magnificent, fragile and vulnerable, but also sturdy and tough.

I think that watching these women perform and seeing their ability to take a song and wring every crevice of emotion out of it was emboldening for Neil, as well. Liza, in particular, was a woman who was born to take to the stage. And now it was Neil's turn.

That year, after putting it off, prevaricating and making excuses for years, the Pet Shop Boys finally went on tour.

A Japanese promoter was keen for them to do some shows over there. Now they could stage the lavish, theatrical spectacle they had always wanted to. We brought Derek Jarman on board to direct the extravaganza and to provide screen projections.

There would be grand costumes and dancers. At one point, the polka dots on the dancers' costumes would echo the Dalmatian spots on the film footage backdrops. This was high-concept

stuff, as arty as you would hope and imagine. They were set
to play Tokyo, Osaka and Nagoya before returning to these
shores for some dates at London, Birmingham and Glasgow.

Let's make no bones about it; the Pet Shop Boys were
terrified of playing live. Their long-held stance that doing gigs
was 'boring' was a pretty transparent smokescreen failing
to hide the fact that they were petrified of doing it. Their
nonchalant would-be cool had always masked a lot of frailties
and vulnerabilities.

Yet, despite this, the shows were a towering success. They got
over their stage fright quite brilliantly. Maybe the spectacular
staging helped. Neil got dressed up as a cardinal for 'It's A
Sin'. Chris even stepped away from the keyboards and danced
on 'Paninaro'. The critics raved, and so they should.

Even so, in the build-up to the tour I had sensed that Neil
and Chris were keeping me at arm's length. I wasn't invited to
the rehearsals. When they were so nervous about performing,
maybe they felt my blunt, brash feedback would have sapped
their confidence? I hope not – I would only have been trying
to help them.

In any case, when I showed up in Japan to see the first dates,
the air between us seemed decidedly frosty. It didn't bode
well – especially as my management contract with them was
up for renewal in a few weeks.

Neil and I had always had a strange relationship. We shared
a sense of humour (slightly withering and slightly camp,
although we never talked about sexuality). We had similar
aesthetic interests. Yet I had always felt an underlying sense of
being looked down upon.

Basically, Neil squirmed at my ('dodgy') acts and my bullish way of promoting them. It was a strength he realised was necessary in the pop business but was still embarrassed by it. Pop stars want the results that me banging on a desk gets them. They just don't want their 'cool' image to be associated with it.

His doubts had come to the fore earlier that year in a meeting in New York where I was valiantly arguing their cause with EMI Manhattan. Neil corrected one of my malapropisms. I had said 'apocolytes', mixing up apostles with acolytes.

It happens. I talk faster than I think and sometimes I make a blunder. Who cares? I still feel that Neil pointing it out in front of a team of record company suits was snooty and churlish. More importantly, it undermined the point that I was forcefully trying to make for their benefit.

I loved Neil Tennant dearly, but Mr Grand Poobah of Upper Buttcrack could be a snooty, condescending bastard. Oh, couldn't he just. The rift between us slowly grew wider.

They gave me my marching orders in the glamorous locale of a Pizza Express in the autumn of 1989. We were having lunch, and Neil and Chris picked nervously at their garlic bread before Neil screwed up the courage to tell me: 'We won't be renewing our contract with you.'

As sackings go, it was exactly as mealy-mouthed as I would expect from him. I stared into my Margherita for a moment and pretended to shrug it off as no big deal. But underneath I was gutted.

Neil and Chris had overcome their fear of live performance and now they didn't need a big front with a big mouth any more. In fact, they felt I had become an obstruction to them. They had so much more confidence than they had five years ago. Mine was no longer needed.

We had come a long way together, from meeting Neil in that dusty old Marvel Comics office with the dishevelled Spiderman costume on loan for Giggles. They were my first successful act after an endless string of flops. I had banged my fists on the right tables and charmed the right people to enable them to make their grand pop dreams a reality: securing budgets and hooking them up with the right musical and visual collaborators.

Yet, crucially, I could never manipulate them. I found that frustrating, but ultimately it made me have an enduring respect for them that I perhaps didn't always have for the more easily moulded acts.

Now it was over.

I took it on the chin, moved on and never let it be known how hurt I was by my dismissal. Over the years, I would let that hurt out via occasional malicious comments and bitchiness. I bullishly asserted that it was their loss and that they had broken a winning formula.

But I always missed the Pet Shop Boys. And I still do.

From the sublime to the ridiculous ... back in the world of Bros, if Matt and Luke were missing Craig they were certainly hiding the fact well.

Without the steadying influence of their common-sense bass player, the Goss twins grew even more wrapped up in their own mythology.

Mike Hrano, who ran their fan club, pursued them for an interview while they were abroad. Mike had been flown out especially and it was soon time for him to go home. But they remained elusive. He couldn't get hold of them and searched the hotel. Eventually he gave up and pressed for the lift to return to his hotel room, defeated.

The elevator doors opened up to reveal Matt and Luke standing in identical outfits, studded leather waistcoats.

To Mike it almost seemed like they were standing in their onstage poses, legs astride, their hands placed on hips with militaristic authority. For Matt and Luke, being pop stars was a twenty-four-hour business ...

Meanwhile, their spending became quite laughably extravagant. I think they had more jewellery than Liz Taylor.

Tragedy hit Matt and Luke's lives when a drunk driver mowed down and killed their stepsister Carolyn. They were driven to their mum's home in Peckham to hear the bad news. They were devastated. The press acted like pigs, hounding the twins at the funeral then printing stories about their 'misconduct' when they retaliated. Disgusting.

Yet the pop star treadmill ground on, giving them no time to grieve, mourn or even take stock of their loss. I was too caught up in my own hectic schedule to really lend any support. After all, there were appearances on *Wogan* to attend.

And that second album to make ...

Given their penchant for the finer things in life, it was inevitable that the second Bros album was going to be recorded in a far more exotic location than London. They decided to make the follow-up to *Push* in Miraval in the South of France, at a recording studio set beside a sprawling vineyard.

My original concept was it was to be called *Pull* and it would feature more Nicky Graham/Tom Watkins songs that followed up those on *Push*. So we would have written 'Now I'm Famous' and 'Now I'm A Man': that sort of thing.

I still think that it was a good idea. There again, I've always been in favour of sticking to a winning formula. If it's not broke, don't fix it, and all that.

Matt and Luke had other ideas. They were by now convinced they were serious artistes with 'longevity' and they wanted their new sound to reflect that. More to the point, if you ask me, they wanted some publishing royalties, too.

They got their way. Muff Winwood at CBS told me they had to have a go at getting involved with the music. I felt this was a disastrous idea and, if I am totally honest, I didn't want to loosen the reins on a phenomenon that I had had a big hand in creating.

On the one hand, it probably was control freakery on my part. On the other hand, once a manufactured band achieves vast success, they often forget the other players who helped to make them big. They view themselves as the sole architects of their fame and glory. And it usually ends in tears.

So Matt and Luke went off to the South of France to the remote luxury chateau studio to work with Nicky on the record. They took with them their new cars and Yamaha quad bikes acquired from sponsorship deals. They soaked up the sun and did a lot of driving around the grounds and the winding cliff-top roads.

Nicky took to the warmer climate well, too. Soon he was sunbathing by the chateau's pool naked; after a few days, he was starkers at the mixing desk. The twins were mortified and desperately tried to look at anything but the appendage they nicknamed Nicky's 'walnut'.

There again, they were hardly the picture of level-headed sanity. At evening meal times, Shirley would sometimes sample Luke's food before spoon-feeding it to him as if he were a Roman emperor.

Indeed, reports reaching me from the chateau suggested that the twins were getting more and more sucked into their own fame. Once again, fan club chief Mike Hrano flew out to interview them on the album's progress.

Bros's session guitarist, Paul Gendler, picked Mike up at the airport. He confided in him that he had to get away for an hour or two as he was going mental trapped in such a secluded location with two such preposterous divas.

As Paul drove into the chateau grounds and headed down the long drive that led to the studio, Mike saw a square lake surrounded by a dense thicket of trees. There appeared to be something white at the far end, lying in the water.

'What the hell is that?'

'Oh, that's a remote-controlled aeroplane,' Paul sighed. 'The boys picked them up in Marseilles. They cost a small fortune …'

Of course, Matt and Luke had both bought one. As with everything, if one of them bought something the other would always follow suit, no matter what it cost. They actually ended up with a few of those crazily expensive model planes. They would crash them just for the hell of it.

Mike set about trying to arrange his fan club interview. He sure had his work cut out. When he first broached the subject, the twins were playing pool.

Matt laid down a challenge: 'I'll play you for the interview, Mike. If you win, we'll do it. How's that?'

Mike liked those odds. He was a regular and skilled pool player.

'OK, Matt, but you know I'm pretty nifty with a pool cue,' he said. He won the game.

'Right, Mike. Best of three,' pouted Matt.

'OK, Matt. No problem.'

Mike won again. Matt was not happy.

'Best of five!'

'OK, Matt.'

After Mike had won five frames in a row and Matt realised that he had been well and truly thrashed, and couldn't challenge Mike again without losing face, he did what so many pop stars with giant, fragile egos do in the face of setbacks.

He went ape-shit.

Matt grabbed his pool cue and tried to smash it against the wall in a fury. Even this tantrum didn't sufficiently relieve him of his frustration at the awful hardship of actually having to do a fan club interview.

So he attempted to lift the pool table up …

Everyone in the room stood aghast, dumbfounded by the comical carnage that Matt had created. Mike finally broke the awkward silence around the table.

'So, you are ready to do the interview now, Matt?'

Mike had a ticket to leave that evening. Not that that bothered Matt in the slightest.

'Nah, let's do it in Germany next week. We have to go there for a few days.'

Eventually, grudgingly, Matt agreed to do the interview. Mike asked the twins questions that fans had written in and the boys gave half-interested, crappy answers.

Mike was by now as mad as hell and wasn't going to take it any more. He leaned into the tape recorder to provide a running commentary. He was joking – but he also wasn't.

'Next time, guys, can you write the questions with big spaces? Luke has to follow the words with his finger. It can take a while.'

Luke, who was always sensitive to any accusations that his intellect fell below MENSA standards, stared at Mike while the penny slowly dropped. When it finally did, he wasn't happy.

'Eh? What the fuck did you say?'

There again, Luke and Matt took their pop star posturing incredibly seriously and didn't appreciate it at all if anyone mocked them. Once again, French and Saunders took the piss out of one of my acts on their show.

The girls didn't just bear an uncanny resemblance to the Goss twins in their make-up and costumes. They also nailed their characters. I had to laugh when Jennifer Saunders, as Luke, turned to Dawn French's Matt and asked, 'I write the drums, don't I?'

Spooky. It could have been the man himself.

Cleverly, the parody that French and Saunders sang, 'When Will I Be Taken Seriously?', lampooned not only Bros's back catalogue but also their craving for credibility. And it wasn't just TV comedians that picked up on this.

After Neil Tennant saw Bros on telly talking about their aspirations of 'longevity', he took a satirical swipe at such pretensions with a song called 'How Can You Expect To Be Taken Seriously?' on Pet Shop Boys' 1990 *Behaviour* album. Maybe he had watched French and Saunders and got some ideas?

Matt and Luke certainly didn't see the funny side of French and Saunders' skit. However, Neil's bitchiness escaped them. They always thought he was such a nice man. They didn't realise he was quietly rolling his eyes at them behind their backs, as he did with so many people.

While Bros were working on the album, I went out to Miraval with Janet, who went through a pile of paperwork from her yoof TV job while sunbathing topless. Matt and Luke decided it would be a good idea to fly one of their remote-controlled planes around her. It hovered around her head, then nose-dived into her reading material.

Janet glared up at the sniggering twins. 'I do hope your dicks are bigger than your bleeding brains!' she barked.

It was never dull being around Janet, but sadly the album that Bros were crafting down in France was pure dullsville.

They had replaced the pure pop of their smash-hit debut with a weedy, middle-of-the-road sound and sub-Jacko bollocks. It was a (very) poor man's George Michael. They clearly wanted a makeover similar to George's journey from Wham! to *Faith* but this crap sure wasn't it.

It wasn't pop. It didn't rock. I thought it was pretty bad. In fact, apart from 'Sister', their beautiful tribute to their late stepsister Carolyn, the album was dross.

As Matt sang a dirge called 'Chocolate Box', his voice seemed to waver as he sang the word 'fool'. At the album playback, I chuckled quietly to myself.

Chocolate in a box? Shite in a box, more like …

Matt and Luke now also seemed to be taking their sartorial cue from Cher's 'Turn Back Time' video. Their obligatory ripped jeans now came with revolting leather jackets with tassels. *Tassels.* I had made Spelt Like This wear tassels in 1985, and look how that had worked out!

The tassels were an ominous omen. At this point, the twins also loved tank tops and Cuban heels. They looked like a right pair of Brigitte Nielsens.

The first single from the album, which was to be called *The Time*, was 'Too Much'. It was admittedly one of the album's better tracks but to be honest that wasn't saying much. It was a bit like being the tallest dwarf. It certainly didn't hold a candle to 'I Owe You Nothing', 'When Will I Be Famous?' or 'Drop The Boy'.

The video for 'Too Much' was the zenith, or, rather, the nadir, of Bros bombast. Luke and Matt were whisked off in helicopters then cruised windy cliff-top roads in posh convertibles. This was all intercut with a live performance where ecstatic Brosettes rushed the stage.

The video featured a love interest for Matt, but really she was a mere cameo to the twins' posturing, which had now swollen to superhero proportions.

To a cheesy guitar solo, there was an aerial view of the Bros twins, each with one arm reaching skywards, their fists touching, by the edge of a cliff. The video looked like an excerpt from a high-octane, unspeakably naff eighties action show like *Cover Story*. Matt and Luke were perilously caught up in their own posing and it was slightly funny and slightly worrying all at once.

Yet the single did OK and we secured a major coup, agreeing to play Wembley Stadium on 19 August 1989. It didn't sell out but ticket sales were OK and not the dismal disaster that some of the press made out. We decided to call the gig *Bros In 2 Summer*. We were well excited about it.

It was a beautiful sunny day. At Wembley, I hung out in the VIP box with Kylie Minogue and promoter Harvey Goldsmith. As the crowd gathered, I surveyed the sight with real pride. *I am managing a band that is playing Wembley Stadium*, I thought to myself. Giddy euphoria filled me.

So where is the fucking tallyman now?

Yet then an awful, empty feeling descended upon me. There was no doubt that this would be Bros's high point. A decline would quickly set in, as it does in pop, and that steep drop would be straight into that dreaded dumper.

Even as the fans screamed and Matt and Luke tore into their set, I just knew that it was all over. I was bored. The twins were draining. And their new music was, frankly, rubbish.

After the show, the brothers didn't stick around to enjoy the lavish after-show party I had arranged for them. Instead, they retreated to their hotel rooms at the plush May Fair to do what pop stars do best – sulk. What about? I didn't know, and I didn't care.

Not long afterwards, Bros left for America to tour, supporting Debbie Gibson, a US teen titan and smut-free mini-Madonna, who had opened for them at the Wembley gig. The trip was an unmitigated disaster.

In no time at all the twins were at each other's throats. They just could not handle life on the road in America as a mere support act. Every night they stared from the stage at kids with their fingers in their ears, desperate for these lame Limeys to clear off so they could see Debbie.

Initially they weren't even given proper soundchecks. Matt was banned from jumping on the ramps at the side of the stage. The record company failed to put anything out in time for the tour, and didn't even know how to pronounce the band's name properly. It was a pile-up of almighty fuck-ups.

They also got a hard time when they stepped off the tour bus in the wee small hours to call at roadside diners in the middle of nowhere. Some pretty hard dudes would be jeering menacingly at Matt and Luke's ostentation.

Pretty quickly their jewellery came off and tracksuit bottoms and baseball caps replaced them for anonymity – and safety. But Matt and Luke without their gold accessories were like Samsons without manes of hair. They got dead miserable.

Naturally, they cheered each other up with crazy spending. On their birthday they went to Cartier and lavished gifts on each other. They flew their family over and dropped £25,000 on the one trip alone.

I also went out to see them and gave them two inflatable replicas of real jukeboxes that I had waiting for them back home. It was my last-ditch attempt to salvage things with Bros in the wake of the Pet Shop Boys splitting with me. It was also a waste of time.

By 1990, Bros and I had gone our separate ways, after a lengthy, inevitable and highly publicised legal squabble. All that I felt was relief. It had been like having the same annoying pop star coming at you twice.

Bros had turned out to be a dire double vision.

A big headache.

The wrong kind of pain in my arse.

Believe it or not, I have no hard feelings towards Matt and Luke now. They have both grown up and are doing well and I'm happy for them. They came out of pop stardom older and wiser; many of my gripes with them can be attributed to the inability of youth to handle the meteoric and hysterical maelstrom of fame. Some of it no doubt can be attributed to me being a fickle, difficult bastard.

But they've both survived. Matt has, if anything, grown into a better singer than he once was, a crooner with regular stints in Vegas. Luke is now a fine actor. Maybe they're not as famous as they once were but they've honed their crafts with tenacity and dedication.

I bumped into them once in Covent Garden a few years after we split. It was frosty but civil, like seeing an old lover that you would feel mean avoiding but would rather not talk to.

There again, that was a veritable love-in compared to my encounters with the dreaded Brosettes. There were a few of those. I will never forget being chased down the street by a pack of them once when I was on my way to Pizza Express.

'You evil, fat bastard, Tom Watkins!' they yelled after me. 'We're going to get you for what you did to Matt and Luke! Just wait!'

I just don't have good luck with Pizza bloody Express, do I?

23

ROUGH TRADE, BIG BUSINESS

So the eighties were over and the nineties had begun. There was a whole slew of cataclysmic events at the decade's end and the new one's start. The Berlin Wall collapsed, as did the Soviet Union. Maggie Thatcher went a bit bonkers and had to resign. Neil Tennant continued to lose his hair.

And for a while, pop music seemed to die with the decade it had been so synonymous with. The acid house and rave boom brought with it a barrage of faceless dance records and one-off singles made by producers who felt uncomfortable in front of cameras.

Smash Hits really suffered. There was a dire shortage of cover stars. Where were the personalities? Across the pond, grunge rock struck an equally anti-star pose. People with lank hair and cheesecloth shirts who'd listened to too much

Black Sabbath and were terribly angst-ridden about being white and middle class.

I didn't get any of it, and I didn't have Bros or the Pet Shop Boys any more. What was next for me? Was it time to quit the music business?

Still, I had other things occupying my mind. My 'eighties boyfriend' and I were over and I had met Darren, the man I would end up spending many, many years with. As those years went by, however, we became more and more distant, so that eventually it seemed like a loveless arrangement. That's all I can say really. Except that he's now married with kids. To a woman! Never let it be said that Tom Watkins can't turn a gay man straight ...

I moved into a Georgian town house in Maida Vale. I love the canal and had always wanted to live in that area. That bastion of London Thatcherism, Lady Porter, was auctioning off the council's acquisitions and I scooped the property up.

I set about renovating the place, installing a basement swimming pool and adorning the walls with massive pop art paintings. Mickey Mouse, of course, was everywhere. Lulu was two doors down the road. It was my little palace and I felt like an emperor.

But of what, exactly? I no longer had acts that were setting the charts alight.

I had had a stab at chart action with a band called Electribe 101. They were fantastic, playing stripped-down house music with the torchy, soulful siren voice of German chanteuse Billie Ray Martin. She had sung on S'Express's hit 'Hey Music Lover'.

I managed to get them a deal with Mercury/Phonogram and they had a couple of mid-chart singles. They went on tour in support of Depeche Mode, but they never took the leap to the next level and the group disbanded during the making of their second album due to that old cliché, musical differences.

Billie and I had not seen eye to eye: she was a talented woman who was very difficult to deal with. And in any case, managing a credible, underground dance act was all very well, but I have always been about POP! I was desperate to get another Watkins group into the upper echelons of the charts.

Nicky Graham thought it would be Faith Hope & Charity, a three-girl group from the Sylvia Young Theatre School. When the school approached us, Nicky thought they were going to be the female Bros and was very excited at the prospect. They were future *The Word* TV presenter Dani Behr (who could be a right princess), the talented Sally Ann Marsh and Diana Barrand.

They were pretty, feisty girls with plenty of attitude and energy and record companies went for them. Before I knew it we got ourselves a deal with Rob Dickens at WEA. Their 1990 debut single, 'Battle Of The Sexes', was a novelty dance record about the gender divide, posing such pertinent questions as 'Why aren't men called slags?'

Deep down I was pretty underwhelmed by it and so was Edna from Huddersfield and the public as whole. The single hit number fifty-three and Faith Hope & Charity went down the dumper.

Was I losing my touch? Would the nineties be a hit-free decade for me? Luckily, no: and my next big success was largely down to a lithe lad from Walthamstow who was dancing behind Faith Hope & Charity when they played the annual *Smash Hits* party.

His name was Tony Mortimer. He danced. He wrote songs. And he wanted to be a pop star.

One night in Walthamstow, Chris Lowe's mate Pete Andreas spotted two cute young lads named Tony Mortimer and John outside a pub. Tony was a great body-popper and loved black American music like, chiefly, Prince, Public Enemy and LL Cool J.

Pete would have mistaken John and Tony for rough trade. In actual fact they were nothing of the sort. Tony was a lot smarter than that, a shrewd little songwriting spitfire who scoured the pages of music magazines and had seen my name as the man behind Bros and the Pet Shop Boys.

Anyway, that night Tony and John were just two naïve lads wasting time on the streets of Walthamstow. Pete chatted to them and before they knew it had lured them to a club in King's Cross off York Way.

John and Tony were entranced by the music and lights and they both grinned at each other at the bar, tingling with the adrenalin you have when you are young and the inside of a club is still fresh, dangerous and exciting. Then they both stared at the whole room – and then they did a double take.

There weren't any ladies here.

They were in a gay club.

They survived this ordeal and Pete put me in touch with Tony, who handed me a tape of all his songs, scraps, doodles and cobbled-together ideas. He did a lot of little raps and I saw potential in him. He was a diamond in the rough, the same as when Bros had walked into my office that summer day in 1986.

The music wasn't exactly great but when I chatted to him I liked his energy, drive and chutzpah. He told me he worked at an oversized men's clothing shop called Trouser Exchange Store in Walthamstow and he could get me a discount. Cheeky sod! Mind you, I'll take it.

When Tony came round to my Maida Vale palace he had no socks on. I thought the poor waif was a street urchin, so I handed little Oliver Twist a pair of Burlingtons. He looked bemused but he took them.

I only found out a while later that it was the current street fashion to go bare-heeled. How out of touch I was ...

I gave Tony the gig dancing with Faith Hope & Charity. The first time he danced he froze with fear, overwhelmed with nerves. *Oh gawd*, I thought to myself, *this kid is all mouth and no trousers (or socks)*. But as I was about to start bawling him out, he bust out some amazing moves like the running man, all the latest dances the kids were doing.

Tony was easily the most magnetic thing on the stage (at least for an old queen like me). Later on at a party, surrounded by a bunch of leering gay men, Tony had clearly had enough of being perved over. He pulled out his enormous dong, waved it at his drooling fans and told them: 'See this? You're never getting your hands on it.'

I think they wanted to get more than their hands on it, Tony. But there you go. It never happened.

Tony had tremendous potential but I told him I wasn't interested in managing solo acts. I loved putting a band together and dealing with a package. In any case, I didn't think that Tony could make it on his own.

He needed a real singer to play against his raps. He was a talented, driven man but he would never win a talent contest with that voice of his. He needed a foil.

So the next time I saw him, he walked in with Brian Harvey, his mate from Walthamstow. Brian was a diminutive demon with just the right angelic voice, a blue-eyed soul brother to play against Tony's white boy rapping. I saw the potential immediately.

Encouraged, Tony came back with two more of his mates, John Hendy and Terry Coldwell (aka the chav Tweedledee and Tweedledum). Musically, this was Tony and Brian's show. Terry and John were there to make up the numbers: we might as well have unplugged their microphones. But they added to the street-tough gang image of the band.

Unlike Bros, they needed little sartorial advice. The latest hip street clobber was their forte. They knew how to dress, had that swagger, and labels like Stussy and Nike were their uniform.

They all came over to my Maida Vale home. Where Tony was upfront and vocal, the other three of them giggled like nervous schoolkids. They probably had had no experience of dealing with an 'out' gay man. They were clearly well acquainted with smoking marijuana, though.

I started by asking them what kind of band they wanted to be and – always jumping ahead – how they should be marketed. Well, what I actually said was: 'So what we need, fellas, is an angle, a twist, something a bit different that sets you apart from being just New Kids on the Block clones. What have you got?'

There was a long, awkward silence

Half-baked, John told me, 'We got a dog.'

Our eyes all shifted to the mongrel they had brought with them, who was sitting, oblivious, on my carpet.

'OK, I like dogs,' I told them. 'Let's use it.'

A drawing of a dog became their logo. We got an ex-convict to spray one around London to garner a bit of an underground buzz. He signed it with the band's name taken from Walthamstow's postcode, East 17.

It was just the right kind of rough, scruffy way to introduce them to the world. Forget hairspray and tassels, now we were in the street-sharp, unvarnished nineties. Time for spray cans and stencils.

The band started recording some material with Phil Harding and Ian Curnow, producers whose careers I was taking care of since the halcyon days of Stock Aitken Waterman had come to an end. I played a dirty little East 17 ditty called 'Deep' to the *Smash Hits* editor, Alex Kadis.

She loved it so much that she made me a promise: 'Tom, if you get them a record deal, we'll put them on the cover.'

We got a deal with London Records. There is no doubt the promise of a *Smash Hits* cover for the band before they had even released a single helped to clinch it.

Their first single was to be 'House Of Love', a banging, slamming bit of techno-pop full of Tony's youthful idealism. It was an impassioned plea for unity, as if John Lennon had done an E then got roughed up by a bunch of Borstal boys. Tony hated the mix and how his song had ended up sounding like the KLF or the Shamen.

'Thanks for fucking up my song,' he told me.

The ungrateful little oik hated how techno it was! Everybody else loved it, including me. I even punched the air when I heard the finished version.

We put the dog logo on the sleeve. It created a bit of an enigma around the band rather than working their image. In fact, it was a bold move for a boy band who relied on their looks and the idea of themselves as 'product' to sell records.

There again, East 17 disputed the notion that they were a boy band: 'Boy bands are fluff. We're rough.'

We made the video super-cheap. It looked like what it was, a low-budget, DIY job. It was filmed outside Walthamstow greyhound stadium with just the dog logo, a few graphics and a baby for props.

The opening shot was a looming, menacing group of shadows. We were establishing that these were bad boys. They hunched their shoulders, leered at the camera, thrust their groins and pointed their fingers, stripped to the waist. These were the kind of boys that mums and dads were terrified of their daughters meeting.

In a funny way, East 17's sexual danger and lusty menace reminded me of how the Rolling Stones had instilled moral panic into the cosy suburban homes of the sixties. This was real lock-up-your-daughters stuff. And girls loved it. Straightaway, they came flocking around the boys.

Well, we all like a bit of rough, don't we?

It seemed even the dour inkies did. *Melody Maker* and *NME* covered the group, clearly seduced by the bad-boy image. It was no doubt a welcome relief from those dour, sexless indie bands that hid behind their hair and instruments. Less shoe-gazing, more groin-thrusting, please!

Alternative music also seemed bored with how self-defeating and drab its scene was. Around the same time as *Smash Hits* gave East 17 their cover in 1992, *Melody Maker* did the same for Suede, calling them 'the best new band in Britain'.

I really liked Suede, who also reminded me a bit of the Stones, although they had clearly listened to a few Bowie records, too. And when you could decipher what singer Brett Anderson was howling during 'Animal Nitrate', it sounded like a song about rough gay sex and poppers.

In Suede's wake came Britpop. I wasn't so impressed. Blur were a 'quintessentially English' band, a bit Kinks, a bit Madness, a lot of mockney and Damon Albarn rolling his eyes like he'd wandered out of Lionel Bart's *Oliver*.

You couldn't get away from them. Believe me, I tried.

Their arch-rivals, Oasis, were fronted by Liam and Noel Gallagher, who were about as glamorous as the Mitchell brothers on *EastEnders*. They banged on about the Beatles but sounded like *Revolver* with all the invention taken out. So *that* was what East 17 would be up against.

Early on in their career we got them a spot on *The Word*, the late-night Channel 4 show co-hosted by Terry Christian. I decided to go on with them, partly because I fancied a bit of my own publicity but mainly because I thought they might get tongue-tied. And East 17 sat there sneering, smirking and not contributing.

I wore a smart suit and had even managed to lose a bit of my bulk, as Terry's co-host Dani Behr kindly noted. To liven things up, I went into my best lecherous-old-bastard manager routine, flippantly declaring that I slept with all of my acts (which is not true, by the way).

At which point, Dani reminded Tony live on air that when he had been dancing for Faith Hope & Charity, he had told her that I was 'a fat poof'. I might be thick-skinned, but even I squirmed for a minute. Backstage after the show, my sister Sally walloped Dani.

While I had been getting East 17 together, up in Manchester, Nigel Martin Smith had been launching Take That via gay clubs and kids' TV shows. They were everything that East 17 weren't: clean-cut, smiley and showbiz-camp in that way that appeals to everyone from gays to housewives. And, Christ, they were dull.

Well, maybe that is slightly harsh. Gary Barlow was a bleached barnet of bland but Take That's other members were a little more magnetic. Robbie Williams, particularly, was like a boy-band Norman Wisdom with sex appeal.

Take That's music was aimed at dance floors, homos and hen nights and was all tacky updates of disco and cover versions. On their first single, a Hi-NRG catastrophe called 'Do What You Like', they smeared each other in jelly in the incredibly homoerotic video.

They even got trussed up in leather gear. It made Gary look like a Village People tribute act from the sticks.

I played East 17 the video ....

'Right, lads, this is your biggest competition.'

After the video ended and after the jelly had been ladled all over Take That, East 17 rolled their eyes in disbelief. Well, that was hardly a competition, was it?

I agreed. And for a while it looked as if we were right.

After their first single's foray into softcore porn, Take That cleaned up their act and started having hits like 'It Only Takes A Minute' and a cover of Dan Hartman's 'Relight My Fire'.

That second track featured guest vocals from Lulu, my neighbour down the road in Maida Vale. Nigel Martin Smith had been around to see her, no doubt to clinch the collaboration.

Shortly after East 17 hit big, Take That leapt out of a van clad head to toe in Stussy. It was a total rip-off of my band no doubt, but at least it spared the world the sight of Gary Barlow in chaps.

Nigel and I loathed each other.

Well, two queens managing two rival boy bands. It was never going to be pretty, was it?

The 'House Of Love' single hit number ten. It was OK, no better, but there was a good buzz building around the band. The follow-up, 'Gold', was a damp squib. It peaked at a disappointing number twenty-eight and didn't live up to its title. It was a bit rusty. Like 'House Of Love', it was a positivist, club-friendly anthem with Tony rapping and Brian singing. It just wasn't as good.

I put the band in angel wings for the video. At the time clubbers had started wearing them. It's not a look that has aged well. They bowed as if they were in the presence of some holy deity but looked like juvenile delinquents being forced to star in a nativity for community service. It didn't work.

The dog got himself in the clip again, though.

'Deep', that song that had got them a *Smash Hits* cover, was their third single and did far better. It was just the right kind of saucy. The video was a lot of fun, a big party with the lads around a piano, playing snooker, dancing and drinking. My nephews were in it.

'Deep' went to number five and in February 1993 East 17's debut album, *Walthamstow*, did a whole lot better. It got to number one.

This was a major triumph. They were appealing to the kind of people who buy albums, not just teenyboppers. We stuck up a few more singles off the record such as 'Slow It Down' and a cover of 'West End Girls' purely to infuriate Neil and Chris.

What's that saying about revenge being best served cold?

Yet my favourite East 17 song was 'It's Alright'. No, it wasn't a new version of the Sterling Void song that the Pet Shop Boys had covered. That would have just been too petty ... wouldn't it?

No, this was all their own, and it was their best yet. Opening like a piano-led gospel ballad, it quickly shifted gears into a fist-pumping club-bound banger. I had insisted that the tune got speeded up to turn the big, churchy sound into a pounding chant.

I couldn't imagine those weedy Take That boys coming up with anything as inventive or surging as this. Released in November 1993, it hit number one in Australia, Switzerland and Ireland, number two in Germany and number three here. Yes, things were alright. Very alright.

Or were they? East 17 had a tight but turbulent internal chemistry. They had a real gang mentality, but their troubled upbringings and wayward personalities made them a lethal, handle-with-care concoction from day one.

Coming from violent, broken homes, Tony had learned to 'shut down', a coping strategy that made him a bit more adept at riding the pop rollercoaster than the others. Brian, abandoned by his mother and left to live with his gran, was the kind of kid who runs to fame craving the love he never got and always gets singed by it. Brian had pain inside him. And he also had music, which is why he was able to access such raw, poignant emotions when he sang.

One clear memory of Christmas 1993 lives with me. East 17's star was in its ascent, the hits were starting to happen, the girls were screaming and they graced many a magazine cover.

It was the golden period for a pop group; that first sweet smell of success. The rush of that first phase is rarely ever equalled. And, coming for them at Christmas, it really felt like a magical time.

There was an unexpected knock at the door of my home in Maida Vale. I went to answer it.

'Awright, Geez? I just thought I'd get you this. I wanted to say a big thank you. Merry Christmas!'

It was Brian. He had bought me a cuddly Mickey Mouse. I took it and smiled. Yes, it was a merry Christmas. And the next one would be even merrier. After that, the giddy carousel of pop would spin out of all control. And Brian Harvey wouldn't be bringing me presents any more.

Yet I won't forget the smiling, mischievous urchin that came to my front door that day, beaming with pride and gratitude.

I would like to remember him that way.

24

E IS FOR EXIT

As East 17 began to think about their second album, their fame continued to grow. We started 1994 exhilarated and ready to consolidate the debut's success.

Thankfully it proved a far more fruitful task than following up Bros's first album. There would be no exotic recording locations to be distracted by, and no trashed remote-controlled aeroplanes. Phil Harding and Ian Curnow were back in charge of the production duties. And even Brian was contributing song ideas.

Brian's sketch became Tony's 'Around The World', the first single off *Steam*, the second album. It was a sweet little song about travelling the world yet wanting to be back home, a perfect pop confection for a young band on the road as much as they were.

It was also based on truth. While East 17 enjoyed touring, jumping in pools, smoking reefers and entertaining countless female fans, some members did indeed suffer away from the loved ones who took care of them.

'Around The World' was another smash, hitting number three. The next single was *Steam*'s title track and was one of their hot 'n' horny anthems, tailor-made for a bunch of Chippendales from the wrong side of the tracks. John Hendy got his top off for the video. It was another top ten hit.

In October 1994, the album came out and sailed to number three. Things were going good. But it was the next single that really changed everything.

Tony had written a song on *Steam* called 'Stay Another Day'. The only problem was that Brian hated it, and made it clear: 'I'm not singing that shit!' Tony was incensed. We had to hold him back from starting an almighty recording studio scrap.

Talk about history repeating itself! It was 'When Will I Be Famous?' all over again. It was a sure-fire hit but the singer just didn't want to record the vocals.

Eventually, Tee Green, the band's vocal coach, was enlisted to save the day and help out. Under duress, Brian delivered a fantastic vocal, wide-eyed and brimming with puppy love.

Once we had heard it, everybody thought the song was going to be massive, even Brian. It was the sort of magical, twinkling, devotional love song that was perfect for the festive season. Phil and Ian worked on it loads, giving it the full kitchen-sink orchestral production. Colin Bell, the managing director of London Records, wanted sleigh bells added to make it even more seasonal.

CHAPTER 24

Well, you can never say no to a shameless cash-in, so the bells were duly added, pealing to all Christendom. To me, they sounded just like the ker-ching of cash registers ringing out.

We shot a video of the band wearing dungarees: it was totally wrong. Then we did another clip that was rather more on the money. We got the four of them dressed up in all-white outfits with furry hoods, Santa's little helpers from deepest Walthamstow. Snowflakes cascaded down throughout the video while the lads tried desperately to look tough miming the song.

It worked. In fact, it worked like a dream. 'Stay Another Day' hit number one and stayed there for five weeks, right across the entire festive season. For the second time in pop history, a Tom Watkins act had a Christmas number one! Once again, I felt invincible …

And yet, just like Frankie's 'The Power Of Love' all those years ago, it would have been so much better had the giddy carousel of pop perpetually frozen at that point. If it had paused on that jubilant seasonal sight of the four East 17 lads, covered in snow, their hearts aflutter with youth's tender romances (and, yeah, preferably with their mouths shut and eyes closed).

Because what was coming around the corner for them was not snow: it was a massive fucking shit storm.

Meanwhile, my Massive Management roster of talent continued to grow. Sort of. We devised a boy band called 2wo Third3, so-named because two-thirds wore the same outfit. I know, inspired moniker, right?

2wo Third3 were conceptualised to be the first 'out' boy band. I thought this was going to be mega. Years before

Boyzone's Stephen Gately or N Sync's Lance Bass came out, they were going to make a whole angle out of being out and proud. Once again, *Smash Hits'* Alex Kadis was up for the scoop.

Only the boys bottled it at the last minute, no doubt worried what their mums would think. After a couple of semi-hits, including the 1995 top twenty single 'I Want The World,' and an East 17 support slot, Epic Records declined to release their debut album. And that was that. 2wo Third3 became zero.

I had loved the idea and I liked their electropop sound. However, I have to confess that once or twice the people working on them muttered to me that they should be renamed Two Turds.

We also had Deuce, a boy-girl all-singing, all-dancing four-piece with real potential. They even had a few hits. The video for one of them, 'Call It Love', featured me making a cameo holding a baby, and lots of babies and grown-ups in cots. It was all about adults acting like toddlers when it comes to romance, you see. The song was campy and catchy, destined to fill the floors of GAY.

I chaperoned Deuce when they went on *Richard and Judy*. I did more talking than they did. The role of high-camp Svengali suited me down to the ground. Mind you, I am not sure why I went on dressed like a flowerpot man on his way to a rave.

Their follow-up, 'I Need You', came close to being our Eurovision entry and hit the top ten. A great single called 'On The Bible' deserved to do better than it did, and when the album only just crept into the top twenty and a member left, London Records dropped them.

Even so, I reckon Pete Waterman had been watching Deuce very closely when he launched Steps not long afterwards.

Is my cheque in the post, Pete? No, I thought not.

East 17 took two singles off *Steam* in 1995. 'Let It Rain' featured an opening sermon from Tony ('In the cosmic corridors we collide') that made him seem like a TV evangelist on the wacky baccy. 'Hold My Body Tight' was more bump-and-grind R&B. They were both big hits.

East 17 were unstoppable … or so it seemed.

Somebody from Massive saw Mark Owen, the choirboy cute one from Take That, in a restaurant. Full of bravado, he swaggered up to him and boasted of East 17's recent success. Only half tongue in cheek, he joked that Take That must be sore that their rivals had scooped the Christmas number one.

Mark was gracious and congratulated him.

He could afford to be. Weeks later Take That released 'Back For Good'. It was a colossal hit, their crossover into housewives' choice radio and a not-too-shabby foray into the middle of the road where bland Barlow felt most at home.

In many ways, it was the tipping point. East 17 were about to be usurped by their milquetoast rivals.

However, the real disaster came a while later. Tony normally did most of the interviews, but wasn't available for a radio slot so Brian took his place. When the conversation turned to drugs, he decided to extol the virtues of Ecstasy and boasted that he had taken shedloads of the stuff.

'If it makes you feel better, and gives you something to do at the weekend, and you go out and have a good time, I don't see why not,' he declared. 'Life is too short!'

He said he had taken dozens of the pills in one night. I doubt he had, he was probably just fronting, but the revelation was a bombshell.

The press descended on East 17 like vultures. This was just the kind of moral panic and scandal they loved to pretend to be outraged by. Their faux-indignation would wind the public right up.

It also all came barely a year after the tragedy of Leah Betts, the eighteen-year-old who overdosed on the drug at her birthday bash. The timing could not have been worse and I knew that Fleet Street was going to have a field day.

Flashing cameras and tabloid hacks immediately besieged the Harvey residence. Poor, bemused Brian came to the door in his Dennis the Menace pyjamas. He was just a kid really, way out of his depth – and everyone was mad as hell at him.

Brian had done exactly what Robbie Williams did when he went to Glastonbury, got drunk and hung out with Oasis. He was rebelling against his status as a boy-band member, displaying his bad-boy credentials and refuting the idea that he was just a puppet in a pre-packaged 'pop' group.

In actual fact, Tony had recently made similar noises in the press, asking why Ecstasy was illegal while alcohol was socially acceptable. But being Tony, he had got a bit hippy about it, saying E increased a person's 'love'.

But that was in the *Guardian* and nobody was scouring the broadsheets. Besides, it was a philosophical statement, rather than an admission of taking it himself.

The truth was that everybody was doing it, along with anything else that was going. But you didn't dare talk about it. Well, maybe if you were Liam Gallagher or Brett Anderson, but not a boy-band member.

Except, of course, if you were Brian Harvey from East 17. Then you hollered it from the rooftops.

We had crisis meetings. Brian issued an apology. Unfortunately, he was pretty obviously stoned when he did so.

East 17 were Going South. Big time. I had visions of Nigel Martin Smith, delirious with glee, rubbing his hands and licking his lips.

Then the House of Commons got stuck in. The band in general and Brian in particular were condemned in Westminster. Even John Major, the Gary Barlow of prime ministers, said it was 'wholly wrong'. Christ, this guy's skin was as grey as his hair! The bloke could have used an E! There again, most of these sanctimonious hypocrites in Parliament could have used an E ...

We caved into the outrage. We sacked Brian. We put an open letter in the *Sun* regretting that 'barmy Brian' had ruined it for us and agreeing how objectionable it all was.

Then the weekend came and we probably did an E. What a bunch of sanctimonious hypocrites we were, too ....

Having said that, Brian had been becoming unmanageable, increasingly erratic and hard to handle. And Tony was just bored. After all, after 'Stay Another Day', where could he go next? He had achieved everything he wanted to.

The third album, *Up All Night*, had a lot going for it. 'If You Ever', a duet with eye-patch-wearing soul siren Gabrielle, was a number two smash. But that gang vibe that had been so integral to the group's appeal had been well and truly blown.

Also, the other band members were getting irked that Tony got paid more than them because he got the songwriting royalties. It's the eternal boy-band dilemma: people who can't write songs being disgruntled that they aren't making money from, er, writing songs.

Terry Coldwell even became peeved that reporters would only want to talk to Tony, thus depriving the public of the Coldwell oracle of wit and wisdom. Yep, it's the other eternal boy-band dilemma: people with nothing to say being disgruntled that people aren't interested in their opinions.

Or maybe I was just becoming a mean, cynical old bastard? After one too many nights of debauchery, the usual orgies and decadent thrills that I hosted like the nineties Nero I was in my Maida Vale palace, I woke up the worse for wear.

And I looked into the mirror.

Who was looking back? It was Tom Watkins, for sure, but the twinkle in my eyes had gone. I never smiled and laughed like I used to. The revelry continued but it felt staged. The truth was I was just going through the motions, bored by an endless procession of pop stars and ponces.

My curly hair had gone, and so had Neil and Chris, Matt, Luke and Craig … and countless others.

Nobody called me Tommy any more. And I wasn't even sure I liked the man looking back at me from the mirror. Truth be told, he was a bit of a cunt.

I was the man who promised pop stardom to eager hopefuls, making them feel like they were getting a free ride in the ice-cream van from Mr Whippy. Truth be told, before long they felt like they were Bob Hoskins stuck in the back of the car at the end of *The Long Good Friday* …

So what next?

East 17 carried on for a while, but really it was time to tell Tweedledee and Tweedledum to put their tops back on and go home. There again, Terry Coldwell always looked so confused and mashed that I wondered if he could find his way home. At least John Hendy could always go back to roofing.

When they finally split, it felt like a relief. They had countless attempts at reforming (and in fact were still at it twenty years later). The last I heard, John and Terry were still trying to keep the band alive, which is a bit like reviving *Only Fools and Horses* without Del and Rodney.

In any case, it had stopped being my business. I was long gone.

East 17 was my last big pop success. After them, for a while I tried fitfully and frantically to find the next big thing. It was a hapless quest. I couldn't find it. Or maybe my heart just wasn't in it any more.

My best attempt was North and South, a band that I recruited via the ancient medium of Teletext. We launched them with *No Sweat*, a TV show, the vehicle that I had longed to use for a pop group ever since Giggles.

Surely this time I would create the Monkees of the nineties!

No Sweat was a big draw on Children's BBC. We got top ratings. In May 1997 they had a single, 'I'm A Man Not A Boy' (OK, it was 'Drop The Boy' redux) that was a number seven hit. Yet it became a case of diminishing returns with every subsequent release.

The moral of the tale was that what was a smash success on TV screens didn't necessarily translate into record sales.

And then North and South decided to tell everyone they hated their music. Ho hum. It was that tedious old case of a boy band desperately hankering for credibility and wanting to be Oasis.

Well, the odds of North and South making the cover of *Melody Maker* and selling out Knebworth were pretty slim. More likely they ended up in a Carphone Warehouse near you.

As ever, I wanted them to just shut up, put up, smile and mime. The problem was that I felt I had the secret formula to build the perfect pop sensation. For a while it seemed like I did.

But as soon as it becomes just that – a formula – it becomes tired and cynical. There has to be an element of magic, a little rogue streak of unmanaged mischief in even the most manufactured act. And my acts had become increasingly uninspired.

Here was the basic problem: I was trying to make chicken soup out of chicken shit.

There was no Neil Tennant and his genius poetry; no Matt Goss with his energy and dramatic vocals; no wild card Tony Mortimer. The control freak – me – had too much control. And he was bored. Let me tell you, Simon Cowell must have a far higher boredom threshold than me.

There was a boy-girl duo called Zoo that I hoped would be the next Dollar. It never happened. There was The Modern, another boy-girl group that I worked on with Stephen Hague. They never got off the ground.

I even patented a cartoon character called Kulkarni, a virtual pop star that I thought would be a chart-shaking innovation.

He would never answer back or want 'longevity'; he would always turn up and do as he was told. But he trickled out into cyberspace, never to return.

But, then again, so did the pop machine that I once knew.

Fuck this, I thought. *I'm quitting this crap and going down the seaside full time.*

And that's exactly what I did.

EPILOGUE

LARGER THAN LIFE?

As the millennium dawned, I got out of London and the music biz. I sold my Maida Vale home and my White House in Fairlight and beat a retreat to the Sussex coast. And then I built not one house but two.

I found a plot of land at Pett Level, right on Winchelsea Beach, between Rye and Hastings. It was remote and idyllic. The first place I built there was a nautical-inspired marvel called the Seahouse.

I had wanted the renowned Memphis movement architect Ettore Sottsass to design it for me. When I met him, he told me I couldn't afford him. He was right. So I did it myself but his influence was all over it. I poured my heart into it because it was my final flight from London and the bullshit of the music industry.

Then I built another one, which got me on the telly. I built a white sugar cube, a Bauhaus-derived beauty called the Big White House, a nod to my first Sussex home. Channel 4's *Grand Designs* documented the building of the property. Kevin McCloud wafted off and on the site. I got a lot of free Siemens appliances. It was a hoot. I still live there.

Most of the locals appeared to welcome the arrival of a new high-profile resident. Except, of course, there are always a few backward-thinking yokels. One of them stopped me when I was walking my boxer dogs along the beach.

'We don't want your sort around here,' he grunted at me. What could he have meant?

'What?' I asked him disingenuously. 'Rich, intelligent and charismatic people?'

To give him at least a little credit, he later apologised. I suppose it is better than being asked if the Pet Shop Boys live in my house. I get that a lot.

Once an entrepreneur, always an entrepreneur. The idle life is not for me. Soon I was itching to get on with something else. I heard another Londoner with a weekend place nearby bemoaning the lack of great restaurants and coffee places in the area.

I bought a rundown pub down the road and turned it into the Ship, an eatery with an annexed butcher's and grocery shop. I made the interiors look a bit like the Seahouse. The walls were bright blue mosaics, a bit like Sarm West. The fireplace was fire-engine red.

Sometimes on Wednesday nights I call the pub quiz there. It's a far cry from my heady, coke-fuelled days in London. Thank God.

And what of the pop world that I was once such a big, fat, lucky part of? What's become of that?

Well, the 'manufactured' aspect of what I did is there still. I can see it in Simon Cowell's creations. For better or worse, I helped to pave the way for what he is doing.

But the 'rogue' element and the sense of mischief are gone. I can't imagine Simon paying an ex-convict to spray-paint One Direction imagery all over town. It's all a bit squeaky clean and sanitised.

Still, there are some certainties we can always cling to. Good old Madonna is still panting and gyrating. And Gary Barlow, like taxes and poverty, is still with us.

The physicality of recorded music has gone. It's all downloads and streams, a world away from my fold-out sleeves, poster bags and picture discs. I miss that.

Music just doesn't seem that three-dimensional any more.

But then, like every other bastard that moans about it, I sit my fat arse in front of *The X Factor* every time it's on. I sit through the overblown spectacle, the strains of 'Carmina Burana', the deified judges taking to the stage. I can't help myself, even though it looks like a Nuremberg rally on pink drugs.

I don't like all the melismatic warbling on there. Sometimes in pop all that you need is a good voice and good ideas. The barnstorming din that gets people clapping nowadays gives me a right old migraine.

Plus the emotions are so stagey and the tears are those of teenage crocodiles. Some of the stories that pass for rags to riches make me laugh.

'You poor sixteen-year-old! You sing like a star. You *are* a star! You are never going back to that horrible Saturday job at

Asda with all those horrible people. Or to that horrible room with the kettle in it.'

It's hardly the stuff of *Great Expectations*, is it? And you know most of these stars will be off Simon Cowell's Syco label and down the dumper quicker than Simon can reach for the fake tan and Botox.

But then, like I said, I watch it every week, so I should shut the fuck up.

What I miss is the weirdos who made British pop music so alive and colourful. You wouldn't get a Marc Almond, a Holly Johnson, a Neil Tennant or a Boy George getting through that panel of judges on *The X Factor*. Let's face it: the golden age of pop's key architects would have ended up in the show's Bloopers section.

Nowadays everyone looks a bit dull. Ed Sheeran. Sam Smith. The former a boring straight bloke, the latter a boring gay bloke. Well, it's nice to know that homos are allowed to be as dreary as heteros now.

To think dear old Louis Walsh once aspired to be me! The former *X Factor* judge and manager of Boyzone, Westlife and now Hometown thankfully stopped short of inheriting my waistline, or lack thereof, but as for his modus operandi ... well, I suppose I should be flattered.

As I was when I went to see Neil and Chris's little musical, *Closer to Heaven*. I sat in the stalls watching as a corpulent, credit-card-waving monstrosity of a music manager started singing a song entitled 'Call Me Old-Fashioned', something I have always said a lot.

I loved it! It was a portrait of a crass, vulgar and utterly crude old lech who collected conquests, possessions (Porsche,

Prada and Starck – Neil knows my shopping list) and money with maximum pleasure and zero guilt. And who figured *to hell with 'artistic integrity'*. So, pretty accurate, then.

Anyway it was a great song and a fitting tribute. Me and the empty seats had a right old chuckle.

Yet, sooner or later, life becomes about more than shopping, sex and three minutes of music. Life gets real. And sad.

Family members become estranged. I fell out with my mum when she stopped seeing me and only saw my money and fame. A Rolex watch, flat and plush caravan weren't enough. She wanted a fur coat, too. The same year. I never spoke to her again.

My sister left the building shortly after. And so did my endless procession of boyfriends. The ones that tried to love were swiftly ditched. The ones that didn't try, ripped me off.

I still have some nice pictures. And I still live in a Big White House. It's just that a lonely wind blows through it sometimes.

It's a bit Charles Foster fucking Kane, isn't it?

I miss the glory days. I would be a liar if I said I didn't. When it was good, it was a right old laugh.

I miss Neil. I miss all the old friends I never see much of. Gary Knibbs. Paul Rodwell is far away in South Africa. I miss Trevor Horn. I really miss Jill Sinclair. She is no longer with us. I never went to her funeral – nor to my mum's.

I always was a gutless bastard when it came to saying goodbye.

And in recent years I have seen the dying of my own light. Heart attacks, liver transplants, strokes: you name it, I've suffered it. I've seen the inside of a hospital more times than you should in a whole lifetime.

Bette Davis was right. Growing old certainly ain't for sissies. They don't bother to tell you that when they are selling you the sex, drugs and rock and roll fairy tale.

Anyway: enough of this maudlin crap! I have had a good life. I got away from the tallyman. I left my fingerprints all over some perfect buildings. I built some perfect pop groups. I helped some of them get places they simply wouldn't have without me (go on, Neil and Chris, admit it).

And I got laid more times than anyone with a tiny penis, a big gut and a lifelong aversion to exercise has any right to expect. Although, looking back, I think that all that pursuit of sex was a waste of time. I could have been having a nice cup of tea with Boy George and Neil.

And I'm not really *that* lonely. In fact, in recent years I've met someone who has shown me companionship and, without getting too sticky, love. My partner Marc has been a rock through all my illness, tirelessly taking care of me day in, day out. When your health falters, when the 'giddy carousel of pop' stops turning, what are you left with? Hopefully a little bit of love. And I'm pretty sure I've found the true meaning of it in the twilight of my years …

So was I larger than life?

Don't be silly!

Life's larger than all of us. Even a rich, fat, lucky, gay bastard like Tom Watkins.

INDEX